The Men *from* The Boys

RAY RAPHAEL

THE MEN
═══ *from* ═══
THE BOYS

Rites of Passage
in
Male America

University of Nebraska Press

Lincoln & London

The paper in this book meets
the minimum require-
ments of American National
Standard for Infor-
mation Sciences – Permanence
of Paper for
Printed Library Materials,
ANSI Z39.48-1984.

Library of Congress
Cataloging in Publication Data
Raphael, Ray.
The men from the boys: rites
of passage in
male America / Ray Raphael.
p. cm.
Bibliography: p.
ISBN 0-8032-3888-6 (alk. paper)
1. Young men –
United States – Psychology.
2. Teenage boys –
United States – Psychology.
3. Men – United States
– Psychology.   4. Masculinity
(Psychology)   5. Identity
(Psychology   I. Title.
HQ799.6.R36 1988
305.3'1 – dc19   88-17369   CIP

For my dad, Sydney Raphael

CONTENTS

Introduction, ix

Introduction

Why are men so nervous about their own masculinity? Male insecurity used to be a well-kept secret, known only to our perceptive female companions who happened to stumble upon it. But now the cat is out of the bag. First came the guilt-ridden reaction to feminism, with hypersensitive men apologizing profusely and confessing their insecurities aloud for all the world to hear. Now we have the Rambo-styled backlash to the hypersensitive male—but this time we're not easily fooled by false bravado. Macho, we now know, is just one more indication of insecurity. Many of us really *believed* in John Wayne, but most of us probably suspect that Sylvester Stallone is little more than a joke. We quietly chuckle when we hear that the undaunted Rocky, who ventured deep into the Evil Empire in the movies, is scared, in real life, to travel to Western Europe. We all can see, on some level, that even Rambo must have had a mother—and for all we know he might be scared to death of women.

The macho man and the wimp—we seem to be shifting helplessly back and forth between these twin manifestations of male insecurity. How do we free ourselves from this fruitless swing of the pendulum? Are we doomed forever to this one narrow arc?

There are very real reasons for men to feel nervous about who they really are, and these reasons are deeply rooted in human experience. But there are also significant methods that various cultures have used to cope with the underlying causes of male insecurity. What are these root causes of our nervousness? And what are the possible antidotes for our deep-seated anxieties?

Infant boys, like infant girls, are tender, vulnerable, dependent. Throughout childhood most boys remain dependent, and they spend their time primarily in the company of women and other children. But when boys turn into men, they are generally expected to leave the nurturing, feminized world behind them. In most cultures, boys must repudiate their prior vulnerability and aspire to a matrix of personality traits more appropriate to manhood: strength, endurance, courage, confidence, self-reliance. Such a transition is bound to be difficult. The ideals of manhood and the realities of childhood are not merely different from each other—they are antithetical. So as a boy strives to attain the fortitude and independence required of manhood, he must also find a way to deny his childish past.

The negation of one identity and the creation of a new identity—these are not easy jobs, and they are not often performed by individuals acting alone. Historically, a youth has rarely been left to his own devices during this difficult time of transition. Traditional cultures throughout the world have often devised ways of dramatizing and ritualizing the passage into manhood and of transforming that passage into a community event. Through the use of structured initiation rites, these societies have been able to help and guide the youths through their period of developmental crisis. By formalizing the transitional process, complex problems of identity formation are translated into concrete and straightforward tasks. A youth might be beaten with firebrands or circumcised or made to perform difficult tests of fortitude, but all he has to do is follow the rules, endure the pain, rise to the occasion—and his manhood is assured. In a finite and well-defined set of rituals, he proves to himself and to others that he has laid his childish insecurities to rest and that he is ready for the roles, responsibilities, and privileges of an adult male.

Often, the trials a youth must endure are extreme:

Throughout their journey the elders belaboured them with fire-brands, sticks tipped with obsidian, and nettles. They arrived covered with blood and were received by a pair of guardians. A period of seclusion followed, during which the boys had to undergo a series of trials. They were beaten, starved, deprived of sleep, partially suffocated, and almost roasted. Water was forbidden, and if thirsty they had to chew sugar-cane. Only the coarsest of foods were allowed, and even these were left raw. All the time the guardians gave them instructions about kinship responsibilities and duties to their seniors. At length, after some months, the priest summoned the supernatural monsters from underground while the other men sounded the bull-roarers. The guardians now taught their charges how to incise the penis in order to eliminate the contamination resulting from association with the other sex. Subsequently, this operation had to be performed regularly. A series of great feasts then took place, and the initiands emerged richly decorated.[1]

This is how a Busama youth in the highlands of New Guinea proves his manhood. As odd as the rituals might sound to us, their impact is forceful and direct: If a youth can make it through this bizarre sequence of mutilation and deprivation, then certainly he can handle the everyday hardships he will confront thoughout his adult life. Dramatically and emphatically, he has repudiated the vulnerability of boyhood while asserting the toughness and resilience required of manhood. In his own eyes and in the eyes of society, he has shown himself to be worthy of adult respect.

Perhaps we have something to learn from this primitive rite of passage. The underlying structure of the ritual is enviable, even if the details might seem sordid. Listen, for example, to a typical reaction of a modern-day man to the crude but gutsy Busama initiation rituals:

I wish I had it that easy. Run through the fire, step on the coals— then it's over and done with. You're a man, everyone knows you're a man, and that's the end of it. For me it keeps on going on and on. The uncertainty of it—at any moment you could be out on the streets. It's all tied up with money. I've got to keep on fighting for money and respect. The fire never stops; I keep running through it every day. (Howard R.)

Introduction

This response points to the basic plight of contemporary males: Without a clear-cut rite of passage, how can we know for sure whether we are truly worthy of manhood? As uninitiated males, perhaps we are all still boys. Surely, this is no small part of our insecurity.

But wait—don't we live in liberated times? Why should we have to prove our manhood at all? As knowledgeable American males in the late twentieth century, we should be able to see that modern social and economic forms have evolved beyond the need for a traditional rite of passage. Since adolescent boys no longer have to be turned into hunters and warriors, there is no longer any reason to subject them to firebrands or genital mutilation or any other forms of primitive torture. A man does not have to learn how to endure great physical hardships in order to operate a computer or meet the insurance payments. A man does not have to demonstrate personal courage in order to push the button that can remove an enemy nation from the face of the earth.

All this is true, yet many young males today still feel an urge, a yearning, a mysterious drive to prove themselves as men in more primitive terms. Even if traditional initiations no longer appear to be objectively necessary, the psychological function they once served is still very real. The psychic needs of contemporary males have not always been able to keep pace with sex-role liberation and a computerized economy and nuclear warfare, all of which contribute to the apparent obsolescence of traditional initiations. There is an obvious gap between our rapidly evolving social forms and our internalized, old-fashioned images of manhood. It is my purpose here to explore this gap between our forward-looking liberations and our backward-looking psyches, for this is the battleground upon which the politics of gender are so heatedly debated. I want to examine the tenuous relationship between a complex modernity and a more basic, archaic heritage.

Caught in this cultural time-warp, we modern-day males may assume ambiguous roles. We write some strange scripts to play out these roles—and the scripts that we write form the basis for this book. *The Men from the Boys* is based upon diverse personal stories, with each true tale, in its own way, confronting some important questions: How does a contemporary youth establish his adult male identity in a unisex world? And how, in this post-modern society, can he possibly learn what a man is, what a man should be, or how manhood can best be achieved? These are perplexing yet compelling issues; they are issues that are being faced by every young man who is coming of age today.

This book therefore serves as a collective self-portrait of a generation of American men—a generation struggling to keep up with the pace of history, or perhaps trying to stave it off. I have conducted in-depth, open-ended interviews with one hundred males between the ages of fifteen and fifty, men who have come of age in the latter half of the twentieth century. I asked these men to talk about the experiences in their lives that helped to define, in their own minds, their adult masculinity. When such experiences seemed to be lacking, I asked the men to explore that lack. During each interview I introduced the term "manhood," but then I let the men define and react to that notion in their own separate ways. I did not have a prepared set of questions; the few questions I did ask were intended only to bring forth vivid accounts of personal experiences. Within the inescapable limitations imposed by human interaction, I attempted to minimize my own influence upon the telling of the tales. My goal was not to shape a set of responses to fit a preconceived hypothesis but rather to elicit a series of monologues that serve as the raw data for this study.

My subjects were not randomly selected according to scientific sampling techniques; instead, I purposely sought out men who appeared, by their words or their actions, to take the transition into manhood somewhat seriously. These are people who have tried to create for themselves some semblance of a rite of passage, although many of them seem to have had considerable difficulty in finding, or passing, their appropriate initiations. By talking with men who have actively attempted to engineer their own transitions, I hoped to uncover some of the problems that so many of us seem to be confronting in the developmental process.

My subjects have not been fashioned from a single mold. I have made a special point of including everyone from a Mr. America body-builder to a believer in witchcraft, from a "right stuff" fighter pilot to a draft dodger, from a self-proclaimed Don Juan to a Super Dad. The only thing which all these disparate individuals have in common is that they have consciously struggled, in the context of their separate and private lives, with the peculiar difficulties presented by coming-of-age in modern America.

I have chosen men of different ages in order to get a feel for the varying stages of the maturation process. Some of the subjects are still adolescents; they tell us about their ideals of manhood and how they expect to achieve those ideals. Some of the subjects are presently in the throes of transition; they give us their immediate perceptions of their self-styled initiations. Most of the subjects, however, are a little bit older. Generally in their thirties, they are now past the normal and expected age of transition. I have focused much of my attention upon this age group for definite reasons. Our modern versions of initiations rarely occur at puberty; indeed, they are often delayed until we are well into our twenties. In many cases we don't really know when our initiations actually end, or even *if* they end. So if we want to find out how well our initiations work—and that is my basic question—we have to wait a little longer. Once men can see their initiation attempts in some perspective, they can begin to evaluate how well they have made their transitions into manhood. Most of the men I talked with have gained enough perspective to interpret their experiences; not only can they now tell their own stories, but they can also dig a little deeper and help us find out what their stories *mean*.

What follows, then, is about to become rather intimate. The men whom I've interviewed have generously shared many of their personal dreams and their secret fears; in many cases, they have made their private lives public. I should hope that we listen to these men with openness and empathy, for it is their first-person accounts that form the heart and soul of this book. Naturally I will be stating my reactions and offering my insights, and I will try to develop some meaningful connections and tenable hypotheses, but this study, first and foremost, is rooted in the individual experiences of the men you are about to meet.

I do not wish to impose some objective definition of manhood upon these diverse individuals, nor do I wish to suggest that an objective definition even exists. I do not wish to imply that we could or should return to the primitive paradigm, nor even that all males, to satisfy some innate imperative, ought to go through a well-defined process of initiation that makes for a clear delineation between boyhood and manhood. My purpose instead is to examine the effects of not having, as the primitives once did, a single definition of manhood or a clear-cut and universal rite of passage. So this is the story of both our initiation and our non-initiation into manhood. It is a first-hand glimpse at the tenuous and often insecure state of the contemporary male psyche. How do we cope with the complex and confusing process of male maturation in the modern world? What kinds of initiation facsimiles do we create for ourselves?

And do these ad hoc initiations work—not necessarily on some objective level, but do they work for us personally? How do they affect our self-concepts as men? Do they help us feel and act as we would like to feel and act?

Of course, any study of a topic as broad as this is bound to be incomplete. The answers to my questions will be tentative at best, for the diverse range of personal experience, particularly in a pluralistic culture such as ours, effectively precludes definitive and comprehensive conclusions. With this natural limitation in mind, I have taken one important step to narrow the scope of my project. Instead of dealing with the complete range of economic classes and ethnic groups which feed into our heterogeneous society, I have focused primarily on young men coming from working-class or middle-class backgrounds—mainstream Americans, as it were. Although interviews with members of ghetto gangs or private clubs for the rich would certainly have been of interest, these sorts of initiations are specific to particular subcultures and might have distracted our attention from the more general questions I am asking: How does a modern-day boy, a child of technology, mature without violating a time-honored male heritage? What options are open to him? What are his possibilities for a successful transition? By limiting our focus to working-class and middle-class subjects in an advanced, industrialized nation, we can perceive most directly the internal dilemmas and contradictions so many of us must face.

Whether consciously or not, young American males live with these dilemmas and contradictions in their daily lives, and they follow some devious paths in their attempts to resolve them. Like Don Quixote with his fire-breathing windmill, many of the men you are about to meet have created some imaginative challenges in order to prove their manhood—and so, I suspect, have you and I. As we listen to the diverse tales which follow, we might well find the reflections of our own personal experiences. The result, I hope, will be to demystify some of the personal dilemmas which are common to our times. We will see that other people, not just ourselves, are caught in the bind between archaic images of manhood and contemporary realities that can impede the realization of those images. To some extent, this realization might help to relieve the sense of individual guilt—a guilt of self-perceived unmanliness—which seems endemic to our times. Our paradox is collective, not individual. Our problems are situational, commonly rooted in contemporary culture.

Once we realize this on both the cognitive and emotional levels, we will be better prepared to overcome our self-doubts, to synthesize the modern with the primitive, and perhaps even to develop appropriate rites of passage of our own.

It is not my purpose here to define men as distinct from women, but only to describe some experiences which seem common among contemporary American males—or, more correctly, to let the subjects of this study describe the experiences for themselves. As the boundaries between the sexes become increasingly blurred, women tend to share many of these experiences. It is not uncommon for a woman today to try to accomplish many of the things that men are trying to accomplish through their ad hoc initiations.

And yet there is a difference. Traditional masculine norms and expectations, although recently adopted by many women, have not been deeply imbedded in the female consciousness by thousands of years of collective socialization. Even when a man and a woman appear to be sharing a common experience, they are likely to interpret that experience rather differently. If a woman, say, decides to prove her worth by going to war or climbing a mountain, she does so more from choice than from necessity. She is not affirming the traditional values of her sex; she is not demonstrating, to herself or to others, that she can live up to archaic norms which have historically shaped the female experience.

A man who goes to war or climbs a mountain, on the other hand, is not only proving his individual worth—he is simultaneously displaying his gender. He is meeting an obligation (some might now call it a burden)[2] which in some sense is imposed upon him by sheer virtue of his being male. The intensity (and perhaps even the desperation) of the experience is essentially masculine, colored as it is by the overpowering weight of social expectation.

In the pages that follow we will hear many tales of striving and winning and losing that might almost have been told by women. But in fact, they were told by men. This is our own collective story, and it is unquestionably influenced by the gender we happened to inherit.[3] While I should hope that women will find enough common ground to be able to listen and understand and even empathize with what we say, this is not an attempt to analyze the male psyche from an outside perspective. Instead, this is the inside story of the male psyche in action. We are who we are, and we are trying to find out what that really means in a world which simultaneously demands and questions our gender-related heritage.

ACKNOWLEDGMENTS

I should like to thank all the men and boys who have graciously agreed to participate in this project. Many of the people I interviewed do not appear in the final version of the book, but I learned from them all nonetheless. Despite claims to the contrary, I have found that men today are often open and honest with their thoughts and feelings, and that they are genuinely interested in sorting out and sharing their most personal experiences.

Some of the subjects who appear in *The Men from the Boys* have chosen to use their real names, while others prefer to remain anonymous. In order that the reader might know the difference, real names will appear in full, while pseudonyms will be abbreviated into fictitious first names along with last initials. In a few cases, identifying characteristics had to be altered to preserve privacy.

Since the viewpoints of the participants are so varied, nobody is to be held responsible for the words which others might say elsewhere in the book, nor does a personal appearance in *The Men from the Boys* constitute an endorsement of my own statements and conclusions. Each person speaks only for himself, and I, as the author and editor of this study, am quite aware that I too speak only for myself.

PART I: RITES OF PASSAGE

CHAPTER 1

The Structure & Meaning of Traditional Initiations

The evolution of male initiation rites has been neither accidental nor haphazard. Throughout human history, cultures from around the world have devised all sorts of rituals to facilitate and celebrate the coming-of-age. Although these rituals display a great deal of local variation, their underlying structure remains remarkably constant from one culture to the next.[1]

Since rites of passage have been scrutinized most closely with respect to primitive cultures, let us start our story there. I do not wish to become nostalgically enamored of primitive initiations, but I do think a quick glance in that direction might help shed some light on our contemporary versions. Despite the obvious incongruities between pre-literate and civilized man, primitive societies, precisely because of their relative simplicity and homogeneity, offer clear and dramatic examples of the male rite of passage in action. Both trained anthropologists and lay observers have long been fascinated by these primitive rituals, and the information that they have gathered might help us get our bearings so that we may place our own particular rituals in proper perspective.

So how do male initiations work?

A basic framework for understanding initiation rituals was provided by Arnold van Gennep in his classic study, *The Rites of Passage*.[2] The central theme of male initiation rites, according to van Gennep, is a change in identity: the death of the boy, the resurrection of the man. This theme of death and rebirth is often treated quite literally. Speaking of some of the Australian aborigines, van Gennep notes that "the novice is considered dead, and he remains dead for the duration of his novitiate." During the rite of passage "he is resurrected and taught how to live, but differently than in childhood."[3] For the Ojibway initiation,

the child is attached to a board and during the entire ceremony behaves as if he had lost all personality; the participants are dressed, painted, etc.; there is a general procession to the interior of the hut; the chiefs-magicians-priests kill all the participants and resurrect them one after the other.[4]

In some West African tribes, the symbolic death of the child is taken to its logical conclusion: youths who happen to die during the initiation process "are considered simply not to have been reborn, and their mothers are expected not to weep or grieve for them."[5]

Van Gennep claimed that the theme of death and rebirth is played out in three phases: separation, transition, and incorporation. During the separation phase, the boy must be severed from all ties with his past. Sometimes his hair is cut, sometimes he is given new clothes, and always he is removed from his home, from the comfort and security of familiar surroundings and from the nurturing world of women. The mothers of the boys, often accompanied by a chorus of other women, commonly engage in ritualistic wailing and moaning at the loss of their sons.

This separation phase—the death of the boy—is enacted very dramatically during the commencement of the initiation into the Poro Bush Society of West Africa. A thick stalk and a bladder filled with chicken blood are tied under the boy's shirt. The boy is then ceremonially killed by spears thrown by masked dancers. The bladder breaks, spilling all the blood. Although the thick stalk acts like a shield to protect the boy, he pretends to be dead and falls to the ground. He is then picked up and tossed over the fence that encloses the private site of the Poro Society. On the other side of the fence one Poro member catches the boy while another drops a log, creating the impression that the boy himself has hit the ground. The women who have been observing the ceremony are supposed to believe that the boy has actually died. They will not see him again until he is resurrected as a man.[6]

The length of time spent in seclusion, apart from the normal life of the tribe, varies from a few days to several years. The absence of women and young boys is apparently critical, for it is strictly and universally enforced. During this time the mysteries of manhood—anything from tribal lore to hunting skills to sex education—are revealed to the boys; these are the carefully guarded secrets which serve to separate the initiated from the uninitiated.

The period of seclusion constitutes the transition phase of the initiation, and it is during this time that the youths must undergo the hazing and tests of endurance that we often equate with initiation rituals. The wide variety of ordeals that initiands must undergo at this point display a sadistic side of the human imagination. An Arunta youth in Australia must defend himself against branches of fire being thrown at him, and he must lay down on green boughs over an open fire. He is also subjected to a head biting ceremony, in which grown men are urged to bite the boy's head deeply:

Their duty is to bite the scalp as hard as they can, until blood flows freely, the patient often howling in pain. Each man may content himself with one bite or he may bite two or even three times. The object of this really painful operation is, so they say, to make their hair grow strongly, and at times the chin may be bitten as well as the scalp.[7]

In South Africa, Thonga youths are continually beaten during their three-month initiation ritual. They are also denied water and forced to eat unsavory foods, such as the half-digested grass found in the bowels of an antelope. They are made to lie naked in the cold winter nights, sleeping only on their backs while being bitten incessantly by bugs in the ground. Should they violate any of the rules, they are severely punished:

The boy must present his hands, put them against each other and separate the fingers. The sticks are introduced between the fingers and a strong man, taking both ends of the sticks in his hands, presses

them together and lifts the poor boy, squeezing and half crushing the fingers.[8]

Why do these trials tend to be so morbid? At least in part, it's for the drama. The tasks at hand are severe—the negation of the weakness endemic to childhood, the affirmation of the strength required of manhood—so the means of accomplishing such tasks must likewise be severe. These are dramatic and visible resolutions to an extremely difficult problem of psychological and sociological development.

No aspect of primitive initiations is more dramatic than the various forms of genital mutilation: circumcision, subincision (the cutting of the underside of the penis to expose the urethra), and superincision (the cutting of the overside of the penis). Societies throughout the world have practiced one or another of these operations as an integral part of male initiation rites. Genital mutilations often constitute an important part of a rite of passage precisely because they produce lasting and visible results. For non-literate people they function as diplomas, marks of distinction that signify that youths have in fact gone through the required ordeals.[9] Of course, any form of scarification—tattoos, the raising of permanent welts, the cutting of ear lobes—will likewise function as a diploma, and in fact these are frequently used. But genital operations tend to have a special force, for they mark an organ integrally linked with the sexual status that the youths are about to assume.

Another mark of distinction available to non-literate people is the changing of a person's name. In the primitive mind an individual's name is equivalent to his true existence as a spiritual being.[10] A change in name therefore constitutes a change in identity, so it is little wonder that a new name is often bestowed upon a youth during his rite of passage. This new name is commonly regarded as sacred, and uninitiated persons are often not allowed to use it.[11]

By using any or all of these techniques—seclusion, hazing, tests of fortitude, genital operations or other forms of scarification, the changing of names—an initiation ritual during the transition phase redefines the physical, social, and spiritual existence of its participants. When the designated period of transition is over, the young men are ready to be initiated formally into their society as adult males. This, in van Gennep's terminology, is the "incorporation phase" of a rite of passage. It is a time of ceremonial splendor, often marked by new clothes, fancy ornamentation, and a spirit of celebration. The boys are now officially men.

Even in this final ceremony, the theme of death and rebirth is paramount. The past is ritualistically laid to rest, for the insecurities of childhood must be banished forever. The graduates of the Poro Bush School, for instance, now run around their native villages pretending not to recognize their families, since they are said to have been reborn as new and different people.[12] The past of the Thonga youths is destroyed by ceremonially burying the remains of their foreskins. The sheds and the paraphernalia used during the earlier stages of a Thonga initiation must also be burned: "All the filth and ignorance of childhood is burnt in this great conflagration." The young men must run away from the fire without looking backwards; if they do look back, if they carry their past with them, "their eyes would be pierced, and they would be blind forever." The initiands are then led into a pool where they bathe and cut their hair, all the while shouting "I am a man." They anoint themselves with ochre, put on new clothing, and listen to a speech by the father of the circumcision: "You are no longer uncircumcised! Try now to behave like men."[13]

Judging by the amount of ritualistic activity in primitive cultures, the transition from boyhood to manhood ranks as one of life's most significant events; it is paralleled only by birth, marriage, and death. But how should we interpret these initiation rites? What do the rituals *mean*?

Mircea Eliade, for one, sees the process of male initiation in its broadest possible context:

Initiation represents one of the most significant spiritual phenomena in the history of humanity. It is an act that involves not only the religious life of the individual, in the modern meaning of the word 'religion'; it involves his *entire* life. It is through initiation that, in primitive and archaic societies, man becomes what he is and what he should be—a being open to the life of the spirit, hence one who participates in the culture into which he was born. For as we shall soon see, *the puberty initiation represents above all the revelation of the sacred—and, for the primitive world, the sacred means not only everything that we now understand by religion, but also the whole body of the*

tribe's mythological and cultural traditions. **In a great many cases puberty rites, in one way or another, imply the revelation of sexuality—but, for the entire premodern world, sexuality too participates in the sacred. In short, through initiation, the candidate passes beyond the natural mode—the mode of the child—and gains access to the cultural mode; that is, he is introduced to spiritual values.**[14]

This is lofty and sweeping language, but the view espoused by Eliade is probably quite close to that which a primitive himself might offer. The purpose of an initiation, in the minds of both Eliade and the primitives, is to enable the initiand to "attain the status of human beings."[15]

There are several other theorists, however, who prefer to look for more scientific explanations that are not likely to be pronounced by the primitives themselves. Most social scientists agree that the structure of the male rite of passage constitutes a recognizable, cross-cultural pattern, but they focus on different elements of that pattern to buttress their individual theories. Why, they ask, do the patterns appear as they do? What can traditional initiations actually tell us about the biological, psychological, or sociological nature of the male *homo sapiens*?

Lionel Tiger chooses to focus his attention upon the all-male groups fostered by initiations, and he sees these groups as genetically based: "male bonding as a biological propensity . . . is the very cause of the formation of those various male groups observable around us." Male bonding, he argues, is "a biologically transmitted and socially learned component of the male life cycle."[16] The need to establish all-male groups—and to initiate young males into these groups—apparently stems from the evolution of men as hunters:

> **Specialization for hunting . . . favored those "genetic packages" which arranged matters so that males hunted co-operatively in groups while females engaged in maternal and some gathering activity. Not only were there organic changes in perception, brain size, posture, hand formation, locomotion, etc., but there were also social structural changes. The male-female link for reproductive purposes and the female-offspring link for nutritive and socialization purposes became "programed" into the life-cycles of the creatures. It is suggested here that the male-male link for hunting purposes also became "programed."**[17]

Tiger's argument is economic and materialistic, since the evolution of hunting is itself rooted in ecological realities.[18] Other thinkers, however, choose to focus their attention on personal rather than evolutionary considerations, and their interpretations of initiations are consequently psychogenic rather than biogenic.

There are two competing psychological views of the male rite of passage, both firmly rooted in the Freudian tradition. According to one of these theories,[19] the hazing and genital mutilations so common during initiation rituals are dramatizations of the Oedipal rivalry between fathers and sons. Circumcision, for instance, can be seen as a punishment inflicted by the fathers to give meaning to the threat of castration if the sons continue to desire their mothers. The punishment occurs at a time when the sons are about to reach physical maturity and might conceivably challenge the fathers for both authority and sexual privilege. Since such a revolt would be dangerous and socially disruptive, the incipient rebellion of adolescent males, fueled by the fires of Oedipal competition with their fathers, must be squashed. The function of initiation rites, in this view, is to re-affirm the authority of the older generation.[20]

An alternate psychological theory attributes these initiation rites to a male envy of female sexual organs and female functions.[21] Through circumcision, subincision, or superincision, men try to imitate the female sexual apparatus. The blood-letting which results from these genital operations can be seen as a simulation of menstruation. Among the Kwoma of New Guinea, raised scars are created on the youth's chest immediately above each nipple, imitating female breasts.[22] The function of the secrecy of initiation rites, in this context, is not merely an assertion of male exclusiveness and superiority—it is also to hide the fact that the desired goals are not actually achieved.

Why would males want so desperately to imitate females? The adult men, according to this theory, are trying to reclaim the boys as their own. Literally, they steal the boys from their mothers; men replace the women as the creators of life. Initiation rites are intended to give "the impression that the boy was reborn by the father, and therefore owes his life to the father."[23] In the Poro bush society, the youths are said to be swallowed by the grandmaster and then reborn—an obvious male simulation of birth.[24]

The difference between these two psychogenic hypotheses, both derived from Freudian principles, suggests an interesting question: Whom are the men defining themselves *against,* the women or the uninitiated boys? Is the rite of passage to be considered a proof of age or a proof of gender?

Of course it must be a proof of both, for the adult male role being affirmed is simultaneously "adult" and "male." Both women and boys are always excluded during at least part of the rituals,[25] although the primary emphasis will shift from culture to culture; some groups focus more upon opposition to women, others upon opposition to boys.[26] And the two Freudian theories likewise choose to concentrate on a primary antagonism: the first sees a conflict between generations, with the men preempting the rebellion of the growing boys, while the second sees more of a gender-related conflict, with the men trying to usurp the biological power of women.

British structural-functionalists eschew any of these psychogenic theories in favor of a more sociogenic interpretation. The primary function of male rites of passage, they claim, is to place the youths within the framework of adult society. The young men are taught their social obligations and then required to assume them.[27] The genital operations, hazing, and other forms of abuse to which the youths are commonly subjected create a sense of personal vulnerability and a consequent dependence upon the larger group. The initiation rite is thus seen as a crucial stage in the process of socialization.

In this view, the suppression of individual freedom during the rituals is critical, for the novitiates must learn to pay full respect to tribal tradition:

In ordinary life he can obey or disobey; at initiation he must submit. He is taken in hand by his elders, treated by them as an object, carried about, gripped in strong arms, and forced to undergo an operation from which he shrinks. His submission is taken for granted, and it would be strange if at this time he did not become aware of the power of traditional procedure.[28]

The prior dependence upon the nuclear family must be entirely negated, for the initiand must be reduced to the state of vulnerability which will eventually lead to submission:

Almost any child in any culture—and most adults, too—would feel abandoned, rejected, vulnerable, and emotionally hurt under these

circumstances. There is no more effective way to deflect a child's emotional dependence away from his nuclear family than to traumatize him and at the same time forbid him to turn to the well-established security and comfort of his family for protection.[29]

A variation of this approach is offered by the symbolic interactionists, who claim the function of an initiation is to stabilize the male sex role by transmitting, through the dramatic manipulation of symbols, the "specific clusters of social meanings" required for a complete identification with the adult male group.[30] Initiations, in this view, occur primarily where men organize cooperative activities which exclude women. Since the loyalty of all grown males is critical in these societies, it is essential that all boys participate in a rite of passage:

> Initiation ceremonies are viewed as mechanisms for maintaining the consensus of the males. If the boys did not undergo initiation or if some were allowed to avoid it, the male definition of the situation might be distorted or weakened. It is for this reason that initiation is required of all boys in a community. The ceremony insures conformity by involving the candidate in an intense co-operation with men in the symbolic process.[31]

Whereas the psychogenic interpretations paid special attention to the meanings of the particular symbols used in the rituals, the symbolic interactionists point only to the functions that those symbols serve in maintaining group loyalties:

> The rituals themselves only remind him of what it means to be a man in his society; in themselves they contain no meaning. In this view circumcision is not different in kind from a gift, a new name, a dance, etc. It differs in degree only insofar as its acquisition has a more dramatic and emotional context.[32]

In other words, the medium is the message. In order that the actors might learn to play out their roles, the whole stage is set for dramatic effect:

> [T]he social meaning of male solidarity must be dramatized in a memorable way and the candidate must participate intensely in the presentation. Furthermore, the rest of the community must be alerted to his new status so they can respond appropriately. What could be more impressive to both the youth and the community than

to be publicly subincised or to be the center of attention of a group of village men intent upon beating him severely?[33]

———

So which theory is correct? Are initiations to be explained in biological, psychological, sociological, or spiritual terms? Are the adult males suppressing the rebellious youths, or are they emulating the role of nurturing females? Do the symbols mean anything in and of themselves, or are they used only to enhance the feeling of male solidarity? Is the individual being socialized into society, or is he being released into the realm of his own spiritual existence?

I suspect that each of these theories encapsulates some kernel of truth,[34] and they might even help us to understand some of the contemporary imitations of initiations we are about to witness. But I must confess at this point that I am not directly concerned with the validity of the separate theories; instead, I am more interested in how to account for our modern fascination with male rites of passage. Why do we look at these primitive procedures with that peculiar mixture of fright and envy? And why do we try, whether consciously or not, to emulate them?

With this end in mind, I think the most fruitful approach centers on the idea of initiation-as-drama. The symbolic interactionists likewise focus upon drama, but they are concerned only with its social functions;[35] I wish to look also at the dramatic impact upon the individual. At a time in history when male insecurity is rampant, formal rites of passage seem to offer dramatic definitions of manhood that are otherwise lacking. They deal with an issue as pressing for us today as it was for the primitives: How does a boy in any culture undergo the transformation from the weakness and vulnerability of childhood to the strength and self-confidence required of manhood? *The primary role of an initiation is to dramatize this change, and thereby to facilitate it. A rite of passage places a difficult problem of personal growth into a social context; it gives a public dimension to private problems; it calls upon the combined force of a culture and all its traditions to help the individual get through this time of crisis.*[36]

The salient feature of primitive initiations, and the reason they continue to hold such appeal, is simply this: *They work.* An individual who goes through an initiation comes out the other side with a heightened feeling of self-worth, for his manly status has been affirmed both to himself and to the group. His individual confirmation goes hand-in-hand with social recognition: he sees himself as a man, the group treats him as a man, and this public support reinforces a personal sense of his own manliness. As obvious as this might seem, it is no small matter. Whatever conjectural explanations we might entertain, this, at the most fundamental level, is what initiations are all about. It is this pragmatic perspective, I suggest, that accounts for our modern fascination with primitive initiations. However bizarre, they seem to accomplish the difficult but all-important task of making a boy into a man.

The function of hazing, in this context, is to provide a threat of potential failure while simultaneously insisting that the novitiate must actually succeed. If and when the youth emerges in the end, alive and intact, he gains a profound appreciation for his own fortitude, a feeling which is enhanced by the honors bestowed upon him. The entire process is both intensely personal and genuinely social; society has in fact helped the individual to become the man he wants to be.

The basic requirement, that primitive initiations must first and foremost "succeed," is not often emphasized in the anthropological accounts, but it is tacitly assumed. In the extensive ethnographic literature produced within the last century there are virtually no first-hand reports of individuals who have actually failed the initiation ritual required by their society. Sometimes there are deaths due to infection from genital operations, but rarely (if ever) does anyone who lives through the ordeals not emerge with the appropriate status of manhood. Failure is reduced to the realm of mythology. There are always dire tales of what happens to the boys who didn't follow the rules or didn't make the grade, but the tales generally refer to prior times. A Thonga youth "is frightened into submission by being told that in former times boys who had tried to escape or who revealed the secrets to women or to the uninitiated were hanged and their bodies burnt to ashes."[37] The boys entering the Poro Bush Society are shown a tray of fingers and toes that were supposedly cut off from errant members of a previous initiation.[38] Under the specter of stories such as these, the novices have no choice but to comply—and succeed.

Perhaps the greatest deterrent to failure—even greater than the fear tactics used by the Poro and Thonga— is the sheer force of ridicule:

The older a boy gets the more acute does his position become. . . ; he is always liable to be the subject of jokes so long as he remains unincised. A person on whom the operation has not been performed

is said by a jesting metaphor to be *mata seni*, blind-eyed, and with this epithet he is apt to be taunted, openly by the boys of his own age, and covertly by the girls. If he passes by a group of these and hears their laughter directed at him, then he guesses the matter of their amusement and feels much ashamed.

The great reason that natives give for compliance with the custom is the *ruma*, the notoriety that is entailed by its omission. One cannot judge of the force of this directly as far as the adult males of the island are concerned, for every one of them has been superincised. But the Matlov mission teacher is said not to have had the operation performed upon him, and in consequence is the subject of sly remarks between the natives—in his absence. Children have actually said to his children in moments of anger, "Go and incise your father"; the thought of such abuse being possibly applied to himself would be enough to upset the equilibrium of any Tikopia.[39]

In homogeneous primitive cultures, it is unthinkable *not* to go through the initiation procedure. There are simply no alternatives, for there is no place in society for an uninitiated male. There exist no such creatures.[40] The expectation of manhood is so strong that it must become the reality. Individual effort is assured through the overpowering weight of social demands. And so, with the aid of the appropriate initiation rituals, the boys are *forced* to turn into men. Manhood becomes a basic fact of life, almost as inescapable as birth or death.

CHAPTER 2

The Uninitiated

But what about us? What happens in a complex, heterogeneous society without a commonly accepted and well defined rite of passage that turns all of its boys, by definition, into men?

The need for personal validation does not necessarily disappear with the demise of structured and obligatory initiations. Unless a youth can find an alternate means of repudiating the weakness and dependency of childhood, he condemns himself to an indefinite state of insecurity; he is likely to experience the normal, everyday uncertainties of adult life as particularly problematic, for he can easily interpret them as threats to his masculinity. Without the aid of a formalized rite of passage, it is harder for a youth to be sure that he has actually *changed* from one state to another. His transition into manhood becomes more difficult—and it generally takes a longer period of time. In the absence of assumed ritual, the delineation between boyhood and manhood becomes obscured.

This is the situation we live with today. The concept of "adolescence"—a prolonged period of development between childhood and adulthood—dates back only a century or two.[1] The adolescent male has physically attained the capability for adult male labor, but he is not yet ready to assume the roles and responsibilities of manhood. For a period of five or ten years, he is a man who is not yet a man. In primitive society he would be considered an uninitiated male, but such a status, for a primitive, could not be maintained for any significant length of time. It simply could not be endured; the social sanction of ridicule would be too great, forcing the youth to become initiated. As Margaret Mead has observed, there is little room in the primitive world for "the unplaced person who has yet come to no terms with his society."[2]

But today we seem to have made room for these "unplaced" youths. According to some observers, adolescence in contemporary society often lasts for more than a decade—perhaps even for a lifetime. In his popularized book *The Peter Pan Syndrome,* Dan Kiley pays special attention to men who refuse to grow up. Peter Pan himself serves as the archetype for such fellows: "No one is going to catch me, lady, and make me a man. I want always to be a little boy and to have fun."[3] According to Kiley, Peter Pan was trapped in an eternal void between boyhood and manhood:

Peter Pan was a very sad young man. His life was filled with contradictions, conflicts, and confusion. His world was hostile and unrelenting. For all his gaiety, he was a deeply troubled boy living in an even more troubling time. He was caught in the abyss between the man he didn't want to become and the boy he could no longer be.[4]

And this, he claims, is the state of countless young males in contemporary America. Men who refuse to assume the responsibilities of adulthood become anxious and lonely beneath their fun-loving façades. Consumed by childish narcissism and troubled by sex-role conflict, they condemn themselves to the Never-Never Land of perpetual adolescence.

A similar but more convincing picture is painted by Barbara Ehrenreich, who chronicles the recent escape of men from the traditional role of the family breadwinner. Both the Playboy revolt and the male liberation movement, she claims, give men permission to spend their money by themselves and for themselves; their earnings are claimed as their own exclusive domain, not to be shared with dependent women and children. Contemporary images of masculinity encourage grown men to remain emotionally unattached and free of any financial obligations, much as they are during adolescence. The emotional task of adolescence (individuation) and the economic function of adolescence (to consume) are buttressed by ideology and cemented into permanent patterns of adult male behavior.[5]

In part, the creation and extension of a developmental period called "adolescence" is a reflection of a casual motif in modern social structures. Just as class and caste distinctions have been blurred in pluralistic American culture, so too have the distinctions been blurred between the developmental stages of a person's life. Of course, the distinctions still exist—there are still significant differences between the rich and the poor, between men and boys—but the delineations between these separate categories are not as clear as they once were. Without titles of nobility or universally accepted proofs of manhood, a great chasm has been created between the extremities of social status. With respect to class structure, that chasm has been filled by the amorphous middle class; with respect to an individual's development from childhood to maturity, the chasm has been filled by a loosely defined adolescence that can appear to have no end.

This casual motif is further evidenced by the decline of ritual and ceremony in a secularized world. Formalized definitions of transition such as graduations or religious confirmations play a relatively minor role in our social life. Unlike primitive rites of passage, they are not consuming events that can alter the everyday functioning of the entire society for months or even years on end. Witness, for example, a typical recollection of a bar mitzvah:

Being Jewish I was naturally bar mitzvahed, so that was my ritual of manhood—but it didn't really have any significance to me. Though we all gave it lip service, it wasn't really part of my life. After I went through my bar mitzvah, my status in the community didn't particularly change. I still had to go back to school and do everything that was going on before. Nothing happened except I got some presents and some fountain pens and things like that and people made a big fuss over me. My approach was only that I wouldn't fail my family or embarrass them when I went through the ceremony. (Ed Lubin)

Ed Lubin's experience, like that of most young men I interviewed who had gone through a bar mitzvah or confirmation, was decidedly lacking in some of the critical components of a traditional rite of passage. There was no separation from family, no transitional hazing; the preparation for the ceremony consisted only of some classes after school. A bar mitzvah contains only one of the three phases of a classical initiation: incorporation. And even that is incomplete, for the society into which the individual is incorporated is limited in scope. The day after a youth is bar mitzvahed or confirmed he still has to do his homework for school, just like all the other boys his age. His period of adolescence is really just beginning.[6]

The function of ritual is supposedly to imbue an event with meaning; in a modern context, ritual seems to trivialize an event instead. Unlike primitive youths, many boys today actually ridicule these alleged rites of passage. As Solon Kimball has observed, "Perfunctory ritual may be pleasant but also meaningless."[7] And yet, as Kimball also states,

There is no evidence that a secularized urban world has lessened the need for ritualized expression of an individual's transition from one status to another. . . . An increasing number of individuals are forced to accomplish their transition alone and with private symbols.[8]

The casual motif in modern society may eliminate the *dramatizations* of the passage from boyhood to manhood, but it does not necessarily eliminate the felt need of the individual to undergo that transition.

The absence of meaningful drama is made possible in part because we have so many alternate instruments of socialization: not only school, but also television and the printed media. These media teach us, either explicitly or implicitly, how we are expected to behave, but rarely do they offer significant personal instruction; they provide images, and therefore expectations, with no means of fulfillment other than the consumption of commodities. The achievement of media manhood entails no sacrifice, no struggle, no hazing; instead, it rewards our most childish indulgences. The boy does not have to die before being reborn as a man—he has only to purchase a different set of products.

Another reason for the decline in formalized initiations is the marked change in our contemporary notions of gender. Male rites of passage are more likely to be practiced in cultures with an extreme and pervasive social distinction, along with a marked differentiation of economic function, between men and women. But in our society, economic and even military activities have become coeducational. Social status is now less polarized according to gender—and so too is sexuality itself. With the traditional notions of the masculine role being called into question, the traditional images of manhood are naturally being challenged. This revolution in values is bound to have a considerable effect upon the initiation process. How can a youth be initiated into manhood when he has no clear concept of what manhood entails?

In primitive societies the image of manhood is clear: men are hunters and warriors, providers and protectors. But the primitive images have been dimmed by the process of modernization. First men turned from chasing wild game to tending tame animals or raising crops; then, with the full thrust of technological advancement over the last century or two, most men moved indoors to factories, offices, or stores. Our modern economic endeavor is the final evolution of the hunt—we still go out to "make a killing" in business—but with the transformation of technology, the traditional economic distinctions between gender become obsolete. A woman, now capable of a man's work, is a hunter too.

The image of man-the-protector, like that of man-the-provider, has also been seriously eroded. Historically, war has been seen as the primal archetype for masculine activity, the supreme example of what men can do better than women. War created the ultimate challenge for the manly virtues of physical prowess, strength, and courage. But today the viability of these traditional virtues is questionable, and the idea that the battlefield provides an appropriate arena for initiations cannot be logically sustained. Modern warfare—even in the "good war," World War II—is exceedingly impersonal, and this impersonal style of warfare fails to fulfill the most fundamental function of an initiation ritual: to provide a structured path towards the achievement of manhood. Since there are no built-in programs that ensure success for those with the talent and the will to succeed, modern warfare can break a man's will as readily as it can strengthen it. In more primitive forms of warfare, in single, man-to-man combat, a warrior was encouraged to develop his strength, power, and courage for good and practical reasons—these virtues were directly correlated with his prospects for survival and victory. Now, the relationship between manly virtue and success is indirect, almost random. Survival depends less on personal ability than on politics or fate. Artillery fired from a distant enemy might or might not blow a soldier to pieces, regardless of his courage or cowardice, his strength or weakness. A warhead on a computerized missile might or might not destroy a man and his family and his entire city, regardless of whether the fellow ever had any aspirations to prove himself as a warrior.

We modern-day males often feel uncomfortable with this loss of our traditional roles. Haunted by archaic images of manhood which are no longer practical or imminent in our daily affairs, we easily succumb to a poorly defined but insidious malaise, a vague sort of questioning of our own masculinity. If we are no longer hunters or warriors, then in what sense are we really "men"? By abandoning our primitive roots, we are not as strong and wild and real as we once were. As Andrew Kopkind observes, "we have sold out to civilization, to the comforts and conveniences of the air-conditioned vivarium." We are "guilty about culture, hungry for the raw but addicted to the cooked."9 The nostalgia for our primitive origins carries a special weight for males, since many of the commonly accepted masculine virtues are rooted in a primitive model. A man in any culture is supposed to be strong, tough, adept, and courageous; clearly that was true of primitive hunters and warriors, but is it true of us? Could a modern-day man, pampered by his civilized trappings, ever hope to make it in the rough, cruel world of the jungle?

The special appeal of the jungle, with its accompanying image of man as a "noble savage," is evidenced in much of our popular entertainment. In *Greystoke* the jungle world of Tarzan and the apes is perceived as somehow more real than the refined world of the English gentry. In *The Emerald Forest* the romanticized lifestyle of primitive hunters is perceived as morally superior to the greed and decadence of advanced civilization. Our Western movies, which in the early days extolled the virtues of the town marshal and the schoolmarm and the law-abiding settlers as they tamed the frontier, now glorify the wild man instead. In *First Blood,* a modern-day Western *par excellence,* civilization is portrayed as corrupt and complacent, self-serving and self-satisfied. Once out in the woods and out of their element, two hundred town boys are no match for Rambo, a lone, barechested savage who learned the art of survival back in the real jungles of Vietnam. *Iceman, Countryman, Walkabout, The Gods Must be Crazy,* and even *Crocodile Dundee*—the list goes on and on. The modern glorification of savage power and primitive survival has become a culturally significant obsession.

There is some sense, then, that we modern-day men are not where we really want to be; worse yet, we are not *who* we really want to be, and that's where the guilt comes in. A *real* man—a man like the ones in the cigarette ads, for instance—ought to live in the great outdoors. He ought to feel the wind against his hardened skin; he ought to hunt and fish; he ought to provide for his family from Nature's bounty and protect them from Nature's dangers. But can he really do all this within the context of his technological lifestyle? Can he possibly live up to the primitive imagery that still helps to determine his sense of self-worth? Probably not, but at least he can try—he can cut wood with a chain saw for the fireplace in his suburban home; he can roast red meat on his barbeque; he can lift weights in a gym to develop the muscles that once came naturally through his work.

And he can also, in the interests of affirming his manhood, seek to reconstruct some semblance of a primitive initiation ritual. In fact, such facsimiles do exist within contemporary society, and they borrow many of the techniques used in the classical rites of passage. Fraternity rushes and boot camp, as we shall soon see, embody the same death/rebirth theme which serves as the basic structure for primitive initiations. Such structured rituals, however, have become less common over the last couple of decades, for we do not have a clear consensus that they are appropriate to a modern and democratic society. The values once affirmed by these traditional initiations are no longer universally accepted. How do we react today, for instance, to this first-hand, real-life description of a typical boot camp experience?

The drill sergeant, a dwarfed red-faced lifer from Kentucky, would mount a platform, thrust out his bony chest like a chicken, and call out the drill in a kind of high-pitched scream as though the words were caught in the back of this throat.

"Think of your life as one long push-up," he yelled to the men lying at his feet, breathing dirt.

He liked to pick on the overweight trainees. "Get your ass off the ground, fatso!"

If a guy was too slow, he'd order the corporal to step on his hand.

The Army seemed to have its own peculiar laws of logic. Halfway through the first long march, the sergeant said it looked like rain and ordered the company to trot a mile back to the barracks to get raincoats. When they got back, he declared with a grin that it didn't look like rain after all; the slickers had to be returned. Three panting

privates made the round trip a third time because they had forgotten the elastic bands for their helmet covers. When one of them later dropped in the line from exhaustion, the men were ordered to walk over him until he dragged himself up out of desperation.[10]

Most modern readers, I suspect, will be somewhat disdainful of this kind of behavior. It seems crude, even primitive—a little like the firebranding initiations of the Busama youths in New Guinea. Our humanitarian sensibilities are offended by the mindless inanities of boot camp. When a single marine recruit was inadvertently killed while being hazed a few years ago, there was a huge national outpouring of sympathy which triggered a movement to reform and liberalize military training. And yet, as we saw by Howard R.'s envy of the Busama initiations (and as we see, too, by the popularity of movies such as *An Officer and a Gentleman*), traditional rites of passage, however inane and sadistic, still hold a definite fascination and appeal, for they seem to provide straightforward solutions to complex and difficult problems. They could make us into men, and there's certainly an attraction in that. On some level we maintain a yearning for the old forms and the old values, as crude as they may be. Our humanitarian sensibilities and our primitive inclinations, apparently contradictory, somehow manage to coexist within us. We are at cross purposes with ourselves.

So contemporary society seems to give us differing and conflicting definitions of what manhood is and how it might be achieved. One definition might require us to do a hundred pushups; another might require us to do the dishes instead. Legally, a boy turns into a man at sixteen when he can drive, at seventeen when he can join the military, at eighteen when he can vote, or at twenty-one when he can drink. In terms of social status, a boy might turn into a man when he holds down a well-paying job, when he moves away from home, or perhaps when he graduates from high school or college. Physiologically, a boy turns into a man when he shaves and his voice changes—or some might argue it's when he can hold his beer.

Traditional, homogeneous societies have precise definitions of manhood upon which everybody agrees; in each culture there is a commonly accepted age at which a youth is expected to undergo the transition and a set of common rituals which lead to an expected outcome. Clearly, we are more at a loss today. With no common road into manhood, and without even a commonly accepted definition of what manhood entails, we cast about fitfully for self-styled facsimiles of initiations in order to express and affirm our status as men. Some of our attempts to prove our manliness bear striking resemblances to formal, primitive initiations; other attempts turn out to be nothing more than personalized experiences which we force ourselves to endure in lieu of well-defined rituals. But whether our experiences are formal or informal, most of us seem to share a need for some sort of proof that we are in fact the men we want to be. Perhaps we feel there is more to prove now that the time-honored methods of proof are not so obvious.

Our quest after manhood might be difficult, our techniques might be devious, success might be tenuous—but the task seems compelling, so we do it. Consciously or unconsciously, we attempt to simulate some semblance of a rite of passage. We construct our own challenges; we create our own rituals. Our choices are many: join the army, compete in sports, get a job, graduate from college, climb mountains, pledge fraternities, screw girls, get drunk with the guys. In the true spirit of American pluralism, the manner of our initiation becomes a matter of personal taste. The paths are many and varied, with each individual choosing his own preferred route. Following in our separate ways, we strive after a catch-as-catch-can image of manhood through a patchwork of ad-hoc initiations.

In the pages that follow we will meet all sorts of American males who have tried to master their coming-of-age in diverse and fascinating ways. But where do their freestyle initiations lead in the end? Do they seem to *work*? Are the boys, according to their own separate definitions, successfully turned into men by their experiences?

PART II: PERSONAL ENCOUNTERS

CHAPTER 3

Reasonable Facsimiles

The formalized male initiation, although certainly on the wane, is not altogether a thing of the past; some semblance of a primitive rite of passage is still available to select groups of youths, at least under specified circumstances. The rituals might be adapted to a modern context, but the underlying structures can occasionally be fashioned in the traditional mold. Witness, for instance, the following true tales of three American youths whose coming-of-age was marked by well-defined processes of initiation.

Will Bell, an eighteen-year-old California surfer, had no particular taste for war, but he happened to be drafted to fight in Vietnam. Whether he wanted to go or not, the army offered Will some sense that it was time to assume his manly responsibilities:

Initially, when I first got drafted into the service, I had this feeling that this is what I do to grow up. I was doing what my father had

done, what my grandfather had done. Somewhere out there they're looking down at me and saying, "Okay, now it's your turn." So I felt when I was done with this thing I would be an adult white male American.

Will's initiation into the military immediately assumed a classical form. He was removed from familiar surroundings, placed with a group of his peers, and ceremonially deprived of all vestiges of his prior identity:

You go through this real heavy anonymity orientation. You begin by following a yellow line through this building, six or seven hours of standing in line for tests and shots. They do a whole physical trip on your body that's real shocking. Right from the first, it's: "Take off your clothes. Here's your folder. Stand right behind that other naked guy." Then you spend the whole day walking through this building naked. Eventually they get around to cutting your hair and giving you clothes, the same color clothes, everything the same.

Then you go off to Fort Ord and it's more processing there, so the first few days of the service are really grueling: You don't get any sleep, you hardly eat, you're always being asked all these questions. They try and plug into you right away that you are all the same and that you will conform to this new system. And uniformity is the code of the system.

The death of the boy was signified by the hair cut and the loss of one's personal clothes; the boys, quite literally, had to be stripped of their personal past. This, of course, is an important feature of the separation phase of the initiation process, and the separation in this case was finalized by taking Will so far away from the comfort and security of familiar and familial surroundings that a retreat towards home became unthinkable:

For basic training I was sent to Fort Knox, Kentucky. That was a real test. When I got to Fort Knox, that's when I realized that this is really happening. I'm thousands of miles from home, not just a few hours' drive. To get home to California would be impossible for me. For approximately twenty-four hours it really gripped me: "I gotta get out of here. There's no way I'm going to be able to do this." I didn't like that feeling. I didn't like that thing right there saying, "I can't make it. I can't do it. I'm going to have to do something really outrageous to get out of this situation." But I couldn't walk away from it, I couldn't fight my way out of it, I couldn't lie my way out of it—which really left me no options. Finally I thought, "By golly, probably the best way to get through this thing is to get into it— really get into the workings of the military system and how it relates to you and you'll breeze right through: shine your shoes, cut your hair shorter, the whole thing." So I started getting into being a good soldier.

The structural mechanism for insuring Will's success was basically the same as that used in primitive rituals: forbidden to quit, he was forced to persevere. He had no choice but to conform.

The army was then free to impose its own stamp upon the blank slate it had created, and this was the beginning of the transition phase of the rite of passage. The birth of the new man was induced by the strenuous and apparently endless series of hazing rituals which are the essence of the boot camp experience:

It's non-stop. Every morning you're up and you have *no time* to get prepared for the day. You're expected to be clean-shaven and have a clean uniform and you don't have time to do all that stuff. Then you run as a group for about a mile to stand in line and have food. Between you and the door to the mess hall there's a set of horizontal bars. There's sixty of them, and you have to swing through there without touching the ground in order to eat. Three meals a day you have to do that. If you fall you have to start over again. For me it was grueling because my hands were real tender. It's a real hard thing to do for a lot of people.

When you finally get in you don't have enough time to eat. You're supposed to eat and get out of there. Then you go back and clean house and be out on the company road to begin the day's activities. Some of the activities are real killers. There's an obstacle course you have to go through. There's physical training, two hours of cal-isthenics every day. That seemed like it was endless. There's hand-to-hand combat, which is real funky because they had it in these big, huge sawdust pits. There's fifty pairs of GIs in there. You throw each other around and it's incredibly hot and you can never take your shirt off so there's all this sawdust inside your clothes sticking to the sweat. That was pretty miserable.

At any time during any part of the day you can be harassed for any number of things: not speaking up loud enough, not standing right, anything like that. Anytime you have a formation there's always an NCO that's cruising around and he'll find somebody who doesn't have his trousers bloused or his shoes tied or some God-awful thing, and he'll stand there and make him do push-ups.

What you work up to is this two-day bivouac at the end of basic training. That's the real killer. You get up early in the morning, carrying full gear—a poncho, half of a tent, your gun, ammunition, your belt, steel helmet—and off you go. You walk probably ten miles in formation, then you go off into the woods and set up your camp. You get with a buddy and set up your tent and dig a drainage ditch around it and arrange your sleeping bag and your chow kit for a big inspection format out in the woods. The guy comes by and says, "This is terrible and that's okay—but we're moving out!" By this time it's just starting to get dark. So you pack it all back up and get in formation and off you go. You go another five miles or so and set up camp in the dark and I think it was about midnight when we finally crawled into bed.

The next day you get up and break camp and hike some more, and that's when they make you qualify with a rifle. When that's done you move on to an infiltration course that's real strenuous. You have to crawl a real long ways on your stomach, then turn over and crawl on your back. The barbed wire is real close to the ground, and you're crawling under it. There's real machine gun fire above you. It's dark and there's tracers flying everywhere. They have enclosed bunkers in this area which have explosives in them, and they're going off randomly. So it's real intense. But when you finally get out of there, you're done. All that's left is to pass your PT test, and then that's it. You've made it through.

After completing boot camp Will went off to radio school, then to "jungle school," and finally he was sent into combat. It was in the morass of Vietnam that Will's initiation started to take on something of a modern slant:

When I got my orders to go to Vietnam I wasn't surprised. I expected some sort of special feeling, but it wasn't there. I didn't really think about it that much, about what I was getting ready to do. To me it was just another place to go. All I thought about was that I had only one more year in the service. I was halfway there. I was almost done. Then I could get on with my life.

In Vietnam I got orders to go to the First Cavalry Division. If you talk to veterans, you learn that it's one of the gnarliest units to be in: forward line, heavy-duty fighting. I was flown in a camouflage plane to a place called Quang Tri City in the northern portion of South Vietnam. You get put in the barracks and then all of a sudden you're expected to be on guard: "Okay, you guys are on guard from twelve to two AM." "Well, what do we do?" "You go out there and sit in that hole between the barracks and wait for something to happen." So there I was out in this hole in Vietnam with somebody I didn't know. It felt ridiculous.

The next evening there was a small attack and we answered it with aerial rocket artillery. I woke up and when I got outside there were several individuals out there sitting around, some of them smoking marijuana and some of them not, some of them drinking, some of them just *there,* watching. "What's going on? What are you guys doing?" "Oh, that's just a Huey shooting A.R.A." I thought, "Wow, so this is what it's all about." I was shocked by the casual attitude. I wasn't really afraid, but I was such a novice, such a know-nothing, that I really wanted to plug into what was going to keep me alive. If being casual and staying up late at night and smoking weed and watching the fireworks was going to keep me alive, then maybe that's what I should do. Or maybe I should dig my hole deeper. Whatever.

As time went on our division participated in a lot of history-making things. There was a Marine base at Khe Sanh that was under siege for four months; for a hundred and twenty days they were attacked every day, relentlessly. It got to the point where three planes would fly in and only one of them would make it out. So the First Air Cav was going to bail the Marines out of Khe Sanh. First there were lots of air strikes in the hills to thin the enemy out, then we waltzed right into Khe Sanh with trucks and jeeps, flew in with helicopters. The Marines left and we set up. For forty-eight hours there were no attacks. Then on Easter Sunday we got our first hot meal delivered that we had had in several weeks: turkey, gravy, potatoes and dressing, and even some green vegetables. That food was there for about ten minutes, ten people got served, and they attacked. The first round hit the chow line and just blew the food all over. Psychologically it was totally devastating. We were attacked endlessly after that. Here we were trapped, just like the Marines. We stayed there for about a week before finally pulling out.

After a couple of other maneuvers I started getting "short"—having less and less time to go before coming home. When you get below a hundred days left you're a "two-digit midget." For some reason you have more reason to be concerned about your health than you would if you had more time left. It becomes more critical, more crucial. Everything is oriented around going back home, going back to the world. That's what it's called, going "back to the world," because you're not in the world here in this hell.

The way I maintained, I always knew that in a certain period of time I'd be home. I wouldn't have to worry about other people trying to kill me. I wouldn't have to be ready to kill someone else all the time. I wouldn't be in a situation where everything was so important because it could be snatched away from me at any time.

The driving force behind Will Bell's experience in Vietnam was individual survival; no more, no less. Will, like most Vietnam veterans, did not seem to entertain any grand sense of national or moral purpose; his only object was to make it through in one piece and then to get on with the business of "my life." Insofar as there was any personal motivation to his role as a soldier, it was simply to put in his time, to endure hardship, in order to become "an adult white male American"—that is, to be a man among men.

The function of war in this context was not to subdue an anonymous enemy but rather to provide an opportunity for a classical male initiation. Implicitly, Will assumed that if he did manage to survive he would be better for the wear, a stronger person, an equal to his father and grandfather and all the other fellows who likewise had put in their time throughout the course of history. And in his particular case, that's in fact the way it worked. Not only did Will survive his tour of duty alive and intact, but he also emerged with a new self-assurance, a heightened sense of his own manhood:

I think the whole idea of being able to survive through danger has given me an appreciation for life that I wouldn't have otherwise. A lot of people just don't have that opportunity. When I got back from Vietnam and met up with old friends who had been in the service but who had not gone to Vietnam, they were still very frightened of life. They were still very uncertain that they were going to be able to survive, that they were going to be able to find a job and hold it. After having gone through Vietnam, I haven't worried since about anything. I've been very poor since then, I've been very opulent since then, and I've been unattached to both of those situations. I feel like I'm going to make it no matter what. No matter how bad circumstances get, I don't think I'll ever succumb. I think my spirit will endure all things and all trials. I don't think any trials will come my way that I can't handle. I'm going to be in there all the way.

At one point in Vietnam I was put in a situation where I had absolutely nothing going for me—and yet I endured. We had to pull out of this place during a big airlift. I had a lot of equipment that I was responsible for, generators and things like that. I got all my equipment loaded on the truck, and then I got all my personal stuff together and loaded it on a jeep and it was all driven away to where the convoy was assembled. Our last job was to destroy our hooches so they couldn't be used by the enemy. There were four of us who walked back to the area to do this. We had no helmets, no guns, just the clothes we had on. We destroyed the hooches, and simultaneously the convoy pulls out without us and it begins to rain and I discover that I have bleeding hemorrhoids. A total breakdown of positive circumstances—no weapons, no radio, no shelter, and an aggravating physical discomfort, to say the least—but I felt it would be okay. Somehow or other, there was this feeling there that it was going to work out. And it did. We just hung out until the other people realized we were missing and the next day they came back to get us. It was another mark to me that my head was in the right place, that hope has genuine power, that feeling can sometimes be stronger than fact. I don't know; maybe I was just lucky, maybe I just slid through. But I really feel strongly that it was because my attitude was good.

All in all, Vietnam was a real positive experience for me because of the intensity of it all. Everything is just magnified so much. It's probably the single most important lesson I've ever had in life. The whole experience was a fantastic initiation. Not being able to make my insurance payment on time, or having a car that's broke down, or the river is on the rise—I know I'm going to do just fine. I can handle all that, because I've handled a lot worse. In fact, I think I've handled *the* worst. I can't imagine any condition, any environment, that's worse than war.

This indeed is one of the major functions of a classical initiation: If you tackle the worst, then you know you can handle the rest. In the proximity of death, life becomes magnified. To taste death yet survive is the ultimate initiation; to meet such a challenge can be seen as the final realization of manhood.

So Will has now been initiated,[1] and his initiation followed the classical pattern—at least up to a point. The separation and transition phases were completed in due form, but Will never did receive a ceremonial incorporation back into the civilian world:

After you get back to the States you just walk out of this building and you're out of the army and there's a bunch of taxi-cabs there. That's it: "Here's your money. Thanks a lot. See you later." You take the cab from the base to the airport and the next thing you know, you're home.

When I got home I fell back into the same peer group. Only two or three of my friends went into the service, and when we got out it was all pretty much back to normal. Everybody just fell into the same pecking order that job or location dictates; I don't think anybody was treated any differently because they were in the war. When I went to leave my home town and go to L.A. and get a job, it seemed to matter a little bit, but I don't think it mattered any more than the fact that I did well on the math test or I was clean-cut and anxious to go to work.

There was no dramatic "before" and "after." I think *I* felt more strongly about it than anybody I encountered when I got back. I felt a significant change, but that wasn't reinforced by anybody else. I was pretty much alone in my experience. For several years I hardly met anybody that had even been to Vietnam; mostly what I heard was detailed stories about how people had avoided going into the service, or if they did go into the service, how they avoided going to Vietnam.

For Will and for all Vietnam vets, a meaningful "incorporation" was not a part of the package deal. If a soldier was lucky enough to survive, and even if he regarded his experience as some sort of initiation, he still returned home without much applause—and without even a significant

34

elevation in status. This, of course, is unlike traditional initiations, which invariably culminate with much pomp and circumstance. The celebration of manhood ensures its recognition; conversely, the absence of celebration opens the door to neglect, and therefore to doubt. When an alleged rite of passage is terminated without fanfare, it becomes harder for the individual to believe in what he has accomplished. This lack of social recognition did not seriously affect Will Bell, but, as we soon shall see, it does affect others. The complete process of initiation—separation, transition, and incorporation—cannot be truncated without cost, and the people who pay the price are the young men whose status has not been socially affirmed.

The lack of incorporation in this otherwise successful initiation is a preliminary indication of significant and sweeping problems with our modern adaptations of rites of passage. The initiation drama is not being fully enacted. There is something amiss in the relationship between the individual and the group, for the group is not validating individual experience. There is something wrong with the *context* in which our initiations occur. But more of this later. First, let us look at two other personal initiations which follow closely along traditional lines.

───

Ken B. always did well in school, and early success led to high expectations. His grandmother, the guiding light of the family, asked him incessantly: "What are you going to do with all this potential that you have?" Driven from within and without to succeed, Ken became president of his high school class and then went on to Harvard, where he collected A's routinely while hardly opening a book. He decided to enter medicine and breezed through the first two years of medical school without much of a challenge. But then the party stopped:

The initiation really started in earnest during the third year in medical school. As third year students we spent all our time in hospitals. We started playing at the real thing. We worked long hours doing "scut work," the dirty work that nobody wants to do: pushing patients to x-ray in their wheelchair, going around and drawing blood, starting IVs. The intensity of the whole thing jumped by a couple of quantum leaps. All of a sudden we were on the wards wearing white clothes. We were dressed as doctors. The patients

called us "doctor." But we didn't *know* anything, because the stuff that we learned in the first two years really was not particularly relevant to clinical decisions that affect peoples' lives.

In third year medical school you're really on the low end of the totem pole in the medical community. The more formal teachers were very demanding, putting you on the spot. The term for it was "pimping" you. You have a team, usually made up of an attending physician, a resident, an intern, and a couple of medical students. You'd meet together on attending rounds. Let's say somebody got admitted to the hospital the night before when you were on call. As a third year medical student, you were the one who was expected to present the case. You'd give the complete history: what exactly happened, and all the things that led up to this hospitalization. You'd go into past medical history, family history, social history, and give the report on your clinical exam and the laboratory findings. You'd make some kind of assessment of the diagnosis and some kind of idea of your plan of treatment.

That's the first part of the ritual. Then the attending physician grills you in a very formal manner: "Well, Doctor, you say that you think this patient has pneumonia, but the white blood count is only twelve thousand with a very modest shift. Will you explain this to me?" Or, "Now Doctor, isn't it true that these findings are also compatible with such-and-such a disease?" His questions would become more and more sophisticated to the point where you couldn't answer them anymore. As soon as he got you to where you were done, you had run out of understanding or knowledge, then he would go to the intern. The questions would then become more sophisticated, because the interns had had a couple of more years of experience. When he got to where the intern couldn't answer any more questions, then he'd go to the resident. Finally he'd find a point which the resident couldn't handle, and then he'd give his little presentation. That was the game as it was played. It was a confrontational style of teaching. They'd grill you, make you sweat, make you jump through hoops.

I always hated it. I can remember somebody asking me a question in this really pointed way, and I would just go into a freeze. I couldn't even answer questions that I knew, especially when they put "Doctor" on it. I don't know why they called us "Doctor," except maybe to get us used to it. It was clear that we weren't really physicians, that we just didn't know enough. Even the nurses, if they had any experience, were often more sophisticated in their understanding.

The similarities between medical school and a classical initiation are obvious.[2] The intended change in identity is induced, in part, by giving the novice a new name and new clothes which are easily identified with the role he is about to assume. His prior sense of a unique, individualized self is challenged by giving him a large dose of routine "scut work." He is humiliated in front of his elders; he is forced to give them respect before he can join their club. And of course he is ruthlessly hazed by the intellectual grilling administered by his superiors.

But that is not all. After medical school comes the internship, and the hazing here takes on a concrete, physical dimension:

The internship is a whole other level, another quantum leap. It's not an intellectual exercise anymore; you really do have the responsibility, and you really can make decisions. It's also the first time you get paid; before that you're paying to do it. That's a pretty major shift.

The first few months of internship were very, very stressful. There were a couple of guys in my training program who later got divorced; I'm pretty sure that the seeds of intense weirdness came during their internship, because it's very difficult to sustain any other kind of a life. The impulse, after you've been up all night and worked the next day, is to not do anything else except be grumpy to whoever's around you because you're so wasted.

I figured it out one time: I spent about a hundred hours a week at the hospital. You could reliably be there from seven in the morning until six in the evening every day, whether you're on call or not. Then you're on call about twice a week, from six at night to seven the next morning. You might not be awake all that time, but you're certainly not home relaxing. You're there at the hospital, and you're necessarily on edge. You get called a lot. On a busy service, you could be up several times in a night. Or sometimes you stay up all night, and then work all the next day.

Being tired was a big problem for most of the guys. From a physical point of view, the exhaustion was overwhelming. By the end of a thirty-six hour shift, if I hadn't gotten any sleep at all (which happened with some regularity), sometimes I had trouble staying awake driving home. There was a lot of discussion about how ridiculous it is to have somebody stay awake for thirty-six hours and then have them try to make a life-and-death decision. But then on the other side people would say, "This is a training program and you're being trained for a situation where you're going to have to be ready to go any old time, night or day." Guys talked about it in those terms, as a kind of hazing rite to toughen us up.

I was once talking to a guy from officer candidate school who was kept awake all night doing some menial, repetitive task as part of his training. The idea was that you would be out there in the fox hole without sleep for three days and then you'd have to make a decision which affects all your men. So they deprived him of sleep and then said: "Now decide, you sucker." They put him on the spot. That was his hazing.

Our hazing was a little different than that. For one thing, we had to do it over and over again. But the work we did all night was interesting and meaningful; it wasn't some stupid, repetitive task. The reason you were awake was you got four people admitted to the hospital that night, all of whom were sick enough to be hospitalized. So you had something there you had to think about. These people might be acutely ill. Right there in the middle of the night you'd have to formulate a coherent picture of what disease process was happening, evolving into some kind of treatment, and then you'd watch them either get better or not get better, based on what you did. Then the next morning you'd have to present the case and justify your actions to the residents and attending physicians.

There was so much going on that you didn't really have any trouble staying awake. But you could easily fall apart afterwards, because all your energy had been drained. This one friend of mine always seemed to have the sickest patients, and he was always the most worried about it. He was trying so hard to do a good job. Once during a period of a few weeks he had a couple of people die and he'd start home to try to see his wife and something would happen and he'd go back to the hospital. He was working there till nine or ten at night, even on nights when he wasn't on call. He finally had a day off, but he went over to the hospital and didn't get back till four in the afternoon. He and his wife went for a walk. This was the first time they had a chance to spend any time together for over a month. She was really upset. Finally they got their energies back together and they went home and they had a nice dinner. Then they were making love later on that night and the telephone rang and somebody told him that another one of his patients had just died.

A lot of the stuff that came down wasn't related to this particular patient or this particular disease. Sometimes it seemed like we were just being badgered, getting hazed, because the guys before us had just been through a hard internship and they wanted to make ours just as hard: "When I was an intern we had to go do all this stuff, so you guys have to do it too." Then after we had gone through the same type of hazing, they'd allow us to join their club.

Did this hazing work? Ken B., like Will Bell, was in fact able to emerge from a grueling rite of passage with a firm sense of his own capabilities. When all was said and done, he was ready to assume the roles and responsibilities for which he had been prepared:

When I went into my internship I was nervous that I might not be able to make it. I had a lot of self-doubt: "Can I really do this thing that I've set for myself to do?" You hear all these stories about how hard it is. The stories, as it turned out, were true. I started right off in the emergency room, and I had some nights there that were very difficult in terms of the volume of stuff I had to do, in terms of the tricky things I dealt with, in terms of not knowing whether I had done the right thing, in terms of getting negative feedback from the people who were watching my work. I remember coming home and being just frightened that I wasn't going to make it through. And there were some people that got fired and didn't make it. That was a clear and present danger, for sure. I thought about dropping out a few times, but by then I could see that the work was really important—or could be. At that point, if I dropped out, it would have been a backing away and a failure to meet a challenge.

Coming out of the internship, coming out the other side, I felt a lot better about myself. Having made it through to the end, I had a sense of victory. I never really doubted, after that, that I could do it. Of course you never have a lock on it. If you pick a path like medicine where the tasks are particularly difficult, there are going to be times when you can't do them. There were times as a resident when I felt sort of inadequate. I still have some tough times when I'm not totally sure of everything, but when I feel inadequate now, it's momentary. I feel bad about it for awhile, then I get over it. I don't have those pervasive self-doubts that I had before. After my internship I always knew, fundamentally, that I was doing okay. I had proved myself to myself.

I think that everybody at their core starts out with a lot of self-doubt. We think: "I really know me, and I know that deep inside I'm really a stinker. I'm not what I project." When I impressed somebody, I used to feel like I had tricked them. Actually, I was pretty good at it. I've faked my way through a lot of situations. I don't know why, but the internship really made a difference in that feeling. Somehow I don't feel like I'm faking people out anymore.

Of course there are a lot of other factors, but I see my internship as a turning point in my own confidence. I'm not exactly sure why my internship had such a profound effect on me. Thinking back on it, I can see that the stakes were high. I had to live up to my image of myself as a successful person. I had been on a career-oriented track since the time I could think. My family are professionals on both sides. If I had failed . . . I can't even imagine what would have happened to me if I had failed. Yet I think it's very important that it wasn't clear to me at the beginning of the internship that I would be able to make it. Success did not come automatically. It was something for me to overcome. That's what really made it a rite of transition: I didn't know that I could do it, I was scared that I couldn't, and I did it. By natural ability, plus the effort I put into it, and sacrifices I made along the way, I got through it. Boy, it's a piece of cake after that.

The power of Ken's initiation derives in large part from its classical features. During the most difficult phase of the internship, Ken was separated from familial comfort and support for days on end. The inevitable hazing could thus proceed free from outside influences which might have weakened his resolve and tempted him to quit. For Ken, as for primitive youths, quitting was not a viable alternative. The sheer force of social expection made failure unthinkable; he felt he *had* to bear with it and make it through, no matter how difficult the tasks might become.

And so he did. He made it through to the end, replacing self-doubt with self-confidence. And Ken B., unlike Will Bell, even had a successful incorporation component to his initiation. He was duly rewarded for his efforts by a permanent change in status: he can now "wear the white" indefinitely, and people will continue to call him "Doctor." The adult role he worked so hard to assume is continually affirmed by everybody around him.

And yet, although the basic structure of Ken's initiation is undoubtedly classical, the *context* is not. Primitive initiations, we recall, are intended to benefit all the young males of a tribe. Those who try must be induced to succeed—and everyone must get a chance to try. This is not the case with respect to a medical apprenticeship. Admission to medical school is extremely selective; only a small fraction of those who want to become doctors will ever get the chance to go through the necessary procedures. In this sense a medical apprenticeship more closely resembles an induction into an exclusive fraternal organization than a rite of passage into manhood. Initiations such as this can help some individuals achieve their desired status, for they help young men to assume their adult roles. But they do not, in themselves, fulfill all the social functions of a male rite of passage precisely because they remain so exclusive. This sort of initiation is limited in its effectiveness by the narrowness of its scope, since it is purposely intended to benefit only an elite handful of participants. One of the primary functions of a professional initiation such as Ken's is to choose who will succeed, not to ensure that all will succeed.

What does medical school accomplish, for instance, for all the pre-med students who will never get admitted? How will their failure affect their personal development and their sense of manhood? We will return to such questions later. For now, let us simply observe that there appears to be a certain incongruity between the success of selected individuals and the overall context in which that success is achieved, and that this problem of context might potentially have significant consequences for the contemporary male psyche.

▬▬▬▬▬

Today, a proper context in which our initiations might occur does not always appear automatically. Professional apprenticeships are not immediately accessible for all young males who wish to prove their mettle, while military initiations are not always deemed desirable or appropriate. So what do the rest of us do, the ones with no ready-made path into manhood? Many of us wind up with our own private versions of initiations—and sometimes even these can approximate the classical form:

When I got out of high school I said: "Enough already; I don't want to go live in a dorm yet. All these people are out there living a real life in the real world. I want to see what this is all about. I feel that I'm old enough that I can handle myself with these folks. I don't want to be cloistered right away for another four years." I felt like somebody had lifted a very warm and suffocating blanket from me when I got out of twelfth grade. It was recess, as far as I was concerned: "Hey, let's go out there and play with the big kids. I've had enough swimming lessons. Spare me the water wings. I'm ready to swim."

The problem was: I dove into the deep end. The water was swift-running in there, let me tell you. It wasn't safe and secure like the ivy-covered walls of academia. My father and my uncle, who works for Newmont Mining, apparently had done some conspiring. Because my grandfather had made them work in the mines when they were young, they thought their kids ought to do the same thing. They decided they would "make a man out of me" by sending me to work in the gold fields of Western Australia. This whole scheme was made more Machiavellian by the fact that my father and his brother married my mother and her sister, so there was double interest from the sidelines.

So I was sent down to my aunt and uncle, who live in Melbourne. I worked for my uncle for six months on his sheep ranch, perspiring side-by-side with authentic paid-by-the-sheep Australian sheep shearers. As the time neared for me to take the train out west, I began to hear more and more horror stories about life on the mineral exploration rigs, where my uncle (who was now sole arbiter of my fate) intended to send me. One night I said to him, "Why do we have to go through this ridiculous routine of shipping me on the train all the way 'Out West'? It's so hot out there. I hear tales of nothing but grief. I can get a job here in Melbourne in a mattress factory. Do we really have to go through with all this?" He just said something to the effect of: "Yes, goddamn it. You're all the way down here and we're going to show you a real slice of life. You going to bloody-well go 'Out West.'"

The day came and he took me to the train station in Melbourne and it was out across the Nullarbor Plains, nothing but scrub as far as the eye can see. After two full days and nights I arrived in Kalgoorlie, which is a small boom town in the middle of absolutely nowhere. Easily for five hundred miles in any direction there is nothing. The guys out there were the roughnecks of the roughnecks. If you picture American drilling gangs in Texas, and you take them back about twenty years and put them in the middle of nowhere with nothing to do and make them about half as literate as the Americans would be, that's the mob I was to be mixed in with.

I got off the train and was met by an older man who was Newmont's representative out there. At the time I still had a pony tail, the vestigial tail of '70s adolescence. The first words I heard, upon descending from the platform, were: "Thet's genna heffta kem auff." So I was promptly trotted off, suitcase in hand, to the nearest barber shop and was given what was called "Short Back and Sides." That's exactly what it looked like, some Marine Corps issue, about half an inch on top and whitewalls on the sides.

I reported for duty to the drilling contractor. My job was called "off-sider," which is to the driller what a caddie is to a golfer. Word had gotten out that the employing parent company was sending along some hoi polloi nephew to get a taste of "real work." Besides which, I was an American, so the stage was set. From the minute I walked in there, I was being sized up.

We would leave Kalgoorlie and strike out on the vast expanse of the Nullarbor Plains. We'd get to an exploration site, which might be a hundred and fifty miles from Kalgoorlie, and we'd set up camp for a couple of weeks. If we were on a "hot hole" we'd drill twenty-four hours a day, but usually we'd drill from about an hour after the sun came up until it went down.

The work was exceedingly unpleasant, to say the least. In your handling of the drilling pipe (and you're always running your hands up and down this pipe for one reason or another, guiding it on and guiding it off), you get covered with these little metal splinters the drillers called "bities." Your hands actually start to sparkle from having dozens of these imbedded in them; there's no time to remove them. You just have to live with it. You can't wear gloves, because you need the tactile feel of the pipe in your hand to be able to thread it properly. I tried to wear gloves, which provided boundless mirth for the drillers. This brief attempt brought forth choruses of "Bloddy poof," which is shortened Strine for "poofter," or homosexual.

At any rate, you're covered with these "bities" and listening all day to a very high RPM diesel engine that drives the hydraulic pumps. You're constantly scrambling from one task to the next: checking all the hydraulic levels, putting on new sections of pipe, that sort of thing. By ten in the morning it's at least a hundred degrees. At one point we were working ten miles from the highest recorded temperature on the face of the earth: Marble Bar, Australia, one hundred and thirty-eight degrees in the shade. So it gets pretty toasty. The working uniform was black cotton shorts, heavy boots with a steel toe, and a hard hat. That's all you could wear, it was so hot. If you don't drink about a quart of water every half hour, you get heat prostration. You're on salt tablets all day long. You're intensely thirsty all the time, no matter how much you drink.

The water comes from wells which are used for the sheep. We'd find the occasional water tank out in the bush, but these were originally kept filled by windmills; American windmills, in fact—the Chicago Aeromotor Company—a name I remember well, as we often had to fill our supply tanks from the well when there was no wind. As Junior Man/American/Pampered Nephew I had the dubious privilege of climbing the greasy ladders on these contraptions and turning the rusty blades by hand for the better part of an hour.

One day Mick Sprlyan, my driller, was drilling a vertical water hole as a favor to the guys in camp. We weren't getting paid for it, so he was in a hurry. I had to get to the top of the rig to fasten a pipe, and the quickest way to get there is to ride on top of the head motor while the driller is working the controls from below. Unfortunately, at the top of the mast there's a stop, like the top of an elevator shaft. If your driller isn't watching, you get crushed when the headmotor pushes you up against this stop. So I just wanted to take the ladder, like usual. Mick said, "Come on, Fred, you Yankee Wanker. Be a man." So I went zipping up the shaft. Thank God he was paying attention.

So there I am forty feet up in the air, hanging on to the rig with one hand and in the other hand I have this three-foot-long wrench which I use to add the new length of pipe. The wrench must weigh at least thirty pounds. I set the wrench on the pipe, and the driller is supposed to spin the motor in reverse to tighten it. Mick said, "You ready?" I said, "Yeah." So he spun the head motor. But I didn't want to get my fingers caught between the wrench and the rig, so I was holding the Stillson wrench pretty gingerly, and the wrench came undone. I'm working directly above Mick Sprlyan, and I'm watching this thirty pound wrench falling from forty feet in the air. It easily would have killed the guy, hard hat or no. I went into stage fright. Finally at the last second I yelled, "Look out!" Without even looking, he dove off to the side. It landed right where he had been standing. If I had killed this guy, all of his mates probably would have descended on me in kind. Shortly thereafter, I noticed this little patch of white hair, about the size of a dime, at the scalp.

One night Mick Sprlyan had to go to a town nearby called Wiluna: two stores and a pub. He left around three in the afternoon and asked me to police the area. To make work, he had me wipe down the drilling rig with diesel fuel. (Diesel fuel is everywhere in these camps: you wash your hands with it, you clean things with it, you power the vehicles with it.) He also had me check the hydraulic fluid and the diesel fuel levels in all the machinery, and to top them off if necessary. Well, I checked all the levels and on this one contraption I noticed that both the hydraulic fluid and diesel fuel were low. So I filled both tanks. When Mick got back he asked, "Did you check everything?"

I said, "Absolutely," knowing that they were spoiling for trouble. "But it's unusual. I sure needed a lot of hydraulic fluid."

Suspiciously, he asked, "What tank did you fill with what?"

I said, "The tank under the seat has gotta have the hydraulic fluid in it, the one on the side has gotta have the diesel, right?"

A look of utter horror came over his face. I had filled the hydraulic tank with diesel, and vice versa. Mick Sprlyan had a fierce temper. He stormed around the trailer for about ten minutes, cursing, calling me every conceivable name. I had to drain the whole damn thing. The diesel fuel was eating away at the rubber seals in the hydraulic system; the hydraulic fluid was gumming up the engine.

You can imagine the flak I caught for that. It got on the radio. Every morning we'd give the base in Kalgoorlie a situation report: "L-twenty-one hole, Newmont Mining, drilled four hundred twenty-two feet." So of course it had to go out that Fred Franger (that's slang for a condom) had gone and filled up the diesel tank with hydraulic fluid, and vice versa. That went out on the radio all over West Australia. Most of the guys thought it was a great joke, but it reflected badly on Mick Sprlyan. In fact, it so disgusted Mick that I was traded off to another driller. The white collar guys back at the base knew they couldn't fire me yet, so they tried to pawn me off on somebody who had a little more patience. This was one of those endless situations where, despite your sterling intentions, every attempt at pleasing your superiors ended in disaster. And, needless to say, they had raised the criteria for being a successful off-sider in my case.

Every day was like an eternity out there. You can't imagine how homesick you become, locked into what becomes a live/work setting with ten of these guys for six months. You're only in anything resembling a civilized town for a total of about six days a month, and even then you're either too hung-over or too tired to enjoy it. On Friday night you get your paycheck and you have two days to get rowdy, romanced, and ready for the next one—like R and R in the military. Prostitution is legal in Kalgoorlie, and there's a greyhound racing track where most of the guys spend the better part of the weekend.

When you come out of the bush, it takes three separate washings and scrubbings in the shower before the water will run off you clean. You have to remember that all of us are absolutely filthy all week long. When you clear the drilling hole you get a huge geyser of dirt blowing all over. All day you get this fine grit and rocks which of course cling to you because of the diesel fuel. You're always in diesel fuel up to your forearms, if not your whole arms. Your hair is just plastered to your head with the dirt and the diesel and the sweat.

The flies are everywhere down there, big healthy flies that are always going for the moisture of your eyes and your mouth. All day long you have a cloud in front of your face and around your head. We also had these funny little bugs like moths, but they didn't have wings. They didn't bite, but they got all over everything. One night one of the drillers got one of these bugs in his ear. His mate, his off-sider, said, "I know how to fix that. We'll put a little warm oil in your ear. Lay down." So the driller lay down and the mate started the oil warming on the little propane stove in the trailer. Well, they had been drinking and both were pretty plastered. The guy forgot and left the oil on the stove too long. When he got around to it again, he poured this near-boiling oil in the driller's ear. The mate came flying out the window of the trailer with the driller in hot pursuit, wielding a rake. It turned into a real melee. The company had to fly out two of the big shots in the middle of the night to get this whole thing quelled. Stuff like that was always going on. These guys were absolutely rough-and-tumble.

After six months I knew I'd had enough. I had survived. I thought I could then say to my uncle, "Hey, I've made it through this little episode. I'm coming back." One day I just got to the saturation point. I gave the drilling contractor two weeks' notice and booked my seat on the train. In fact, I made it a surprise. I showed up at my aunt and uncle's house in Melbourne wearing my hard hat and my blackened work shorts with greasy singlet (which I'd packed in a plastic bag, lest I be thrown off the train), and called out, "Eh, got a bed for the night?" I'd done it long enough that I guess they were relieved and proud. They probably realized that it was a little too much, but I didn't kill anybody or get killed, so I made them happy.

There's a family tradition of getting this ritual hazing. My cousins got the same thing. My first cousin worked in the mines in Colorado. We all had to go through this rite of passage, which, however dreadful, I think is invaluable. If I have kids, they'll get a taste of it too. It certainly makes any white collar job seem delightful; not being physically beat at the end of the day or filthy all day is nice—but you ought to know what real work is like, if nothing else. I'd give my kids a year of it, not just six months. It's good for everybody for awhile. Strenuous, dangerous, belittling, intimidating—all of which is good for you, and tends to prove the old Nietzsche axiom: "That which does not kill me makes me stronger."

I think everybody ought to be made to put in some hard labor, or a turn in the military, or something where you're forced to put up with hardships all day, every day, and you can't, for whatever reason, quit. You can't go to your driller when you're an off-sider and say, "Gee, it's really unpleasant out here in the sun. I don't like the ambiance of the drilling machine." You wouldn't even think of saying that. You wouldn't dare. It's beneath contempt, unthinkable. You just put up with unpleasantness. You're on your own, partner. It's every man for himself.

I certainly came away from it with a different outlook, and a lot more patience. I met a client on my last project, head-to-toe Dressed For Success. He was nitpicking every detail on the building I was representing, and remarked that he didn't like the mood created by the skylight in the breakfast nook. I had to smile and think about Kalgoorlie. I wish I'd been able to show him the ambiance of the breakfast nook on Hole No. 736 North for Newmont Mining, somewhere near Peenabarra, West Australia. (Fred Searls)

Fred's family certainly took the separation phase of his rite of passage rather seriously: they sent him half-way around the globe, and from there hundreds of miles into the desert. The Australians, on their part, provided him with a difficult transitional phase of the initiation process. The usual haircut and change of clothes, accompanied by an assortment of new names, signified a dramatic change in personal identity; the arduous hazing, coupled with the psychological teasing, helped Fred adopt a masculine posture and live up to masculine expectations. Despite his discomfort, and despite the apparent inanity of the experience, Fred came to accept the basic premise of his family's traditional initiation: Through overcoming hardship you develop the physical strength and moral fortitude that puts you "on your own, partner."

And Fred even managed to come up with his own version of an incorporation ceremony: he returned to Melbourne while still wearing his "uniform," having clearly put in his time. And yet this incorporation was limited; although his family now accepted him as a man, he never did gain acceptance by the all-male world of the Australian roughnecks—nor, for that matter, were most of the people back in the States likely to give him any special regard on account of his adventures in the Outback. In the end, Fred's initiation was no more than a private affair.

Of course an individualized rite of passage such as Fred's still counts for something, or at least it *can* count if the individual buys into the basic premise, constructs a reasonable initiation facsimile, and then goes on to succeed at the appropriate challenges he (or his family) has set up for himself. But as we begin to stray farther from the standard group context of traditional initiations, the results will become more tenuous. The individuals perform increasingly bizarre tasks, and they perform them to increasingly limited audiences. This privatization of our rites of passage, we shall soon see, causes problems, for there seems to be more to prove when there is nobody around to approve.

CHAPTER 4

Freestyle Variations

oger G., like Fred Searls, felt compelled to leave home with dramatic flare upon graduation from high school. Unlike Fred, however, Roger had no family tradition of initiations— so he had to invent his own:

When I left home at seventeen, I realized that the choices I wanted to make were the choices that made my life exciting, not that made it dull or ordinary or humdrum or day-to-day. My choices had to do with personal challenges, with engaging the world. So when I left home I took a trip to Mexico on my own, which was a watershed experience. Mexico is the developing world; it's certainly much more of a challenge to go to Mexico than it is to go to Europe. There was a kind of empowerment in that. Maybe by "empowerment" I'm just talking about feeling good about yourself. When you feel good about yourself, you feel like you have power in the world. Just the fact that I could move, that I could function, that I could hitch-hike, that I could travel cheaply—it tested my mettle and my patience and my ability to know myself. I got busted for marijuana when I was in Mexico and I spent a few hours in a Mexican jail. By some act of mercy or absolute good fortune, I was released. But dealing with challenges like that, dealing with experiences like that in foreign countries, the romance, the intrigue of doing things illegally in foreign lands . . . these are all experiences which had to do with my coming of age, and it was all based upon my getting away from home.

Roger is talking here about the first stage of a traditional rite of passage: the separation from family. But unlike primitive youths, and unlike Will Bell and Ken Bigelow, Roger has chosen to undertake this separation alone; he is not joining some existent organization or participating in a prescribed community ritual. And Roger pays a price for his independence, for he is not likely to receive the tutelage and organized hazing that are common in the transitional phase of a traditional initiation, nor is he likely to have much of an incorporation ceremony upon returning from his journey. His personalized rite of passage is therefore cut short; it certainly includes a powerful separation, a decisive repudiation of his childhood dependency—but that's as far as it goes. What actually happens to Roger in Mexico, what he makes of what happens, how he is received when he comes home—all this is very open-ended. Perhaps his experience will make him stronger, or perhaps not. It's really up to him. There is nothing in the process itself that is geared to help him with his growth, so his journey cannot be construed as an initiation in the classical mode.

But why should Roger, or any modern-day male, be tied to some ancient apparatus? Does a youth always need a formalized structure, complete with separation, transition, and incorporation? Why should he have to depend upon community ritual if he can somehow manage to prove his manhood, pure and simple, all by himself?

Today, many young men actually prefer to undertake their initiations all by themselves. From the standpoint of an avowedly individualistic culture, this seems like the most admirable way to proceed. A youth would appear to be more manly, not less, if he can not only *endure* his rite of passage but also *create* it; such an approach is certainly more in keeping with the frontier ethic of rugged independence still closely linked with the masculine mystique in modern America.[1]

But where can a young man go, in this technological and interdependent world with no more frontiers, to prove he can stand alone? Roger G. chose to travel by himself in an exotic foreign land—and he also chose to retreat into the wilderness:

> **After I left home I started experiencing the real disjuncture between civilized life and wilderness life. I liked the danger out in the wilderness, the sense that anything could happen and I had to be constantly aware. I also felt that I achieved a kind of animalness, a kind of wildness, when I walked by myself for a long time, when I wasn't in touch with other human beings. I became increasingly sensitive to the signs. Like five days out, I started seeing animal trails a lot more than I did at first. I started seeing disturbed places where things had been. I started smelling deer. I started fishing in the streams with my bare hands, catching trout by trapping them underneath the rocks in the little pools and pulling them out. At one point I got so crazed that I actually ate it raw out of my hands. It was a spontaneous act, an unconsidered act, one continuous motion. I caught the fish with my bare hands and pulled it out and bit it. It tasted very alive, the freshest fish imaginable. That kind of connection . . . like running across a bear face-to-face because we both came around from the rock at the same time, with mutual surprise and respect. That kind of aloneness and contact with wildness.**

Out in the wilderness, separated from both comfort and culture, a young man can experience the primal experiences, the life-and-death realities, that are obscured in civil society. He can prove himself to himself without the interference of social distortions; he is a man apart, and he must make it through on his own. He convincingly frees himself from the strongest yet most confining of all social units—his family—by abandoning the entire edifice of human society. By sacrificing the security of home in favor of the uncertainty of the wilds, he dramatically negates his prior status as a weak and dependent creature.

And while repudiating his childish past, a youth simultaneously affirms his archetypal image as man-the-survivor. He declares himself wild, not tame. Instead of being continually nurtured within the safe and secure confines of modern civilization, he recreates the presumed vitality of the primitive hunt:

When I was younger I worked at some very sedentary jobs: middle-management, the service department, sales. About three or four nights a week I would go out after work with my bow. I put a lot of effort into it, good enough to where I took quite a few deer with a bow and one bear and lots of small game. If I was in Orange County I'd go out in the orange groves and shoot jackrabbits. If I was in New Jersey I'd go chasing woodchucks, jackrabbits, squirrels. Here in the Bay Area I'd hunt brush rabbits and jackrabbits up in the hills. Almost every night I'd take two or three arrows out and prowl the hills and hunt rabbits. I'd eat the young ones and the older ones I'd give to my dog. I always used almost everything I took. I'd make leather articles out of animal skins. I'd take home possum and cook it up—not the best food in the world, either. I enjoyed using it, but I didn't really need the meat. It was mainly for recreation. It was what I had to do for my own emotional needs. Hunting helped me keep focus.

It took a lot of fine tuning, physical tuning and spiritual tuning, to get with it for a hunt. I never really felt quite with it until I rubbed the charcoal on my face and hands to cut the shine. I also liked to take a cold bath in the lake or river the night before. The Indians frequently did that. You get rid of the body odor, but it's also neat just to do it. I've taken some cold ones. It's stimulating. It's a way of knowing you're alive.

This last summer I discovered that apparently I have a great-grandmother who was Indian. It was a neat thing to discover that, that I probably do have some Indian blood in me. When I was a kid sometimes I'd get lost in a store and people would say, "Whose little Indian boy is this?" I looked very much like a little Indian fella, dark-complected, straight black hair. My brothers are all lighter haired, some of 'em almost blond. I had a reading one time, and the mystic decided that in my prior life I was an Indian. That was kind of an affirmation of some things about me; I didn't come by my interests artificially. (Dick Byrum)

Dick Byrum's hunting was clearly a matter of style, not necessity. He used charcoal "to cut the shine," but its real purpose was certainly more symbolic and personal: It made Dick *feel* like a hunter. Even if all he killed was possum, he still managed to put meat on the table. Through hunting, the most traditional of all masculine activities, Dick formed an important bond with his alleged Indian ancestors.

As one of the ultimate male traditions, hunting constitutes an ideal form of self-initiation. Although hunting can be, and often is, performed in groups, all it really takes is a party of one. In this sense the hunt is more accessible than war for a youth who wishes to initiate himself by re-discovering his primal masculine role. A youth cannot simply decide, all on his own, to go off and become a warrior—there might not be any wars to fight at the moment—but he can, if he so chooses, go out to the wilds and pretend he's a primitive hunter:

One of my most interesting challenges was to run the savannas, the high plateau in East Africa. I mean, what's it like to run with the game, to run after the game? What's it like to hunt primitive style with a club? I'm talking about running after gazelles, which are just a bit faster, most of the time, than cheetahs. Once I was stalking a group of about ten of them and there was another group coming from another area running towards me. I wondered, "What's chasing *them*? It certainly isn't another guy with a club like me. There's gotta be a cat running after them, either a cheetah or a lion or a leopard." It was two hunters passing, me and that cat. I was hardly in a position to take on a lion or a leopard with a club, so what was going to happen if that thing started coming after *me*? There's something heightened that comes out of that kind of danger. It's really electric, the thing that goes on. I was out there running with the most dan-gerous animals in the world—the cape buffalo, the lion, the leopard, the elephant, the rhino—and there's no taxi to get me out of there. The baboons were peering out of the bush like that Rousseau paint-ing. There was a live Rousseau painting right there in front of me, and I was in it. If I ran the wrong way or did the wrong motion, maybe they would have jumped out after me. What's in front of me are a lot of images in my mind of what can happen, and how am I going to take care of myself? How am I going to co-habit this space with these animals?

I was trying to make contact with a more primitive aspect of my-self. That's why I went back to the place in the world where we think the first man came from. To my way of thinking the Garden of Eden is right there in East Africa, probably somewhere in Kenya. Some people say that the first time we picked up a bone and used it as a tool, that's when we were first men. Well, I ran by stacks of bones out there on the savanna for three weeks until I finally picked up the bottom leg of a giraffe and said, "Hey, you could use this as a club." Early man, he probably ran by bones for ten thousand years before he said, "Wait a minute, we could use this. We need something. We're not as fast as the gazelle, so we need something." The bone became the weapon, the neutralizer of the speed and strength of the other animals. I found that out for myself, not reading about it in some library. (David Smith)[2]

The appeal of David Smith's adventure is twofold: the fantasy and the challenge. The challenge is obvious; by putting himself in a trying situation which tests his strength and endurance and courage, he affirms to himself his ability to cope with danger and adversity. But even the fantasy is real. Since civilization has removed the element of immediate danger from the modern struggle for survival, David has to recreate that danger on his own. Most modern-day males receive regular wages and salaries at predetermined times; they are protected from starvation by insurance companies and the welfare state. For young men like David Smith, this nine-to-five routine is not nearly so attractive, nor so masculine, as chasing elusive game through the woods or across the Savanna. So David refuses to accept his fate as it is given to him; he conjures up instead a more vital image of what it means to be a man in the world. He fabricates his own drama, his own initiation, and then he proceeds to play out his part.

This all adds up to a feeling of power, primal power. It feels good, it feels *real*, to achieve power like that. In fact, it feels so good that it can easily become a habit. David Smith, for instance, has turned his personalized, self-styled initiations into a way of life. Addicted to the authenticity of physical adventure, he seeks for himself an unending set of difficult and challenging ordeals which enable him continually to rediscover and reaffirm a classical sense of his own manhood:

When I started getting into adventure, I didn't know that there were underlying reasons that made me do it for a rite of passage. No one ever told me that, 'cause I'm not an Indian. They didn't say,

"Okay, prepare yourself for this thirty day trial. You're going to go out and come back a man." I didn't realize I would come back more of a man.

It started with an old dream that I had, a goal: swimming under the Golden Gate Bridge. I think that swim—it happened on my twenty-sixth birthday—was a baptismal. It was what I now call my "call to adventure." The challenges got progressively more difficult, but I was progressively more in contact with my capabilities. Swimming one mile across the Golden Gate, where many people have swum, got to twenty miles down a river, thirty miles down a river, sixty miles down a river, and finally to the point where I looked at the world and said, "Hey, I can connect these continents."

In fact, I wound up swimming from Africa to Europe. I found out that it was impossible to swim there, and that was the challenge to take. People continually tried to do it but nobody ever succeeded, so finally they said, "This just must be impossible." There's a sea captain down there who goes across from Tangier to Gibraltar every day. The guy said to me, "I don't know why you blokes come over here all the time and try this. This is impossible. There are times when I can't even get my ship through this current."

Some people would say to that, "Okay, I guess you're right," and turn around with their tail between their legs. With me it made my motivation even stronger; it was more of a reason to do it. I just knew I had to take more time, more discipline. I had to get my body more prepared, and I had to get it together upstairs: "How am I going to do this?"

I actually wound up doing it twice, because the first time I didn't hit the coast right at Gibraltar and I passed out as soon as I hit shore in Spain. I had gone from Africa to Europe, but I wanted to do it in perfect form. I was searching for something that happened to me in my first swim across the Golden Gate. It was what I call "tapping the source" or "getting a peak performance." I was successful in my other swims, but really what I got was a lot of pain in the water. I didn't slip back into that experiential warp, that other plane. Finally I got it again in my second swim to Gibraltar, where I just felt like I had hooked into another energy field, a sort of a universal charge that came through me and made everything right: I could do whatever I wanted to do.

After that swim I decided it was time to do something else, create new tests for myself. Maybe I could "tap the source" in a trek across the Sahara. So that was one of the next things I did: I walked across the High Atlas Mountains in the Sahara. Again I confronted a great deal of negativity; people thought I might be robbed or killed by the Berbers who live up there, the "Lords of the Atlas," who are pretty tough guys. People had their fantasies of what might happen to me. They said I needed a gun. If the Berbers didn't get me, there were big cats up there that could wipe me out. Snakes, the viper, all that stuff. That was just in the High Atlas. Then I'd go off the mountains and into the Sahara and I'd have to deal with the heat and the water and things like that. So practically everyone said I couldn't do it. Even the Berbers themselves, once I got up there, warned me about the robbers. When we tried to communicate through charades, they would always mime a guy grabbing someone around the throat from the back and stabbing him in the chest. I can't even tell you how many guys went through that pantomime with me. But I did the trek, and I survived.

When I create a challenge for myself it's usually in a foreign country, so whatever I'm doing there involves a cross-cultural communication with the people and the terrain. Instead of going to a place as a tourist and just looking at it, I become really involved. Once I took a pilgrimage to Hunza, the Shangri-La paradise in *Lost Horizon*. I was doing a piece for *Geo* magazine. Most of the time when I do an adventure I write a story about it or do a lecture series or something like that, and I usually take a photographer along with me. While I was there, the local swimming champion challenged me to a race across a freezing Himalayan river. The water temperature was thirty-nine degrees Fahrenheit. They told me four people died in the last race across the river, so of course I took the challenge. I wanted to see if I could stand up to a tough mountain man in his own environment. Neither of us died, and I won a yak in the race.

The way I look at the world, I'm like an old-fashioned explorer. I'm still looking for challenges to overcome, just like they used to do. When I find a place in the world that interests me, I think: "What can I do with that particular terrain?" Last month I was down in the Virgin Islands and I created a triathalon for myself. First I swam from the United States Virgin Islands to the British Virgin Islands. When I went down there I found out: "You're either going to get eaten by sharks or that current is not going to allow you to get across there." I responded to that: "What d'ya mean I can't get across there?" The second part of the triathalon was to take a mountain bike over thirty miles of mountainous terrain, some of it straight up and down. I went up this thing called Joe's Hill, about a quarter-of-a-mile mountain, that people *know* you can't go up on a bicycle. Well, I had an eighteen speed mountain bike and in fact I did go up it. There were areas where I even passed my support vehicle, a Land Rover. Then the final leg of my triathalon was a five-mile kayak trip out to another island.

That's an unusual triathalon. It was my own. There was only one competitor, and he was competing against himself. He was challenging: Can this be done? It's great to design your own challenges. It's setting something out there that you can train for, and then you go play it out. It has a whole cycle, an identity in itself: "This is something I want to do and I want to put some energy into it. I'm going to prepare for it, I'm going to do it, and then I'm going to debrief myself, find out what I got from the experience."

I think people have to create their own challenges, and then prepare for them and go out and do them. The first one doesn't necessarily have to be a real tough one—if you're afraid and intimidated by the wilderness, then go camp out in your back yard. But you have to be creative about what you do; it has to come from yourself. I may be the only person that ever donned the cover of *Sports Illustrated* for a creative athletic event. The piece was about a pentathlon: jumping out of a plane over St. John, then swimming from St. John to St. Thomas, then going underwater with a lung, then a run, and finally a trail bike to the top of a mountain. It was pretty much totally creative, except that I actually did the physical part of it too.[3]

David Smith, with his perpetual string of real-life adventures, has taken the initiation experience to its logical conclusion: If it feels that good, why not do it all the time? But the initiations, he says, only work because he has chosen them on his own and because they are hand-tailored to meet his personal needs. For David, the individuality of the experience is critical. Not only does he leave his boyhood behind, but he seems to leave the rest of humanity behind as well. In effect, he initiates himself into a society of one.[4]

And yet there is a catch. David might perform his individualized feats first and foremost for himself, but he also takes a photographer along with him to document his experiences, and he writes articles for magazines to share his private triumphs with the world-at-large. His various accomplishments, although avowedly personal, must also be socially recognized.

This might seem contradictory or even somewhat contorted, but it is really quite normal. Traditionally, primitive initiations always occurred within a group context; personal validation was augmented through social recognition. The status of manhood was dramatized and proclaimed publicly so it would be constantly re-affirmed in all subsequent situations, interactions, and relationships. When a youth went through his rite of passage and became a man, everyone else would know about it and treat the fellow accordingly. This public recognition does not necessarily occur during the individualistic initiations we create for ourselves today—unless we take a photographer along with us or choose to write an article about our experience or wind up on the cover of some magazine. A young man can go out and prove to himself he's a hero by performing impossible feats, but when he returns to ordinary life people might not accord him any respect or regard him any differently. The personal proof of manhood and the social status of manhood are no longer synonymous when our initiations are turned into private affairs.

What David Smith has done with his articles and pictures is to re-introduce the idea of public display into his private rituals. Even when he confronts challenges primarily for personal reasons, he is not always totally isolated; his individualized life-and-death adventures inevitably take on a social dimension. He might swim from Africa to Europe just to prove to himself he can do it, but he is still likely to wonder: "Will my accomplishment get the recognition it deserves? Will I receive any applause for my efforts? Will I get rewarded for my courage?"

And of course: "How many other people could perform a task like this?" David Smith's individualized initiations are explicitly intended as non-competitive events—"There was only one competitor, and he was competing against himself"—but has he really been able to abandon the idea of competition altogether? I think not, for he seems to use competition as a further means of recognition. A competitive tone permeates David Smith's saga despite his avowed claim that his only opponent is himself. He races with the Hunza swimmer; he beats the Land Rover, a *machine,* to the top of Joe's Hill. He takes on tasks that no other mortal has been able to do, tasks that are thought to be impossible, and when he succeeds at these tasks, he implicitly proves himself superior not only to all the other athletes who have failed before him (like the four Hunza swimmers who previously died in the freezing river) but also to all of those who once doubted his ability to perform impossible tasks.

There seem to be two different levels of competition at work here. First, David proves his superiority to willing competitors, to the men who have consciously tried to accomplish these various feats of strength and endurance. Second and just as important, he proves his superiority to all the common people who would never even think of performing his superhuman acts. In yet another of David's perpetual string of challenges, he ran the Khyber pass between Pakistan and Afghanistan in one hundred and fifteen degree weather; it was a day, he reports with unwitting conde-scension, when "five hundred people in Pakistan died in the heat. I don't know how many died in Afghanistan."

Both types of competition are present in many of our freestyle initia-tions, and this need to compete constitutes further evidence that our individualized experiences are not quite so private as we might like to believe. Witness, for example, the initiations of Matt and Bob Beach into the supposedly non-competitive world of mountain climbing:

Matt Beach: **I started climbing with Bob and a couple of friends and I realized I was pretty good because I could do things pretty easily. Like we went to do a tricky little climb on a wall here in the city and I found I could do that and then I went to Yosemite and it's been uphill since then. I met a partner and we talked each other into doing an El Cap [El Capitan, the famous vertical cliff in Yosemite National Park] route. It was a real severe route. It takes four days, overhanging most of the way. When you drop a water bottle down from fifteen hundred feet, it lands fifty or sixty feet away from the wall. That was a real tough climb. Once we had done it, we were accepted by some of the big boys down there.**

Some of the routes that I've done, there's only a fraction of the people in the world that could physically and mentally put themselves

through it. A small fraction, too. The retreat rate on some routes is like ninety, ninety-five percent. Only five or ten percent of the people can make the ascent on the first try. Me and my partner, I was seventeen and he was nineteen; I'd tell people in the Valley that we had done the Zodiac and they'd be mind-fucked. Some people would really be blown away. It's great. It got around that these two young hot shots did the Zodiac.

Bob Beach: I've been climbing twice as long as my brother. I'm twenty-one and he's only eighteen. He's gotten really good really fast. I'm still a better climber than him, but this route, the Zodiac that he did on El Cap, is something that I've never done anything comparable to as far as commitment is concerned.

Matt: We could've got killed, but it's really fun. There's nothing like getting out there and getting really scared. You'll be up in the corner nailing petons and the crack'll get thinner and thinner and thinner. If one piece pulls, the next one will pull and the next one will pull and the next one will pull. You take a thirty, forty foot fall. No problem. Then you might slam out on a ledge or something. Once you do it. . . .

Bob: It's really cool to talk about a fall—a gripping situation where you almost died and you can come down to the bar and joke about it afterwards. That's what good falls are, if it makes a good story.

Matt: You listen to all the stories that collect down in the parking lot. Me and Bob like to bullshit, I have to say. It's so great to be able to talk about it: the big fall or the rad route. It gets so hung up in ratings, it's sick. It's so easy to get caught up in it, especially when you're down there in Yosemite. It makes you wonder about all the ethics. It started off: "Lets all go down and have a great time." But now everyone's just out to do the hardest stuff they can, and do as much of it as they can, and be as good as they possibly can. I'm plugged right into that. It's hard not to be.

Bob: I remember when I first came down to Yosemite. I was really intimidated. I guess I was around fifteen. I had been bouldering every day in San Francisco and I got to be a good free climber, especially for my age. Then all of a sudden I was hanging around Camp Four, that's the camp for climbers in Yosemite, bouldering with guys who were a lot better than me. Where I once had a real contempt for them and the whole competitive talk-it-up atmosphere, when I finally got accepted by the locals it was just the greatest: "Hey, this kid is a pretty good climber." All my contempt went by the wayside.

Matt: The competition gets pathetic, really bad. It's so obvious in climbing: if you can't get up a certain route and someone else can, then that other person is better. People aren't up in your face about it, but it's just the hierarchy.

Bob: Once we were watching a guy free-climb Ugly Duckling. The guy was getting all nervous and didn't want to do these really hard moves. This friend of mine called up. "Go for it, you sniveling wimp!" So the guy goes up and tries to do the moves and falls and my friend walks away. Intimidation tactics. I would never do something like that. But I guess my friend thought it was funny to egg him on and see him fall.

Matt: I hate to say it, but I noticed this year in Toulemme when I was watching people climb that it would be so much more exciting to watch them take a screamer than to just casually finish the route. It's terrible, 'cause you're sitting there watching them with the worst intentions. Then after awhile you realize, "Fuck it, who cares? It would be great to see it anyway."

Bob: I don't know if I agree. I don't want to see anyone come close to dying. That's kind of morbid. But there is this friend of ours, David, who climbs just about at my level and we're really competitive. When I watch him do a climb I sit there and say, "I hope he falls." I don't want him to take a big one, but I like to see Dave fall—particularly if I've already done the route. If other climbers can't do a route that you've already done, that makes you feel like you're a better climber.

Matt: The same way with me and Jeff. He'll watch me fire up on something and hope that I can't do it. And I'll do it too. It'll get terrible: we're not doing each other favors, like handing over the rack. Everything turns into the wrong reasons.

Bob: They say climbing is a non-competitive sport, but it's one of the most competitive sports there is.

Matt: People like John Bachar, he's a famous free solo artist. He climbs without ropes or anything, so if he falls he dies. He does nothing but climb, three hundred days a year. In Tuolemme Meadows he wrote in the gym there that he'd offer ten thousand dollars to anyone who could free solo as good as him. He wrote this up on this big blackboard. He pushes it to the limit.

The Beaches themselves seem disgusted by all the competitive gaming, although they readily admit to playing the game themselves.[5] Whether they like it or not, the need for social recognition appears to dominate their more personal motivations. But isn't there more to rock climbing than telling "a good story," being "accepted by some of the big boys," or getting "hung up in ratings"? At least in theory, rock climbers are responding to the "call to adventure" in its purest form: they challenge themselves for the sheer sake of the challenge. They climb a mountain "because it's there"—and because of the feeling they get inside when they prove to themselves they can get to the top. Through climbing they induce the "can-do" attitude which is so crucial to developing egos; they affirm their sense of self-reliance and independence; they come to believe, at least for the moment, that they do in fact control their own destinies:

Bob: After you go down and you climb for two weeks things just start to click and it's the greatest feeling. You have this confidence and a real feeling of power. You come back to the city and you see people walking and shopping and bustling around and you feel so much more sane than them. When you come back down from a climb, all those little things just don't matter at all—like if it's cold outside or the cashier is in a bad mood today.

Matt: After you've been up on a wall for awhile you'll come into the Valley and everything is a lot more trivial. You can just accept things easier. Someone says to you, "Are you cold?" Cold, yeah, but are you going to freeze to death? They're two totally different things: Are you comfortable or are you going to die? You get really into being a hard man on walls. Like these couple of friends of mine spent seven or eight days stuck on El Cap in a storm. All day they'd eat one meal, half a peanut butter sandwich and two raisins. It's so cool when you can just dish it out—not be uptight, just be able to sacrifice and pull it off.

Bob: When you get back down, you're above the whole trivial world. But it doesn't last. You gotta go climbing again.

Matt: A wall is the ultimate experience for me. You're always in your slings; you're never off the rock; you're never standing on firm ground. Four days is a pretty long time. You start to focus on everything with a totally different perspective. You're living for the moment. You're doing things all the time in this continuous motion, and after awhile instead of being totally scary you've got it honed down just to the adrenalin part of it.

It's such intense physical abuse that it gets real heavy duty. You shred your hands apart, rip them up. Your legs cramp up, your stomach cramps up. Then when you get off the top of your climb, using every single muscle in your body, it's as hard physically as it could've been and as hard mentally as it could've been, you're totally pumped to the limit, you're right on the edge of it—it's a good, good feeling. There's something about it when you pull your head over the top of a four-day climb that's just so bonus.

Free soloing does that too, in a different kind of way. It's a real rush. You're committing yourself totally. You eliminate the rope, you eliminate the doubt. Free soloing works out your impurities. It makes you get your sight at a pinpoint, real concentrated. You know that what you're doing. . . .

Bob: You can't be thinking about girl problems.

Matt: Yeah. You don't let yourself get strung out. When you do a free solo, a severe one, or a severe wall, it's a level . . . like a graduation, I guess.

Bob: A plateau you've reached.

Matt: Yes, a plateau you've reached. Climbing the ever prominent ladder of "the right stuff." Then you know that you've got your head together that much.

Bob: Each time you climb a wall it's a new challenge. Then you graduate to a more severe route. It's great. It's a total rite of passage, to bag walls.

The adventures of Matt and Bob Beach up in the mountains are simultaneously significant and trivial. On the one hand, they are dealing with very real problems of ego development which are played out in the context of profound life-and-death situations; on the other hand, they participate in the various petty diversions of interpersonal rivalry which seem to have little or nothing to do with their more important tasks. How do these apparently contradictory aspects of their experience—the petty and the profound—coexist so well? My suspicion is that they share a common root: a feeling of personal power and superiority, of "being above the whole trivial world." The profundity of a truly heroic endeavor helps them to feel powerful and superior, while the need to feel superior is certainly related to a perfectly normal sort of human pettiness.

As we saw with David Smith, Matt and Bob Beach oscillate between the satisfaction of private goals and the need for public validation. Historically, the public and private realms have been irrevocably intertwined; one major function of a classical rite of passage was to provide personal validation through social recognition. But the privatization of our free-style initiations makes that function more difficult to fulfill, since a young man's separate and isolate initiation experience need not be acknowledged in the rest of his everyday life. Up on the ledges of El Capitan Matt and Bob Beach can be real men, but once back down on the ground they have to behave just like all the other boys their age. According to Matt, "When you come back down to the city and homework piles up you just have to go, 'Fuck, I don't wanna be here.'"

And why, indeed, should Matt be expected to define and affirm his manhood all by himself? Individualized initiations add an extra dimension to an already difficult burden of proof; feelings of confidence and self-reliance are naturally harder to sustain when they are not reinforced by normal social interactions. Perhaps this is why, despite their better judgment, the Beaches let their stories take on the importance of actual events and turn their very real adventures into competitive games, for they crave the reinforcement that their private initiations, in and of themselves, cannot provide. Competition appears to offer an element of social drama necessary to the initiation experience; notions of winning and losing substitute for the dramatic gestures present in primitive rituals. Initiations, after all, just don't seem *complete* without some form of public display:

Matt: **I want to take a good four or five years doing nothing but climbing for three hundred days a year and just getting severely good and doing all those really extreme things that I want to do. If I did a lot of climbing for a long time I could maybe put up a new route on El Cap. That'd be great, something like that. I'd like to do some incredibly cool shit, desperate stuff. Right now, as it is, I'm known as one of the young semi-hot-shot rads down there, but now I'm eighteen and it's getting to be a lot more big-time. Unless I start really committing myself and doing the real severe stuff and getting my picture in *Mountain* magazine. . . .**

How do we relate to Matt's unabashed desire to have his personal accomplishments reported in the media? It would appear to be somewhat less than admirable, or at least in partial violation of the allegedly individualistic nature of the actual experience. By setting up the privatization of initiations as a separate ideal, we box ourselves in; we want to appreciate our internal victories for their own sake alone, but rarely are we able to evidence such extreme self-reliance. And so it is that Matt Beach and David Smith seek the impersonal attention promised by mass media, since the more intimate and significant forms of social reinforcement are lacking.

But what happens when our self-styled adventures never find any audience at all?

When I was eighteen and just out of school I left home with a pack on my back and headed for the Rocky Mountains. I was from New York City. The closest I ever came to a wilderness experience was a walk through Central Park. I wanted more than that. I wanted something really *wild*.

I guess you could say I found what I was looking for in the mountains of Wyoming. I hitch-hiked around and had a few minor adventures, and finally I wound up in a genuine A-1 wilderness. To hike from one end to the other would take me a couple of weeks—and that's just what I wanted. I had the sense that my whole life up to that point was a sort of preparation for this one special event.

The beginning of the hike was an ascent of a mountain pass which took me two-and-a-half days. The hike was pretty hard but nothing really scary or sensational—just a lot of woods and rocks and watching where you put your feet. Then around noon of the third day I reached the ridge, and it was totally as glorious as I had imagined. The clouds were rolling past me just a few feet over my head. The meadows were teeming with flowers and dotted with these dramatic rock formations. As far as I could see in all directions there were mountains and mountains and more mountains; it was July and lots of them still had snow on top.

I felt like I had finally arrived. This was it: the world, the real thing. I felt like I was someone special because I had managed to escape and come all the way out here and find it. They didn't make things like this in New York City. It was like I was being reborn—not just a city kid anymore, but a real man. I could puff out my chest and breathe the pure mountain air and feel the wind against my weathered skin. I had found some kind of personal power up there in the mountains.

Only one thing bothered me: There wasn't any background music to highlight my personal transformation. Whenever something like this happens in the movies, the music swells and then maybe the credits flash on the screen and the whole thing is over. Everybody in the movie theater can appreciate how wonderful everything is and what a hero you are. That's not the way it was for me. There was no one around to appreciate my experience, nobody to share in the glory or to look at me and tell me that I had really changed.

So I walked on down the other side of the pass into the heart of the wilderness. I was out there for twelve more days, but the scenery was never again as spectacular and I just became more and more absorbed in petty details: how my freeze-dried food was holding out, how to keep the mosquitos off me, stuff like that. By the end of the trip I had to admit I was more bored than exhilerated. And then when I went back into civilization it was just the same old thing—cars speeding around, people talking about nothing in particular, and nobody paying me any special attention.

Was that some kind of an initiation I had up there on the mountain pass? I sometimes wonder. I want to think that it really was something significant, but then why didn't the feeling last? Why does everything feel just about the same now as it did before? (Jerry P.)

The problem of public validation seems inherent to any self-styled initiation that takes place off in the wilderness, far away from the watchful eyes of human society. Surely there is personal power to be gained by these experiences, but by removing the initiations from any social context a youth makes it harder for that power to be sustained. It is therefore quite understandable that many young men try to refabricate the context which is lacking: they compete with others, they brag, they publicize their private events in any way they can. If the arguments on their own behalf sometimes seem a bit forced, that is only because they have no choice but to sing their own praises when the rest of society refuses, or at least neglects, to sing their praises for them.

CHAPTER 5

The Quest for Male Validation

Perhaps the task of public validation is more difficult when our freestyle initiations occur in the wilds, but any youth who creates for himself a personalized initiation has to deal in one way or another with the interplay between the private and public affirmation of his manly status. By their very nature, freestyle initiations can occur in any location, situation, or context; the only requirement is that a youth set for himself a series of goals which, once achieved, will prove to his own satisfaction that he's a man. The question is: How will he define success? *Who* will define success? If he's unable to validate the results exclusively by himself, then what other forms of validation will he seek? How can he translate his personal achievements into socially recognized events?

For Chuck Sipes, a world-famous body builder, external rewards clearly enhanced the internal affirmation of his manly feelings:

I started working out with weights in high school and it didn't take me long, maybe a week, to know: "Boy, this is for me. I like this." As

my body began to develop, as my strength became stronger, that became an ego trip for me. For as long as I can remember, when I saw somebody with big arms and a nice physique, I admired that and I wanted to be like that. So I trained all during high school and I started reading the muscle magazines and visiting a few gyms. Also in high school I was a boxer, and I did pretty well at that. I liked punching people out; it didn't bother me at all at the time. In fact, in one of my fights I knocked the fellow out in the first eleven seconds of the bout. That was proving to myself I could whip somebody.

When I got out of high school I went into the service, and after that I didn't really know what I wanted to do with my life. I ran a gym for approximately three years, and then I got it into my head that I wanted to go work in the woods. I had the fantasy of a lumberjack out in the woods working hard and working out with weights and getting even stronger, because I really wasn't still satisfied with my strength. I felt my strength could become even better. So I worked as a lumberjack for a couple of years, and then finally I entered the Mr. America title and I won it. I was on top of the world. I had trained for a solid year to prepare myself for the contest, and I won it the first time I entered it.

After I won my Mr. America title, I realized how much I enjoyed the attention I was getting from being a winner. I enjoyed the thrill of victory in front of a big auditorium of people, and all the people clapping for you, and all the notoriety—I liked that. So that's one of the reasons I decided to go on and compete for other titles. I had the feeling that I wanted to be the best in the world, and they would remember Chuck Sipes for many years to come.

Two years later I won the Mr. Universe title, and I said that was enough. But a few years went by and I said, "Wow, I still have that yearning to compete again." I don't know where that came from, but it was there deep down inside of me. I wanted to be a triple-crown winner, to win all three major titles in body-building. So that's what I did. I devoted another year to my training and I won the Mr. World title. That was the ultimate. I was the strongest; I was at my utmost best in body-building and strength.

One thing I should probably mention is that many body-builders win titles and they're not very strong. They train by pumping the light weights to develop a fantastic physique. For me, I didn't just want my physique to look good—I needed that strength and that manliness to go with it. That's why I did a lot of feats of strength. I used to break chains; I used to lift automobiles; I used to blow up hot water bottles and burst them just with the power of my lungs. Once I lifted a Ford pick-up that weighed twenty-four hundred pounds; I lifted it off the ground and they took a dollar bill out from underneath the tire. I traveled all over the world with my feats of strength. I went into the high schools with the Marine Corps; I was a feature attraction in a lot of different shows. I did these feats of strength to prove that I was strong. Besides *looking* strong, I wanted to let people know I *was* strong.

So now I've accomplished just about everything I wanted to do. I set my goals early in life. I wanted to win those titles: Mr. America, Mr. World, Mr. Universe. And I did it. I'm one of the few triple-crown winners in body-building, winning all three. I still feel good about it, because that's Chuck Sipes.

Just recently I had one of the most honored moments in my life: I was put in the Hall of Fame in my high school. This was to cover the last hundred years. There were over two hundred nominees that were looked at, and I was one of the twenty-four who were put in the Hall of Fame. At the time I was going through high school, I had no idea that someday I'd rank in the Hall of Fame. For me, the educational part of high school was not the main thing, and some people looked down on my body-building: "That guy's a muscle-head. He ain't got no brains." So when I was recognized in the Hall of Fame for some of my physical contributions, it made me feel really good. I was put there alongside of Ernest and Julio Gallo of the wine empire, a brain surgeon from back in Michigan, some admiral in the Navy, a movie star and an opera singer, a lot of people from all walks of life.

I like all these honors that people give to me, but there's more to it than that. I've proven my manliness to *myself,* that I could develop my strength to almost a superhuman degree. After I won these titles, and after I proved to myself that I could become very, very strong, I could see then I was a man. Up to that point I wasn't so sure. Now, I don't really have to prove anything to anybody any more.

Chuck aspires to a well-defined image of manliness, and then he presumes, once he matches the image, that others will respect him for it.

There is positive feedback here between private and public validation. Chuck's personal motivation led him to accomplish tasks which were socially rewarded, and this in turn spurred further personal effort, which of course led to more rewards. He trained for a year by himself before each contest, and when he won that event "in front of a big auditorium of people" his success was confirmed. A confirmation such as this is reminiscent of the incorporation phase of a classical initiation. The challenge he had set for himself had been met, everybody could *see* that it had been met, and the whole experience left Chuck with the feeling that he had convincingly and decisively proved his manhood.

Yet there is still an air of boastfulness to Chuck Sipes's tale, much as there was with the saga of David Smith, the creative adventurer. Throughout my interviews I noticed two major tones: self-congratulatory and self-doubting. I will speak of the doubters later; for now, I shall focus on those who like to publicize their private gains. For any of our freestyle initiations—whether they are performed to an audience of one or in front of an auditorium full of people—the restating of personal achievements serves to confirm and enhance manly feelings.

Even in the realm of sex, where manhood is encountered most privately, I noticed a tendency to boast. Where I anticipated shyness or reserve, an unwillingness to disclose personal lives, I found instead an almost obsessive desire to make the private public. Sexual prowess was reported as a form of masculine achievement which, however intimate, still awaited social recognition:

When I joined the Police Department in San Francisco, those were my real playboy days. I had a car and a nice apartment and money and a good job. I was out hunting women virtually every weekend. That was my hobby. I had real good techniques. On Friday nights I'd go down to Perry's on Union Street—that's *the* place for the in-crowd to be, the swinging singles. I'd go down there and my little technique was to wait till the girls left the bar, going from one bar to another one. You get 'em between bars. In the bar, everybody's watching and there's a lot of pressure and you could hardly talk. So I'd wait till they left, and they don't want to go to the next bar alone anyway. I'd walk up to them and talk to them on the street and generally what I'd say is, "I hope I'm not being too rude, but I'd sure like to meet you. Can I buy you a drink down the street here?" That was a real good technique.

What I'd try to do on Friday night is get phone numbers. I'd meet girls and if I liked them I'd say, "I've got to go to work, but can I get your phone number?" I'd collect about four, six, eight phone numbers. I'd pick the best of them to select from. I'd ask them out Saturday night if I liked somebody, or if not, I'd do the same thing on Saturday, just to get some phone numbers.

That was really the flowering period of my screwing around. Two things I used to do were devastating. One would be, almost always, bring a dozen roses on the first date. Now that sounds corny, but almost nobody does it anymore. I've had women more than once break down and cry when they open the door on the first date. It softens them up, it sets you apart. The other thing was I take a girl home, to her house or my house, and I try to get her to bed and we're kissing and the girl knows what's coming. We're embracing and I pull my arm away as if I'm going for her breasts—and then don't go for her breasts. Just go behind her neck or something like that and then go back. You do this a couple of times and it gets her off her guard. And then when she goes into her standard rap—"I wouldn't feel comfortable going to bed with you on our first date. I don't know you well enough"—I'd listen and listen and listen and say, "Okay, I understand. We'll just go back to kissing." There's no fighting. I'm not pushing them so they don't have to resist. I had more success than if I were real pushy.

My thing was just to go after them until I had them. I'd stay with them for a night or two, but that was enough. If she didn't measure up, I'd still like to get in a position where she's crazy about me and then I could end it. I would do all kinds of things to get her really infatuated with me and then I'd break up with her. Until she's crazy about me, I'm still after her, I'm still pursuing her. Once I've got her, then I can make a decision about what to do with her. I can't make a decision until I've got her.

This went on for seven, eight years. I only had one real romance during that time, a girl I stayed with for about a year. When that didn't work out, I was happy to go back to my bachelor hunting. I wasn't in any great hurry to give it up. I wanted to get married eventually, but I was having a great time. There were dozens of girls, maybe hundreds.

This may sound like bragging, but I've had almost every single woman I ever really wanted. With my determined pursuit and my sneaky techniques I could generally pull something off, so I always thought it was worth a try. It's an accomplishment I'm proud of, a track record, a hit-and-miss ratio, a statistic. It's a skill you get good at, like having a good batting average in baseball or like going to school and saying, "Yeah, I made straight A's."

I take pride in that. I'm happy about it, but that's not really important. What's really important is that I haven't missed out on things, that I've had some really beautiful women. I don't have regrets like, "Gosh, I wish I had this one there." Some guys I know have never had a beautiful woman, but I've been through all types of women. I know the whole thing; I know what I think is the entire field, the whole selection, so now I can make a rational decision. When you haven't tried them all you don't really know which one is the best. (John F.)

The picture of sex presented here is distinctly unromantic, and John F. would be the first to admit it. He is talking about achievements, not relationships, and he is using those achievements to reinforce his own masculinity. Sexual encounters such as these easily masquerade as initiation rites, as proof positive of a manly status, but like many other freestyle initiations, they lack an intrinsic element of social recognition. By reporting his success, John takes a step towards supplying the recognition that is lacking.

But who is John trying to impress by his tale? Certainly not the ladies. His female partners are unlikely to relate John's masculine prowess to the world at large; indeed, they are more likely to take offense at his attempt to publicize his conquests. John impresses women with roses; his stories are clearly intended for men.

And isn't this quite natural? Traditionally, only men have had the power to bestow manhood upon other men. Classical initiations invariably occur in all-male surroundings, far away from any and all female influence. This, of course, is impossible for young males who use sexual exploits to affirm their manhood; women are inevitably involved. But if the exploits are to function as a substitute for initiations, the role of women, ironically, is minimal. It is other men who must be made aware of the achievements in order to grant their masculine approval.

During adolescence, a time when sexual status is seriously in doubt, boys are particularly dependent upon validation from their peers. Sexual conquests during this time are readily interpreted as affirmations of manhood—but in order for a conquest to function as a rite of passage, it has to be recognized and acclaimed:

From the second grade up till today, I've been the horniest guy, always horny. In grade school I always liked girls, I was attracted to them, but I didn't know what to do with them or how to handle them. I dreamed a lot and fantasized a lot and looked at girls and had a lot of ideas, but I never did anything. Then when I was eleven my family moved to Mexico City. In Mexico the cab drivers would generally point things out: "This is a whorehouse." Sometimes my friends and I—we were all Americans— we'd go down and look at girls who we thought were prostitutes and talk about it.

Then one time a friend of mine stole some money from his father. He said, "Let's do it." So we went down to this little whorehouse at about three o'clock in the afternoon, which is not peak time. We stayed out in front because we were afraid to go in. "You go in." "No, you go in first." My big fear at the time, I can remember it clearly, was what do you say to the guy behind the desk—"Hey, I want a girl"? Maybe he'll kill me or arrest me or something. I was terrified. I just didn't know what the right words or procedures would be.

Finally a girl opened the door and looked out and saw us there. She smiled and she said, "Come on in." We went, "Oh no, we're just standing here." So she went back inside. I thought, "Oh God, I missed my big chance. This was it. Chickened out at the last moment." So I said, "Mike, I want to go in. Just follow me." Finally we opened the door and there's girls all over, just hanging around on couches and chairs. I walked right up to the little window, the little desk that they had, and I said, "Any girls here?"

So this girl came over, she was nice enough to come over to us, and she said, "Do you guys want to do something?" And then we had to talk about business stuff. (I think the money was thirty pesos each, which at that time was about two dollars and forty cents.) Then the three of us went upstairs into a little room with a swayback bed. We gave her the money. She wasn't very pleasant or anything; she was real businesslike, just a working-class, a low-class, whore.

Mike said, "Well, you go first." But I didn't know what to do. She said, "Is this your first time?" "Oh, no. Of course not." I was afraid to take off my clothes, not out of embarrassment but just because I thought there might be a trick here somewhere. I wasn't sure about this whole situation. Someone had told us, some guy with a big brother, that one of the things these prostitutes do with young guys is that you don't actually get inside them. They put their hand down there and you're actually screwing their hand. So that was something we had to watch out for. We had talked about that before: "She's not going to give me a hand job."

Anyway, she took her clothes off, everything but her bra. Finally I took my clothes off and I got on top of her and there I was and we were doing it. I enjoyed it at the time, finally getting to do it. One thing that didn't help, though, was my friend Mike at the foot of the bed making remarks like: "Hey, you look like a frog!" And he kept saying, "Now hurry up, hurry up. Are you through?" I said, "No, I'm not through. Leave me alone." Finally, when I was through, he said, "You're through," in a very knowing voice.

We went back to school, Mike and I, after going to that first whorehouse. We were probably the only two guys in the class that had done it. We were celebrities. We had crowds around us when we'd tell them all the details, how great it was, what studs we were. Some guys said, "I bet she gave you a hand job." "No, I checked. She had both hands around me."

My reaction to all this was it wasn't really very exciting. After all the talk you hear about it, all the writing, all the pictures, all the taboos about sex, I thought, "For this? This is what it was about?" I was so disappointed. I thought it would be a lot better. I could do better myself, just masturbation—I've had better feelings doing that. It wasn't something bad; it just wasn't nearly as exciting as I thought it would be. But we thought, "This is a good chance to learn," so we went back several times. Then we went to some other girls, other whorehouses, but they were all about the same because we couldn't afford much better.

I can remember keeping count; it was an important thing at that time. Guys say, "How many times have you done it?" You say,

"Three." Or whatever. Most people would lie. I can remember up to eleven, but I can't remember after that. It just sort of blurred away. I always thought I'd keep count all my life; that was part of what being a man was all about. (John F.)

Why does John go back to whorehouses over and over if he could do it better by himself? It's certainly not for romance, nor simply for the physical sensation; he gains instead a public antidote to his private insecurity. He is no longer perceived as a shy and struggling adolescent; he is now, according to the acclamation of his peers, a sexual warrior who has counted coups. He has managed to transform a troublesome personal problem of adolescent transition into a social accomplishment.

And this, of course, is an important aspect of the initiatory experience: to help an individual through his time of crisis by providing him with the appropriate social context. In many primitive societies, sexual instruction formed an integral part of the initiation curriculum; in some cases, sex was ritualistically performed in a group setting. From this perspective, John and his friends were not really acting that strangely by transforming their early sexual encounters into public events—but from most modern perspectives, such behavior is seen as morally questionable. Sex today is basically a private affair; attempts to make it public, such as John F.'s escapades in a Mexican whorehouse, are generally perceived as pornographic. A fraternity "gang-bang" or single men masturbating in the back rows of adult theaters—we see these semi-public displays of sexuality as blatantly kinky, not well-integrated facets of a normal and healthy sex life. Indeed, most of us perceive even the "personal ads" which seek out sexual partners as somewhat perverse, for they place our private needs on public display.

So where does this leave a young man who is struggling to affirm his manhood while simultaneously fulfilling his sexual needs? It leaves him torn between competing and contradictory values. On the one hand, he is told by the dominant culture to keep his sex to himself. Sexual lessons are to be learned alone, or at least not in the presence of other men. On the other hand, an informal male subculture encourages a youth to share his most private deeds:

When I was in high school we had a scale for how far you could get with a girl. It started with a hundred points for holding hands and ended with a thousand points for going all the way. Each act was very

specifically defined. There were all sorts of fine distinctions between under and over the clothes, touching and looking, things like that. After a date we'd always have to announce how far we got. I remember in my freshman year I had reached five hundred. I don't really remember what that entailed, but I do remember setting a goal for myself, a sort of personalized program for sexual initiation: I would advance at a steady rate of one hundred points a year until I reached the limit. And that's pretty much the way it worked out, a little more each year. I finally scored a clean thousand in my sophomore year in college.

Looking back on it, I've wondered why we didn't just make the scale from one to ten, or even from ten to a hundred. I think those extra zeroes gave the thing a little more weight. We wanted to feel we were really getting somewhere.

The whole process was a continuing game of numbers, which I guess made the emotional stress easier to take. One year when I had just turned fourteen I went to summer camp where there were a whole bunch of us sleeping in a dormitory. At that age most of the guys were masturbating pretty regularly, so instead of trying to hide it they made it into a quasi-public event. In each room, posted on the wall, we had a "BTMS" chart—"Beat The Meat Sheet"—with everybody's name on it and the number of times they masturbated. This one kid, David Watkins—he was a pimply-faced guy with a sharp wit—he won the competition hands down. He did it two or three times a night all summer.

Towards the end of the summer the camp director somehow found out what "BTMS" stood for. The shit really hit the fan. The poor director (he was in bad health anyway) treated it like some sort of scandalous perversion, which I guess it was if you wanted to look at it that way. But it was also perfectly appropriate behavior for adolescent males deprived of any real outlet for our instincts. We actually managed to turn our horniness, which was a sort of curse we couldn't escape, into a status symbol. David Watkins was one of the most respected guys in camp.

The only problem for me with the "BTMS" was the first half of the summer, whenever I tried to masturbate, nothing happened. I was a little late in maturing and I didn't ejaculate. So there I was with nothing next to my name on the "BTMS"; it didn't count unless you could come. (I guess there were ways of validating whether you came, although I can't remember that it ever got that kinky.) Then finally, somewhere around the middle of the summer, I actually did it. I came. It felt great physically, plus I made it onto the "BTMS." There was a general feeling of satisfaction in my room that I had finally joined the club; before that, I think people kind of sympathized with my embarrassment, since I was the only blank on the chart. I managed to get three or four more entries before the camp director tore the sheets down, so I ended with a respectable showing. Of course most people had twenty or thirty or forty, and David Watkins must have had at least twice that, but at least I was there somewhere. I had made my mark and been counted.

Another game we played in high school was judging the attractiveness of girls. Maybe we kidded around about it, but it really did mean something to us. At least it did to me. As badly as I wanted sex, it would have been totally obscene, maybe even dirty, to do it with someone who didn't rate high enough on the scale.

Actually, we saw ourselves more like liberal reformers than male chauvinists. The standard one-through-ten scale seemed too simplistic; it didn't give enough room and credit to the personal idiosyncracies of each individual girl. So we designed a system with separate categories for "face," "figure," and "personality." That seemed to allow for more individuality. A girl who didn't have a pretty face could score well on her figure, and vice versa. It just seemed more respectful to do it this way.

The particular stroke of genius to our system was in our weighting of the numbers. We gave up to eight points for face, eight for figure, and nine for personality, giving a grand total of twenty-five points for the perfect girl. (Nobody I knew ever reached the twenty-five mark, although I think we did come up with a couple of twenty-threes, maybe even a twenty-four.) How many other rating systems have ever given such importance to "personality"? It was the supreme mark of our liberalism that personality could actually account for one more point than each of the physical attributes. Somehow we managed to ignore the obvious fact that the combination of "face" and "figure" accounted for sixteen of the twenty-five points.

Once there was a girl I liked. I was very attracted to her for some mysterious reason, but objectively she didn't rank very high on the scale of twenty-five. According to my friends, she was way down around fourteen or fifteen. That was beneath my dignity and I never did go out with her even though I wanted to. She would have been an embarrassment to me. (Ralph W.)

However crude these ratings might appear, there is some traditional wisdom in Ralph's quest for an external validation of his sexual status. It's a lot to ask of a young and insecure male that he tred the troubled waters of adolescent sex without any tutelage or support, and it is therefore quite understandable that he seek the informal aid of his peers.[1] The concept of "scoring" serves to mask unwanted subtleties and insecurities, while it simultaneously channels the uncertainties of sexual maturation into the more comfortable arena of competitive gaming. All of Ralph's games, in their own strange ways, mimic that critical function of a classical initiation: to turn difficult personal struggles into public events whereby young men can help each other confirm their incipient masculinity.

So in the absence of formal structure, it's the informal male subculture which serves to validate manhood. John F. and Ralph W. try to impress their adolescent buddies with their sexual acumen; Matt and Bob Beach strive for the recognition of their fellow climbers; Fred Searls hopes not to make a fool of himself in front of the Australian roughnecks. Typically, a youth seeks to establish his manhood by participating in the symbolic acts of an exclusively male world:

My first job was with a very small construction outfit. I was one of two laborers, and the other laborer was a black guy by the name of Charlie, a big, husky, muscular guy who spent most of his adult life in jail on moonshining charges. Totally rough and rowdy. And I was just a white, skinny kid who just didn't know my ass from a hole in the ground.

The first day on the job we were building a garage for somebody out in the suburbs and I was up on the roof. Charlie would pass the plywood up to me and I would pull it up. A four-by-eight sheet of plywood is a real easy thing to handle once you get familiar with how to handle it, but when you don't know anything about it, it's real clumsy, particularly when you're up on the roof. It was made more difficult by the fact that Charlie had introduced me to the joys of chewing tobacco. I had gotten a plug from him at lunchtime and I got up on the roof after lunch and I started getting dizzy as hell. I'm standing on the edge of this fucking roof, chewing tobacco and getting dizzy and trying to grab these four-by-eight sheets of plywood and wrestle them up there. I just about fell off.

Charlie introduced me to a lot of things: playing the numbers, gambling in the lottery. He was my mentor. I played poker in the union hall on rainy days, watched the girls at lunchtime, just did the whole thing. Drinking a lot. Charlie introduced me to my first moonshine; he made some great stuff. So there was this whole introduction to the macho side of life, to the man's side of life. (Ray W.)

The initiation here has little to do with any formal organization; it is more a matter of lifestyle. It can be administered in a bar or an army barrack or out on the street, anywhere that grown men tend to congregate. For Ray and for many others, this informal "introduction to the macho side of life" is all that remains of a male rite of passage.

Our popular culture abounds with images of this informal hazing into the world of grown men. Advertisements for beer, for instance, show a younger man performing some difficult task under the approving eyes of his immediate elders; when the job is done, he is allowed to join their club and they all celebrate his initiation by drinking a particular brew. This imagery might seem trite, but at least it has a populist bent: insofar as we accept the images as they are presented to us, manhood can be attained simply by purchasing the appropriate product. The manhood we achieve in this manner is admittedly superficial, but it is also attainable—and this, of course, holds a special appeal. At least in a casual sense, we can all appear to be "real men."

But how casual can we afford to get? Does a loose and informal participation in "the macho side of life" really *satisfy*?

For those who want something more, this all-male subculture can actually be formalized. College fraternities, for example, attempt to reconstruct the vitality and authenticity of a tribal band. In the absence of an organic and significant community of men, fraternities actually fabricate their own facsimiles; they create makeshift tribes for the sole purpose of validating each other's manhood. They might not serve much of an objective function—they are certainly not necessary for collective survival—but they do provide that social context which is so often lacking in freestyle initiations. They help young men carve out a well-defined and distinctively masculine niche in an otherwise loose and amorphous culture:

At the beginning of your freshman year they have a thing called rush week, where you go around and visit a number of different fraternities. Then each day the fraternities issue invitations to people who they want to come back. When you go visit a fraternity, they generally invite you in to have dinner. At Beta Theta Pi, which I finally pledged, they all sing at dinner, seventy men singing together in the same room. They sing real well, and they obviously like to sing. It's an incredible feeling, the way they show you the brotherly affection between members. And it is certainly true. It's present. It's fantastic. It's a commune of men.

After dinner they show you around the fraternity house. They've got it really cleaned up, I mean *polished*. The windows are washed, the lawn is mowed. In my fraternity, you go in and there's a waiting room that's got all red leather couches and chairs around it, a low coffee table by the fireplace, wood paneling, indirect lighting, and the big fraternity crest over the mantle. Then they show you the den, where they have photos of all the famous Betas from that chapter. There were guys who were like the javelin champion of the Pacific Coast Athletic conference in 1936. It goes way back. They've got guys who have these funny little leather football helmets on, and guys who received all these various awards.

They give you this fraternity magazine. It has pages on the history of the fraternity, pictures of the fraternity house, and features on particular people in the fraternity. Like the governor of the state at that time was a Beta Theta Pi. He was a Beta at another college, but he was still a Beta so his picture is in there. They have people from all across the nation—senators, supreme court justices. Or the Sigma Chis, Milton Canniff was a Sigma Chi, so they always had Steve Canyon, the comic strip, in their rush book. They had Steve Canyon talking about fraternities.

Then they take you upstairs. Here's all the individual study rooms which people have decorated—but people don't sleep in their study rooms. At night everybody goes to this all-glass sun porch which is like a bunk house. So all the men in the fraternity sleep together. They have two of those sleeping porches, about thirty-five guys in each room. There's the noisy porch and the quiet porch. Once you move into the fraternity, you make your choice. On the quiet porch, you can't ever talk, even if you go to sleep in the afternoon. It's always quiet. But on the noisy porch you can stay up and bullshit all night long, or sing, or whatever you want. You can't tell someone to be quiet if you sleep on the noisy porch, but you can move to the other porch if there's extra space.

When I moved in the next year, I went on the noisy porch with the boisterous bullshitters. We had a guy who would read stories to us, sexual case histories, when we were all in bed. It was some kind of encyclopedia of sex with stories about people with particularly curious stuff, like someone with a big cock or something. He'd read these case studies and we'd all howl and laugh and then we'd all go to sleep.

After I accepted with the Betas, one night a week during my freshman year I went to a class. The whole pledge class had dinner at the house, and they taught us the history of the fraternity. We had tests. We had to be able to recite things. There's actually a hardbound book that's published by a national office. It has things like where the first chapter was, and the year it was formed, and who the founding fathers were. You have to know their names and their birthdates. It's just like Washington, Jefferson, and Madison. You're taught their personal histories, what they were interested in, what they did after they graduated from college. And then you have to learn songs each week. You all sing together as a pledge class, and you have to be able to write it out as well as sing it on the test. Like,

> *Marching along in Beta Theta Pi,*
> *Marching along we'll rend the air*
> *with song. . . .*

Can't remember the rest. That's a walking song. You walk with one arm on the shoulder of the person in front of you. The whole fraternity walks out of the house that way and will go into the street singing this song, kind of shuffling along. It really sounds great with seventy or eighty men singing together. You'll go to a sorority and serenade them with three or four of these songs.

There's another song called "Pass the Loving Cup Around." That's a sentimental, emotional one. It's for when someone is married or pinned or something happens to them that they want to celebrate. They'll do a Loving Cup, which is a great old trophy that's been around the fraternity for seventy years. They fill it with brandy or bourbon and ice and pass it around. You stand in a circle and you start singing:

Oh, pass the Loving Cup around. . . .

It's a nice solemn song about brotherhood. And for each person, the man on your right and the man on your left takes one arm of the Loving Cup and they lift it to your lips and you drink from it. You don't touch it. Then you pass it on and you help it to their lips. It goes all the way around the fraternity.

So you learn these rituals, and you learn how important it is on the campus to be who you are. Your circle of friendship is your pledge class. Even though you live in different dormitories, you come together for all this training. On Saturdays you go to the fraternity to clean up the grounds. That's your responsibility as a pledge class.

In spring, just before your formal initiation into the fraternity, there's this thing called Hell Week, where you have to go through one week of punishment. Some things were already illegal when I was there, like the use of hack-paddles. What my fraternity used instead of hack-paddles was ice-cold showers. You go upstairs to the bathroom and take off your clothes. They turn the water on cold and make you stand under it for a prescribed amount of time. It might be fifteen seconds, thirty seconds, a minute. The longest one is three minutes. Three minutes in a cold shower is really intense. And then you have to sing a fraternity song or something while you're in the shower.

Hell Week is real psychological, all the way through. Before it started, they were telling us that the univerity had been making stringent rules and Hell Week was changing. They said it was not going to be a physical problem for us, that they had become more reasonable. They had decided that the fraternity would be modern and progressive and that our Hell Week would be shortened to four days instead of seven. They would be a model of sophistication and maturity for all the other fraternities.

They pretty much had me convinced that was true. They said we would leave our dorms and move into the fraternity on Wednesday night. We would have a banquet, then we would go to our normal classes on Thursday and Friday. On Saturday we would do a service project for the community, and on Sunday there would be a party for us. That's what initiation week was going to be. They had us bring nice clothes for the party. They gave us a list of what to bring: "Bring your favorite pillow, because we want you to be comfortable. Bring a nice blanket, and we'll make your bed for you."

So we came over there on Wednesday evening, and everyone was incredibly cordial. I remember it was such a warm feeling. They had a special dinner prepared for us. Then after a nice dessert they let us study in the study rooms and different people would come by and say, "It's really nice having you here." They had made beds for us, like the seven dwarfs or something. We had this special area of the quiet porch so we would be able to get a lot of sleep and get to school on time and do real well in our studies that week. We all went to bed at ten o'clock.

Then at about ten after ten, just as we were going to sleep, all the fire alarms went off in the building. We didn't know what was going on. Guys came running in and said, "All right, out of bed! Go to your study rooms right now. Don't say anything." Then they came around to the rooms and said, "All right, take off all your clothes and line up in the hall." So we line up naked in the hall, and all of a sudden they were very antagonistic. Anybody in the fraternity could walk down the line and tell people things they didn't like about them, make fun of them physically. Like: "You've always had big ears. That's why people call you 'ears' behind your back, 'cause your ears are so ugly." They told me I was skinny. They'd make comments about the size of people's cocks. I had a foreskin, and that was one element they focused on because that made me different. Not so many people had foreskins; maybe I was the only one. So they would call me "foreskin" and they'd point that out to anyone in the fraternity who happened to be walking by.

Then they came around and gave everyone an onion tied to a piece of string. They made you hang the string around your neck and tie the loose end to your cock, with the onion hanging down on the other end. So if somebody tugged on your onion, it would pull your cock up. Then any time anybody wanted to speak to you, they'd pull your onion, which pulled on your cock. That's the only time you were allowed to speak, if someone pulled your onion. And they told you that any time they wanted you to take a bite of the onion you'd have to. Personally, I had never liked onions that much anyway.

Finally they said, "All right, enough of this shit. All of you back to bed." Now we're getting kind of mad: "What is this crap, anyway?" And they're telling us, "You're not going to be able to take it. This is what it's going to be like for the next four days. Any time you hear that bell, off with your clothes, line up in the hall." We all got back into our pajamas and they put us in bed. Half an hour later, same thing. All night long, same thing. The bell rings, you run out of the sleeping porch, go into your study room, take off your pajamas, find your onion, tie it on your cock, throw it over your neck, run out into the hallway, and find your place in line.

And they're giving us these new names. Different people give you different names, and you have to remember them all in case they speak to you. You have to be alert. If you forget one of your names or mess up on any of their orders, the penalties are you have to eat your onion, or you have to get down and crawl, you have to do imitations of animals, you have to sing by yourself in front of all the other guys. They'll ask questions like, "We want you to tell us about your favorite way to masturbate." Some people would be so afraid they'd just go ahead and bare their souls. Other people would get hard and say, "I don't masturbate."

They'd try any way they could to break down your defenses. It was always changing. You'd just get used to one routine and they'd change it on you. They would have us do all sorts of things, like clean the kitchen at 4:30 in the morning. Sometimes you'd have clothes on, sometimes you wouldn't. They'd do that to us all night long, then in the morning we went off to classes. We'd have to report in at different places on the campus at certain times. They didn't want you to run, they didn't want you to get away, they didn't want you to try to quit. They were checking up on you all the time, watching you. There were different ways that you'd have to take your hat off or bow to them on the campus. Other people wouldn't notice that you'd be subjecting yourself in an inferior posture, but people in the fraternity would know. And when you saw a member around the campus, if they asked you to do something you'd have to do it: carry their books, or go to their car, or walk their bicycle. They had a rhyme—I don't remember it, something about your onion and your cock—that you had to repeat to them if they asked you.

After going around to classes all day we were really tired, but the next night it was the same thing again. They started giving us regular tubbings. In the basement of the fraternity they had a dark, eerie room. In it was a large concrete tub. And written on the walls, like graffiti, were the names of people out of the past, by classes. They'd have everybody's last name and it'd say, "Class of '41." That was all the people who had made it through their Hell Weeks and the rituals they had to go through.

They had blocks of ice sitting around the room and a cold water hose. They'd take us down to the tub room and give us a song to memorize. Then they'd leave, and we'd be in this room. Then they'd come back in and ask different people to sing it. If anyone couldn't sing it, you'd have to get in the tub or you'd have to sit on a block of ice without any clothes on. Sometimes people would balk at getting in a tub with ice floating around in it. But if somebody just couldn't take any more tubbing, someone else could volunteer to do it for you, and that would develop a sense of brotherhood. There was this incredible feeling of people helping each other in that situation.

Sometimes they'd say, "We need someone to sing 'Marching Along with Beta Theta Pi' sitting on a block of ice while they're being sprayed with the hose. If we don't have a volunteer by the time I count to twenty, then we're gonna have two people do it. If we don't have a volunteer by then, we're gonna have four people do it." So I would volunteer for things like that. All the time I'd be taking the water, people are cheering, they're applauding. You build up prestige by volunteering, and everybody starts doing it. It's a chance for everyone to become a hero among your fellow people, your closest friends. And under that kind of intensity, you don't ever forget it. If I would see those people now, I would flash back emotionally to those times. I would still want to relate to them with that kind of tightness, that kind of kinship, that we developed.

I saw people change during these rituals, where people I hadn't liked very well would do things to help me personally. Like there's this one guy standing next to me in line who just didn't want to hear any more crap about foreskins. He was really huge, and he'd almost get violent about it when some people would say that to me. And they would back down a little bit, 'cause if he would have become violent he could have torn their heads off. So I had that kind of help from someone right next to me.

For myself, I was finding out how tough I really was. I had always thought I was weak and the other guys were strong, but I was finding out that it was hard to break me. For one thing, I had a sense of humor, and I would always think of what assholes *they* were, the fraternity guys. They would reinforce that idea every time they would do anything.

On Saturday morning they had us do a service project together where we painted this children's home. We hadn't had any sleep for three nights, but we had to go out in the public representing the fraternity. They told us that this is an important service project and you'll be in the newspapers and we want you to tell them that this service project is what we do during our initiation week, that we're not keeping you up or depriving you. So you have to be able to lie for your fraternity; you have to be able to suffer for your fraternity.

That night they told us they were going to take us on a moonlight, midnight hike to the top of Spencer's Butte, which is the highest mountain in town. They told us that on the top of Spencer's Butte they had put out rocks to spell the Greek letters, BTΠ. It was our job to hike to the top of the mountain, pick up the rocks, and reassemble them back at the fraternity by dawn. That would be our group challenge, to put the rocks back in just the right order on the fraternity lawn.

So they had us put on all these clothes because it was really cold out. They asked us kindly, "Are you sure you have enough clothes on? Will you be warm enough? Would you like to borrow a sweater or coat?" They totally duped us by playing on our sympathies and using the brotherhood angle. See, there was this phone room in the fraternity that wasn't very big, just enough room for four telephones. Maybe it was about five feet by ten feet, with a fairly tall ceiling. They said, "Before you go on the hike, let's just for the fun of it see if you can all get in that telephone room." So we had to figure out a way we could all pack into this tiny room. We had to sit on people's shoulders, but somehow we managed to do it. We were still bundled up with all these clothes on. Then they gave us two twelve-inch cigars and closed the doors and put towels around the cracks and we had to smoke those cigars in that room before we could go on our hike.

Well, that was terribly claustrophobic. I got pretty sick from the tobacco.

Finally they just opened the door from the outside and we fell out and they took us to the foot of the mountain and let us off. I started getting into it again, hiking at night and going up this mountain. The challenge was great: "Let's go get these rocks." When we got up there I figured out a way: I gave everybody a number, and we all stood with our rock in the shape of the letters. There was one rock for each of us, so everybody walks off this mountain in the middle of the night with a rock in their hands. We get home and we put it together just right on the lawn and they have us come in for hot cider. We go back out, and they've changed it around. They've torn up the letters while we were inside. Then they tell us to put it together again. Some of the rocks were so similar we couldn't tell them apart. Maybe they even put some different rocks in. Anyway, we couldn't do it, we couldn't get it back together. We had done it right the first time—we *knew* we had put it together right—but it didn't matter.

So it was down to the tub room. We were really depressed. But after our tubbing they told us there was only one more thing we would have to do and we would be through with Hell Week: we had to meet the Mystic Dragon. The dragon is the symbol of the Beta fraternity. The dragon's name is Wooglin. I don't know where the name comes from, but it's a really neat dragon. And we're called the sons of Wooglin, the sons of the dragon.

So they got us all together and said, "Prepare to meet the dragon." They took us down to a room where they had cardboard all over the floor and a great big cauldron in the middle. They had everyone kneel down around it and they said, "Before you can meet the dragon, you have to chew up three blocks of tobacco and spit it out as an offering to the dragon." So we chewed tobacco and chewed tobacco until we could fill up the cauldron with our spit. People started getting sick and throwing up. That's why the cardboard was all around, for people to vomit on. They hadn't fed us for awhile, so it was like having the dry heaves with nothing in your stomach. I went upstairs to the bathroom. I remember lying on the tile floor throwing up into a urinal.

They helped us then. They let us take showers and put us downstairs. Then they'd take us away, one at a time, to meet the dragon.

Every once in awhile you'd hear a big scream, followed by a loud shout, and then they'd take another person away. You didn't know what it was.

I was one of the last ones 'cause I'd been sick. I was really frightened. They put a blindfold on me and led me into the room where I was surrounded by men. They were silent, but I knew they were there. There were officials at the end of the room, and they said some stuff in Greek. They took me to different positions, to the four directions. A guy would say to me, "I am the Brother of the East who brings you the blessings of light and knowledge." And, "I am the Brother of the North who brings you strength and fortitude. Now prepare yourself to meet the dragon!" So they took me over to what they called the dragon's balls, some kind of round, smooth spheres. They told me to take my pants down and lean over to grab hold of the dragon's balls. Then they took my blindfold off and showed me this huge guy with a polished hack-paddle, wood, about two feet long. They told me that my final test would be to take one hack with that paddle. They told me he'd run all the way across the room and wind up and hit me. They said that people had been injured in the past, so I'd have to pull my balls up and cup them with my hands. So I pulled my own balls up and leaned over. The guy walked real slowly back to the other end of the room. I realized that's what I'd been hearing: everybody's scream when they got hit. My knees just started shaking. There was someone on each side of me to hold me up. They told me, "It'll hurt, but we'll help you. Just let yourself fall forward when you're hit and we'll catch you."

So the guy starts running towards me. Everyone in the room starts going, "Mmmmm," louder and louder. And then . . . then he doesn't hit me. It's incredible. He just taps me lightly on the butt, and another person slaps something close to me to make a sharp noise, and another person screams, so the other guys outside the room think that that's going to happen to them.

After that, it's all: "You made it! Congratulations!" You stay in that same room, but they want you to go along with it when they bring the next guy in, so right away they have you doing it to your own people. You're a member now, and you pretend, and you help to scare the other guys.

When the whole pledge class is done you're all given this warm welcome. Everyone is open to you. You're there in the chapter room, this special room in the basement of the fraternity where only members are allowed. It's beautiful—all paneled, polished, carpeted, with cushions all around. You're haggard, you haven't slept, you haven't been allowed to shave—but now you're through. You're done with your Hell Week. It's a fantastic feeling of relief. I went back to the dormitory and all I wanted to do was sleep.

The effects of it . . . when I saw people the next day I began to feel proud of myself. I did it. I survived it, along with all these other people. I wanted to paint my name on the wall of the tub room, to have our names there and the year we did it. Everybody was really into that.

The formal initiation was really nice. It was a week later, on a Sunday. We wore suits and ties, and everyone in the fraternity had on a suit and tie. Only members of the fraternity were present. Some older members came, some business-types from around town. We had a formal dinner and we went down into the chapter room. We went around to the four directions, and they revealed to us these charges for you to consider yourself as a member of this special elite group. We were given our pins with diamonds in them. And we were each given a fraternity number. I think I'm eight hundred and two, or something like that. You'll always be that number. Your name goes on this huge roster, with all the people before you. And your name goes into the national organization. You start getting a national magazine. And you're eligible to stay at any Beta Theta Pi fraternity in the United States. You can go to Yale or Stanford or North Carolina State and you can stay in their chapter house.

I have good, strong memories of the comradeship that the fraternity developed. We had a real acceptance of each other. You did not have to prove yourself anymore—after you had proven yourself during Hell Week. It seemed like you could get away with about anything once you were a member. If you flunked a class, that was okay. Whatever you did, it was just the nature of your personality, your character.

People tell you stories of other Hell Weeks before you have your own. They're laughing about it, they're sharing it. Then you have *yours,* and that's your contribution to the whole history. And we do have our names on the wall. If you go up there today, my name

should be painted right on the tubroom wall, along with the other twenty-nine names from my pledge class, and along with all the other guys before and since. (Joseph A.)[2]

The most important and sweeping function of a primitive initiation was to provide a youth with a sense of his own personal significance within the context of a greater world. In becoming a man he took his place alongside his fathers and forefathers; by discovering his tribal heritage he became connected with the ongoing flow of life. He was transformed into a spiritual being as he joined his ancestors in a universal brotherhood that cut through time.[3]

Fraternities, in their own inimical manner, manage to simulate this function. They offer a true initiation in its classical form, where the power of the tribe is paramount and personal growth is carefully engineered. The ancestors—the football stars of yore, the names on the tub room wall—gaze down upon the neophytes, encouraging them to shape up and belong. The members sleep together, eat together, sing together, suffer together as they learn what it means to be a man among men.

As with the primitives, these modern-day novitiates must deny and transcend their prior and separate identities before they are allowed to join the tribe. To accomplish this monumental task, the fraternity barrages and assaults their individual egos until they acquiesce. The youths are ridiculed for their personal idiosyncracies, their ears and their foreskins, which set them apart. Their privacy is mercilessly denied as they are stripped of their clothes and ordered to perform all sorts of ridiculous acts. They are humiliated at every turn. They are given new names, as if their old names were not good enough. And of course they are frightfully hazed. They are deprived of sleep and incessantly harassed. They are forced to endure extremes of hot and cold. Their minds and their bodies are tossed about till they almost shatter.

How are the initiands taught to cope with such duress? In true classical form, they are given two invaluable aids. First, they are actively discouraged from giving up: "They didn't want you to run, they didn't want you to get away, they didn't want you to try to quit." The fraternity is not merely testing the pledges to see if they are strong enough to endure; it wants and *needs* them to make it through, for without new members it has no reason to exist.

Secondly, the pledges are encouraged to help each other out in times of stress. By volunteering to suffer individually on behalf of their brothers, they can become true heroes at nobody else's expense. They prove their courage not by aggressive displays of personal superiority but rather by coming to the aid of the group. The ideal of interpersonal competition is superseded by that of service. Group loyalty and personal caring —these are the values that the fraternity wishes to foster through its communal hazing as well as through such powerful rituals as the passing of the "Loving Cup."

All this is done, of course, with an abundance of traditional male imagery. There's cigar smoking and tobacco chewing and communal drinking and the telling of sexual tales. There's a focus upon genitals to the point of obsession. Pulling on onions which are tied to cocks—the symbolism here is blatantly reminiscent of the genital mutilations practiced in primitive initiations.[4] Then of course there's the Mystic Dragon, the *beast,* the primordial challenge to male *homo sapiens.* These symbols are not chosen randomly; they are powerful references to the most obvious and dramatic aspects of primitive masculinity.

And somehow it all seems to work. The whole process, admittedly bizarre and occasionally even obscene, really does accomplish the desired goals. Joseph A. feels better about himself—and, presumably, so do his fellow pledges. He no longer feels encumbered by the burden of proof. Now that he has endured he is free to be himself, but this time the image of "himself" has more of a group context. He is a Beta. He can paint his name on the tub room wall. He is one with the ancestors.

But who are these ancestors, anyway? Just a bunch of college boys from the early twentieth century who saw fit to create theatrical representations of a traditional male culture. The drama they fashioned is rich in symbols from other people's history, but it is strangely out-of-synch with our own. In part, the Beta initiation must remain secret because its various and sundry antics might be construed as reprehensible in the context of more public mores. Indeed, our self-conscious body politic often tries to stop these fraternal activities as soon as it learns what is really going on. The only event which does not remain secret is the day of service, a perfectly normal and acceptable offering to respectable society. All the rest of it—well, it's more than a little risqué.[5]

In the past few years there have been several deaths, duly reported in the media, attributed to fraternity initiations: young men falling off cliffs and suffocating inside the trunks of cars. These tragedies are clearly not intentional, nor are they indications of weakness or failure on the part of the men who are killed; they are caused by rank amateurs who are not sufficiently versed in how to conduct the rituals. The college boys are "playing initiation," much as small children might "play house" or "play doctor," only this time the stakes of the game, or at least the dangers, are much more serious.

Joseph A., who obviously understands and appreciates all the classical imagery, still retains a trace of ironic distance from Beta's carryings-on. And it is small wonder that he does. The initiation might be classical in theme and structure, but there is no escaping the obvious fact that the whole thing is little more than a caricature of itself. What it all boils down to in the end is just a series of pranks. Fraternities, unlike primitive initiations, allow a youth to retain his childish ways while simultaneously laying claim to a more manly status.[6] Even when he joins the club of "the good old boys"—well, "boys will be boys." It's an attractive but slightly vacuous sort of manhood that emerges in the end. The men are not preparing to defend the tribe or go off on a hunt; the endurance they evidence serves no objective purpose. But they do recognize a need that is not now being fulfilled in a more natural manner: the need to belong, and simultaneously to prove that they are worthy of belonging.

College students aren't the only ones to conjure up history in order to promote group identity for modern-day men. Our pluralistic culture is replete with choices; we can select from any number of different "tribes" which are based on an eclectic assortment of traditions. Each of these groups offers us an invaluable opportunity to belong, yet each also reveals a gradual evolution from integral to incidental forms of male bonding. This movement from the significant to the trivial is no small part of our collective experience as males.

Witness, for instance, Ryan J.'s initiation into the Masons:

Once you've been accepted by a Masonic Lodge then the Master and his officers put together your first degree. You're given the basic instructions as to what the organization is about. You have to take one obligation which is given at the altar. You swear to keep the secrets of the organization. You then have to sit and listen to a lecture that's presented by the officers about the basic tenets of Masonry.

During part of the ceremony you're blindfolded so you can focus in on what's being said to you.

Before you could be advanced to your next degree you would have to commit to memory a question-and-answer prologue of about twelve hundred words. It's in middle English, because this all comes from back around five or six hundred years ago. It's pretty difficult; I mean, try reading your *Beowolf* sometime. So some people don't make the grade. They drop out, they're gone.

None of this is written down. All of the Masonic ritual is taught, mouth to ear. I really can't tell you all the different things that are in it. The last guy that revealed the secrets back in the nineteenth century wound up dead in the Hudson River.

After you've recited your part in front of the officers and the members, then the Lodge advances you to the second degree, which is when you learn more of what goes on within the organization and about the historical significance of the Masons. You're blindfolded again for a while and you take another obligation. You get eighteen hundred words of stuff to go learn with your coach. Again it's in Middle English 'cause they haven't changed any of the rituals since it was first put together back in England.

The third degree is the ultimate thing in Masonry. It's divided into three parts and it takes about three and a half hours. The first part is another obligation, similar to the first and second degree. Then the candidate takes part in a play, which is very difficult because you're blindfolded all the time and you're led around the room. It's taken out of the Old Testament, dealing with one of the master architects who was building King Solomon's temple, things that happened to him. Then the third section is a lecture where you're told all of the secrets of the organization and they're entrusted to your care. This results in your becoming a full-fledged member of the organization from that point on. You are recognized as a "true and trusted brother." You promise to keep the secrets of a brother Mason, murder and treason excepted. You promise to help and assist brother Masons, their widows, their orphans.

After I got my third degree I went "up the line" to become a Master. It takes eight years; there are eight offices and you spend a year in each spot and you get advanced to the next one, ultimately being the Master of the Lodge. You have to learn the different speeches and different parts of the rituals for each of the offices along the way. Then when you get to be a Master you know all of the Masonic ritual. That in itself was a great experience for me, because I never used to be able to talk in front of groups. I used to stutter and stammer. But to put a candidate through the third degree, the Master has to do forty-five minutes of solid talking. You're the guy that gives the lectures. So before you can advance up the line to being Master, you have to be able to give this stuff perfectly.

I found it personally rewarding to go through all that. I felt I had to prove to myself that I could do it. When I first started up the line, I used to go to the Lodge and I was a nervous wreck. I didn't have a very big part in those days, but I'd still be a nervous wreck when I'd have to get up and give my three or four paragraphs because the older guys were really critical if you just missed an "and" or a "but." It might not sound like such a big deal, but they were into every word had to be *exactly* right. They would insult you publicly about it. I remember one time I was going to be Officer of the Lodge and we had to be in full dress and I had to go to the Goodwill for six months before I could find a set of tails to wear. I gave my part for the first time and I didn't do a terribly bad job but I was nervous and I didn't do a really super job either. So there I was in my tails talking to the Treasurer of the Del Monte Corporation and the District Attorney of the City and County of San Francisco and up comes this guy who was a steam fitter who was the officers' coach and he completely blew me away for not saying the part absolutely correctly. It was really a put-down.

I found that really hard to handle. So finally when I became the Master and did the third degree part, that was the big payoff because I was able to do that and learn that and show these other people who had been giving me a bad time for many years that I could do this just as well, if not better, than they did it. At the time that was my motivation for doing this. I look back on it now and it was probably kind of stupid, but at the time there was a lot of fulfillment in it because I had had such a hard time memorizing all that stuff. I was never a football hero in high school or head of the debating club. I wasn't in any ambitious sort of thing. For me, being a part of the Masons enabled me to prove to the older men (and by proving it to

**the older men I was able to transfer it to society in general) that I had
arrived and I'm a real person to deal with.**

The success of these fraternal orders is due to their inherently social
fabric. Not only do they offer particular images of manhood, but they also
provide viable settings in which those images can be realized. This is no
small feat in an individualistic culture where young males are often left to
their own devices to prove they are men. When a group—*any* group—
offers a well-defined set of norms and goals, along with a method for
living up to those norms and meeting those goals, we are given at least a
semblance of structural support for our transition into manhood.

Fraternal fellowships therefore help us place our personal struggles in
a larger context. By joining a group we move beyond our individual
limitations and share in the collective power of a body of men. And the
groups themselves generally try to exceed their own narrow boundaries,
claiming access to the universal power of *all* men. The symbolism used by
the various fellowships is replete with archetypal images. At least through
ritual, each group wants to extend its scope, to connect with life's most
fundamental realities, to gain a sort of ceremonial power over the world.

To affirm for itself this transcendent sense of self-importance, each
fellowship tries to establish its historical roots, to tie itself to a significant
tradition. Beta Theta Pi takes its name from the ancient Greek alphabet,
while it self-consciously attempts to turn its own founding fathers into
important historical figures. Jokingly but meaningfully, it even refers back
to the era of dragons, a time when a man in search of honor and glory
could supposedly find for himself a challenge to meet all challenges. The
Masons refer all the way back to the Old Testament, and they ceremoni-
ously conduct their rituals in Middle English. Each with its own theatrical
style, our modern-day fellowships use the sheer weight of history to
transform apparently petty antics into emotionally significant events.

When viewed from the outside, however, the nostalgic imagery of
these various rituals seems at best only quaint. If bar mitzvahs or confirmations appear today as merely trivial, the initiation ceremonies of college fraternities or the Masons can be perceived as contrived and contorted. Unless we can somehow manage to suspend our disbelief, we are
likely to interpret all this mustering-up of tradition as a futile attempt to
return to archaic images which have little or nothing to do with contem-

porary realities. Dragons, the Greek alphabet, Middle English—what, we might ask, does all this have to do with a man's coming-of-age in the late twentieth century? But when we cast about for a group to join in our attempts to gain access to the brotherhood of men, these strange adaptations of ancient imagery are about all we will find. Our forced and unnatural air belies desperation. We reach back to other people's history precisely because our own contemporary lifestyles seem to be lacking in resonance or appropriate meaning.

CHAPTER 6

Single Combat

erhaps the most convincing way to join the brotherhood of men is to become a warrior, a protector of the tribe. In order to join our fathers and forefathers, we have only to do what they once did: put our lives on the line in a display of personal strength and valor. Will Bell, the Vietnam veteran, joined the Army to do "what my father had done, what my grandfather had done"; this, he felt, entitled him to become "an adult white male American." Evan R., likewise, wanted to live up to his masculine heritage:

My dad was both in the Navy and the Army. When he was seventeen he enlisted in the Navy for World War II and served four or five months. The war ended and he was discharged. When the Korean War came around he had not served his full obligation so he was drafted for the Army. As a kid growing up, I had a familiarity with the fact that there was a military: the cruise book from his recruit class, some of his old uniforms laying around, that type of thing. I imagine that's a common enough experience.

I viewed the achievements of my dad as significant. He was a high school jock and had been to war and I hadn't done any of that. Basically, I had made no mark on the world. I had got through school on a nip and a tuck and finally graduated, but the edge was taken off of it because I didn't do real well. I still needed to prove to myself that I had some excellence, was capable of excellence.

There comes a point in time when you say, "Gosh, school is going to end. What am I going to do with myself?" I wanted to join the military, and I thought I'd really like to fly. As a kid what I always wanted most was to be a pilot, and the kind of piloting that was exciting was tactical airplanes, fighters—let's drop bombs, go fast, look cool, that kind of stuff. Fighter pilots are somebody; they're neat, they're glamorous, all those things that little kids apply to heroes.

The thing that makes air-to-air combat so interesting is it's man against man, using an airplane. Nobody else is flying your airplane except you. If you screw it up and get shot, then the guy that was flying the other airplane is better. It's very simple: he shot you down. It doesn't matter whether you're a good father or he's got halitosis or he's got warts on his nose—if he flies better than you and shoots you down, who gives a rat's ass for all the rest of it? It's personal combat. I'm into that. Let's have at it. There's a time and a place for personality, pleasantness, for being kind—but when the other guy is trying to deprive you of your life, that's not the time to be anything except successful. Either you win or you die.

This is the traditional image of warfare: "Let's have at it." It's single combat, "man against man," the survival of the fittest. The strong will destroy the weak, for that is the way of Nature. Fighter pilots who have the skill and the guts to outwit, outfly, and outshoot their rivals will live on; those who don't will perish. And the ones who survive, of course, are the real men, while the ones who fail don't quite have the "right stuff."[1]

But is this how warfare really works in this day and age? Could young Evan R. simply join the armed forces and then go out and challenge the nearest enemy to a personal contest of skill and courage?

When Evan finally did become a fighter pilot he was in fact forbidden, by the dictates of international politics, to "have at it" with a real, live enemy. Evan came along just a little too late for Vietnam. Nobody was trying to deprive him of his life, so it was not quite a question of "you win or you die." Despite four years in ROTC and seven years in the Navy, he never did see active combat.

This is not to say that Evan failed to prove his manhood through military service. The Navy did have something to offer him—the opportunity to rise through the hierarchy and gain some self-respect:

They put me through AOCS, Aviation Officer Candidate School. When you're there they intend you, and they force you, to exceed anything that you thought you could ever do, to find new levels of endurance, to go beyond pain. And it works. You feel like a real superman when you come out of that program, because it's the toughest thing you've ever been through. You come out of there with a sense of elitism: "Hey, you're somebody special." And in fact you are; statistically, ten thousand people apply for the one position that they graduate. So you're already better than all those others. In the program itself, depending on the class, less than half the people make it through. So it is quite a challenge.

After going through that training, I felt like that was a significant accomplishment. I had been selected on the basis of my achievement. I was making my mark on the world. After all those years of feeling like I was a nobody . . . click, I was now a somebody. I had done something that measures up not only to my own expectations, but to other people's expectations. My dad was extremely pleased that I could be an officer in the Navy.

But was that enough? Thousands of new officers are commissioned every year in the U.S. Navy, and Evan R. quickly learned that just being an Ensign is not "the end-all to end-all." He wanted to do something to distinguish himself from "those who are green and not worthy of respect."

So you go on: what level of accomplishment do you have to have to gain respect, to get the fulfillment of the need that you feel inside? To me, it was getting my wings. To get Navy wings is a bona fide big deal. That classifies as major league, there's no doubt in my mind. That's what I wanted to do, so I set out to do it.

To get his wings, Evan had to learn how to land a jet fighter on an aircraft carrier, which of course is no easy task. He failed his first test and felt crushed, but he went back into training and finally made the grade.

I don't think I've ever been happier than when I found out I qualified. The sense of self-worthlessness that I had felt when I had failed was now erased. I felt good. I was *somebody*.

But you'll see again that this all gets deflated. At each point you find out that you're not such a big shot after all. You're commissioned as an officer, then you find out there are sixty thousand officers. So what? You land on the carrier, and again: So what? There are two thousand fleet aviators on the East Coast that land on carriers on a regular basis. Big deal. You haven't shown me anything, because landing on the carrier is just like learning how to start your car.

So now I went into ACM, Air Combat Maneuvering. You learn how to shoot air-to-air guns; you shoot at a banner that another airplane drags through the air, and then you come back and they count the bullet holes. I got through ACM—didn't break any airplanes, didn't kill myself, didn't kill anybody else. Got good enough grades and got my wings. At that point you're designated a Naval Aviator, and that is another significant achievement. That's more exclusive. Getting your wings is joining the club.

But the climbing goes on. I graduated and went on to the fleet squadron thinking I'm a big, bad fighter pilot, and I find out that I'm in a bigger pond with bigger fish, and you're suddenly a small fish in a big pond again. You find out that in fact you don't know everything there is to know about being a fighter pilot, that you aren't the baddest dude in the whole world.

What does all this have to do with real-life warfare? The closest approximation of a real enemy which the Navy provided for Evan R. was a banner being dragged through the air. The challenges which he finally overcame turned out to be institutional in nature; ironically, Evan was able to prove his individual merit only by climbing the ladder of a bureaucratic organization. The military hierarchy insured that Evan's drive for masculine self-respect, a drive which could not realistically be satisfied by single combat, could still find an acceptable and accessible outlet: he could climb to the next rung of the ladder; he could eke out a little more authority and prestige in his perpetual battle for ascension; he could find a social context in which to affirm his incipient manhood.

This rechanneling of aggressive energy into institutional forms is not particularly surprising. Despite the frontier mystique of rugged individualism which we Americans still embrace, and despite our desire to prove our valor on our own, our real military structure is inevitably interdependent, with no single individual—not even at the higher levels of command—enjoying much autonomy. The most important warriors of today, if we are to be honest with ourselves, are not individualized heroes but coordinated teams of highly skilled technicians and engineers—nuclear scientists, computer programmers, logistical experts—who are the architects of our military might.[2]

The advanced and impersonal technology of the military affects us all in one way or another. The automation of war implies that fewer soldiers are actually needed to wreak havoc upon an enemy; prospective warriors, in effect, experience the same type of "unemployment" endemic to any automated technology. And even for those who manage to hang on to their military jobs, there is not always an appropriate opponent. The entire military machine is reduced to perpetual preparation for events that we hope will never occur.

So whatever happened to Evan R.'s original ideal of single combat? Evan himself managed to adapt to the times, but how does the bureaucratization of warfare affect other young men who might, in different times, have proved their manly valor in battle?

Many of us—perhaps most of us—are in no great hurry to go out and join the army. Indeed, we feel blessedly relieved of our traditional masculine burden.

Why should I join the army? You've got to be crazy. I was on a football team once, and that was bad enough. I've got better things to do with my life than do push-ups and get yelled at all the time. Why should I give up my freedom? Isn't freedom what it's all about? (Cyrus W.)

Yet some of us still seem to long for that special intensity of military experience—and in the absence of real battles we are tempted to fabricate facsimiles. At least through fantasy we hope to salvage something of a warrior's initiation. We transform war into an illusion, mere play:

As early as I can remember, I played survival-type games with toy guns, dart guns, BB guns, pea shooters, rubber bands and paper clips, pointed fingers. When I was in the police we played them with plastic bullets. So I've played them all my life in one form or another.

When I read an article in *Time* magazine about the survival game, I thought, "This should be fun." I called up the place in New Hampshire to get the paint guns and a rule book so I could play it with my friends. I didn't realize there was a structure to it, like a dealership. They said, "No one's doing a game in your area. Do you want to put on the games yourself?" They gave me the exclusive right to put on the games in my territory. So I organized it just so I could play the game. But I don't really like organizing it, keeping track of all the stuff. My wife does most of the organizational work.

We lease a hundred and sixty-seven acres up in the hills, but we only use about twenty acres. The original idea was to use a larger area and to issue a compass and a map to everybody, but then it became a game of hiking, not a game of shooting people, which is really what's fun. So we narrowed it down to an open field of a couple of hundred meters, together with the hills and all the vegetation surrounding it. You can make a direct run through the center of the field, but you'll be seen. So usually you go into the vegetation to make your attack at the flag. The object of the game is to capture the other team's flag and return it to your flag station, or to eliminate the other team. Then the game is over and you blow a whistle for everybody to come in and you start a new game.

The way the games work is somebody will call here and sign up to play on a certain date. We'll write their name down and they'll pay in advance with a check or a credit card number so we'll know they're coming. Sometimes they come individually or sometimes they come as a group, as an entire team. We have some companies, like the Hilton Hotel, that just want to come and play each other.

I go out there and set up a table ahead of time and get the equipment out. They sign in and I give them a uniform if they need it, just a camouflage thing so they won't be spotted so easily. A bunch of guys bring their own camouflage stuff, the guys who are real serious about it. Then when everybody's ready I hand out the pistols and we discuss their operation. I go through the basic rules. The first rule is never take your goggles off during the game. That's very important, because the pellets that these paint guns fire can damage your eyes. So I make a big speech about that. The next rule is if the pellet doesn't break on you, it doesn't count as a hit. If the pellet does break you'll get paint on you, and that's clear proof you've been hit and you're out for the rest of the game. In championship games they're real strict about that; if you have a drop of paint on you anywhere you're out. We're not quite that strict. But some problems do occur; for example, when a guy gets hit in the back he doesn't know whether it broke or not. So a lot of it is people yelling, "Hey, I got you!"

"Where? You didn't get me."

"Check your holster."

"Yeah, I guess I didn't feel it."

You're always yelling back and forth like that: "Did I get you?"

"No, you didn't get me. You came pretty close."

If there's a dispute then somebody calls a freeze. Everybody yells, "Freeze," and then the guy walks out in the open and says, "OK, where am I hit?" Then when that's settled you go back to where you were and you say, "One, two, three, go," and the game starts again.

When you get hit you're generally real angry. Here you were attacking and doing a great thing and suddenly you're dead, you're out, you're no longer playing. You might have to wait for an hour before the game is over, and all you can do is sit and watch. It's a real disappointment. Some guys get mad. You hear a lot of yelling: "God-damn son-of-a-bitch!" Guys are walking out of there cursing all the way. But it's not like you're really dead: there's so much anger and disappointment that you know you're really alive.

We get a wide selection of people wanting to play. A lot of professional people: accountant, lawyer, psychologist, all that kind of stuff. We also have young guys, blue collar workers, macho types. They're real hot-heads: they get mad if they don't win, and they take it real serious. Some of these guys are more into the war aspect of it. They come out there with big knives and everything, make them feel real military. That kind of attitude usually doesn't last, because it's really just a game.

The game is open to women, we're happy to have them, but very few women actually play it. And the ones that play—they go out there once and they're exhilarated, but they don't want to do it again. It's just a thing they've done to see how it is, like going on a roller coaster. It does not appeal to most women, for whatever reason. They don't like getting dirty, they don't like breaking their fingernails, they don't like getting paint in their hair. It's very clear once you've played it — men like it and women don't, essentially. Very few women have the aggressiveness. They take less joy in shooting people. They're worried about hurting someone. When they shoot somebody, they'll say, "Did I hurt you?"

But the men, they'll generally go, "Ha, ha, ha. I got you!" It's friendly, but they like shooting people. I shoot a real pistol in competition. The main rule in competition shooting is you never point your pistol at anyone. It's an absolutely cardinal rule you have to obey, and you get it deeply ingrained in your brain. It's so deeply ingrained in me that I wondered in my first survival game whether I could actually point a gun at somebody who was not a real enemy. I thought I might have some problems with that. But I got to the game the first time and—bang—I shot a guy and it felt great. No problem whatsoever.

I get a real charge out of it. I've been in the real thing, and the excitement is the same. There's an excitement that comes with danger that's very attractive. What you don't have in the survival game, but you do have in the real thing, is fear. The fear you have in the real thing often overwhelms the excitement and makes you sick physically. Your stomach is in knots. You'll be walking through vegetation looking for somebody, just patrolling, and anybody could be sitting anywhere and shoot you. You can walk for days, and you never know when someone's going to shoot you, plus the added concern of stepping on a mine or contacting some sort of booby trap. So you have that continual fear which you can't shake. That's what's nice about the survival game: when it's over, it's over. You can relax; there's nothing more to worry about. Everybody has a big pow-wow— "Hey, remember when you were hiding behind the bush over there?"—and you can do it all again. Then at the end of the day you get your picture taken, filthy, with big blotches of mud and paint all over you, and you go home with your bumper sticker: "I Survived the Survival Game."

Some of the most exciting times you can have in the survival game is just waiting. You're waiting for someone to walk by and you hear them coming. They're coming slowly and being real cautious. Sometimes the excitement is almost overwhelming. It makes you physically

tremble, 'cause you're just waiting: "Come on! Come on!" You got
your adrenalin up, especially in a hazardous situation. You can only
watch through a certain area where the brush is open. You can hear
them coming, but you don't know exactly where they're coming
from. They may be coming from behind. You have to make a decision, which way you're going to watch. You can't watch both ways
because if you move you make noise. So as you're watching, waiting,
looking in this direction, you think they may be coming from behind
you and they'll shoot you first. Some people can't take it. They lose
their cool. They can't sit quietly and hold their emotions. What
happens is they panic: they jump up and start shooting or run away.
They just can't take the excitement.

If you like sneaking around, that's the important thing. I like being
able to hide, I don't know quite why. There's no other game you can
do that in. It's an ability, an art form: being able to camouflage
yourself properly, to know how to conceal yourself well. It's hard to
do. There's no other place that appreciates that, other than the real
army. And war games in the army are nowhere near as much fun as
this. Generally they're logistical wars: who can move the most equipment to a certain area in the minimum amount of time. There's very
little individual shooting; it's mostly just a big map game. That's
what they have to do to prepare for real wars, because that's what real
war is about these days: moving a lot of equipment.

What we're doing in the survival games goes back to a more primitive type of warfare. Really, it's just hunting. When you're sneaking
through the brush, waiting for someone to walk by, you can either
shoot him or you can spear him and eat him. If it was a deer you'd be
eating him. It's the same sort of thing. It's a primitive feeling, being
able to sneak up on somebody like that.

For some people it's sort of a manhood ritual. I'm thirty-six, and
when I grew up virtually everybody went into the army. You had to
because you were drafted. Now, there's been no draft for the last
twelve years. So there's a lot of kids—eighteen, nineteen, twenty—
that say to me, "Wow, were you in the army? You really *did* something." A few years ago, just because you were in the army, it didn't
mean you *did* anything. But now they think you're somebody, you've
done something, like you've climbed a mountain. A lot of people miss
it. Being drafted was one of our rites: you got to go in the army, you

went through basic training, and then you were a man. Now we don't have that. For some of them, they want to experience this stuff—and the Survival Game is about the closest thing to the military that they can do. It's really important just to have done it, even if only once. One of the great questions of being a man is: "How will I react in combat?" That's what people want to find out in the survival game: "Will I cut and run, or will I stand and fight?" (Alec Jason)

Alec Jason's Survival Game offers us the opportunity to play-act a drama that has gone out with the times. It personalizes the experience of warfare; it brings it back down to a human scale. It returns us to the ideal of single combat—even if it's only make-believe.

The Survival Game, a self-conscious simulation of warfare, is the archetypal competitive sport, but other athletic contests can likewise be seen as simulated battles. In the absence of personalized warfare, we construct a series of mock battlefields upon which we can challenge willing enemies to tests of strength, speed, and skill. We throw balls instead of spears; we swing bats instead of clubs; we fight with fists instead of guns. We play games and we play them for keeps—but the games do not destroy. In sports, our harmless metaphors for war, the winners can revel in victory but the losers are never killed.[3]

The attraction to sports is particularly strong during the formative stages of development when boys are seeking a standard of manhood. Since professional athletes serve as the most visible models for adult masculinity in American culture, the perplexing tasks of personal growth easily get translated into the imagery of sports. When a youth is trying to establish his identity as a man, sports give him a sense of who he is and tell him where he stands.[4]

Fifteen-year-old Alex Lash, for instance, is in the throes of adolescent transition. Intelligent and personable, Alex is a straight-A student who could probably forge a career in the professional field of his choice—but all he really wants to do when he grows up is play baseball:

I want to play in the big leagues because that's the highest level you can be. That's the top of the pyramid. If you get to the big leagues, you're the best. And there's nothing I'd rather be the best in than baseball—just for the sake of saying, for my own satisfaction, "I'm one of the best."

For the last eight years, that's been my major fantasy. The recurring dream is: two outs, full count, bottom of the ninth, and they bring me in from the bullpen in the seventh game of the World Series. I swear I've had that dream a couple of times. It sounds corny, but I have. But I never find out what happens; I guess the pressure is so intense that I just wake up.

Whenever someone asks me, "What do you want to be when you grow up?" I say, "A baseball player." I've always said that. For some reason, that's just the first thing that comes into my mind. I am interested in other fields—science, literature—but I can't see myself being a professor or an English scholar poring over old dusty volumes in the library. I *can* picture myself being on a baseball team and playing in the major leagues. It seems like a childish fantasy, something that most people would outgrow. I guess I just haven't outgrown it yet, even though I'm almost sixteen.

The biggest thrill for me is pitching. I'd even rather pitch than go up to bat. There's something about being up there on the mound and all the attention is on you. You know that everything depends on you. It's individual competition, just you against the hitter. If he gets a hit he's one up on you, but if you strike him out you're one up. I'm not really into degrading people, but it's that one-on-one—it's real intense. For just a few minutes, you're up against that one batter. You know that every camera, every focus, is on you and on the batter. It makes me nervous, but it also makes me really high. It's like a euphoria to be out there. The grass is green, the sun is shining, the uniforms are pressed and white and you're ready for the competition.

Alex's ambition, really, is a perfect example of the precious American Dream: by winning we achieve success, we make our way to the top. In sports this dream takes on a peculiar slant, for success on the playing field is easily equated with the process of maturation. If ever a fellow does make it to the very top, manhood will certainly be achieved; it will be, almost by definition, an accomplished fact.

And yet the manhood he achieves remains somewhat fantastical. In classical initiation rites, a young male must first discard his childish ways before becoming a man; in our society, a youth can supposedly prove he's a man by mastering a game that is most often played by children. Ironically, childhood activities such as baseball and football are never fully acknowledged until they are played on an adult level, so boys are tempted to prove their manliness by continuing to play at their games. This makes for a peculiar but attractive method of initiation. We can have our cake and eat it too; we do not have to give up being boys in order to become the men we would like to be.[5] For Alex Lash, this is certainly an appealing prospect:

> I think everyone's a little scared of growing up. I think you wouldn't be normal if you were not scared, after living seventeen or eighteen years at home, by suddenly going *out there*—paying your bills, making your own bed, doing your own laundry, cooking your own dinner, doing your own shopping. I don't want to. I'd rather have my mom go out and do the shopping. I don't want to have to pay for the house, the roof over my head. It's definitely scary. But if I could pay for the roof over my head by playing baseball, that'd be the best way to do it. That'd be the ideal way.
>
> I've never really talked to a major league baseball player, but from what I gather they're just men who still have that little competitive, mischievous, boyish nature in them. They want to go out on the weekends and roll around in the dirt and dive in the grass, except they are a little better at it than most people so they do it for a living. My dad is sort of like that. I can see him still being a baseball player, because he still has that sense of fun, that sense of mischief. At times he really reminds me of a little boy. Whenever his back doesn't hurt, he still loves going out to the schoolyard with me and playing strike-outs. It's like having another fifteen-year-old to play strikeouts with.

In a world where single combat can be found only in games, it is difficult for men to outgrow their childhood fantasies and their adolescent visions of competitive achievement. Paul Z., for instance, is an unattached laborer who was pushing thirty when he tried to make his debut in professional football:

> It was the year all the kickers were missing all those field goals in the NFL.; it was the year a lot of people decided, "Hey, I can do better than that." And so I thought, "Well, I'll try it. I'll work on my kicking."
>
> I called the Raiders up and said, "Hey, if I can kick fifty-yard field goals every time, will you give me a tryout?" They said, "Yeah." So that was my goal. I went out to South Fork [High School] and

practiced kicking there. A kid came up and was fielding for me and I told him all about it and I gave him my autograph. My first, my one and only, autograph. The dream was growing.

I jumped on a plane to New York and got a room in the Y and was practicing kicking into a mattress. Then I went out to Central Park and was practicing there, but there was no goal post so I had to go up to Azteca Lumber on 79th and Amsterdam and I bought all these two-by-fours and I made a goal post in Central Park and put it up in a garbage can. I just kept kicking in the snow in Central Park, even in the middle of the night.

I figured by then I had to be able to kick fifties in the snow to really make it. I'd get to forty-fives and boom, boom, boom. No problem. Get to forty-seven, get to forty-eight, and invariably right around forty-eight I just couldn't do it. That was my limit, basically. So that was it. I figured, "Forget it. If my goal is to kick fifties, I just can't get it together."

And that's basically as far as I got. I went to the NFL office in New York and talked to the guy who worked there. He wasn't real encouraging. I wrote to the Cleveland Browns, but I never sent the letter. I was writing these fantasy stories about me kicking in the Park and the Brown's coach's daughter discovering me. Then I guess reality just reared its ugly head.

A couple of years later I was listening to KGO and they said they were going to have a contest: "Kick for Cash." You could kick a forty yard field goal and win a thousand dollars after the Cal Berkeley game. That would be easy for me. So I made out two hundred postcards. There were twenty people whose cards were drawn, and of course I was one of them. They gave me tickets to the game. At the end of the game half the people leave the stands, but there's still about twenty thousand people left. When it came my turn to kick, I said, "I'm going to kick this baby *hard*." I kicked it hard and I kicked it further than anybody else kicked it, but I was way wide. Twenty thousand people went, "Oooo . . ." At least they cared. So that was it. I had only one shot.

Then the next year, last year, it's the same contest basically except you get two kicks and you win five thousand dollars if you make them both. I had my cousin put in about thirty cards for me. Sure enough I got picked again.

This time it was only thirty-five yards. I'm the first kicker. They gave me a totally brand new football, which is hard to kick. Anyway, I just got into my rhythm. I go, "Don't try to kill it. Just a nice flow." Well, it was lousy, like it landed on the goal line and the goal posts are ten yards back. They said, "You get another try. You can still win the bike." So this time I just pounded it through and made it. Twenty thousand people went crazy, and I won the bike. That was about it, basically. I still have the bike. I ride it to the laundromat now and then.

Why do adult males continue to play these games, long after the age when boys in other cultures have already asserted their manhood? What is it that we really hope to *prove*? And why, so often, do we try to prove it through sports?

Although the ideology of athletic contests is based on Alex Lash's "one-on-one," our games also offer that dramatic social context which we have found to be lacking in many of our individualized initiations. Twenty thousand people boo or cheer as Paul Z. attempts to kick his field goal; "every camera, every focus" is aimed at Alex Lash as he attempts to mow down the batter. Sports provide a public arena, a ready-made structure, in which we hope to validate our worth. Team sports provide us with an approximation of a tribe; even individual sports provide at least one opponent who serves as our "public." There is always someone around to approve (or disapprove) of our deeds. However superficial and contrived, sports are simply *there*—they are present in our lives, ubiquitous in American culture, and it is therefore little wonder that we turn to them so readily when we cast about for a suitable context in which to prove our mettle.

Athletic contests hold a special appeal in an automated society which limits other forms of personal interaction with the physical world. In the absence of traditional contexts, they offer an attractive and accessible definition of manliness. Strength, speed, endurance, finesse—these are all very concrete and "real." They harken back to that primordial struggle for survival that still captures our fancy: The strong will survive and the weak will not. In the words of Mr. America, Chuck Sipes:

I don't feel superior to anybody, but people do look up to me wherever I go. I can't help that. People admire strength, and if they're looking at a male that's the first thing they look for. That goes right back to the beginning of time: The strongest survive and the weakest perish. That's the way it is in nature, right? Especially when you're young. A young animal, that's his most trying time in the wilderness. If he isn't strong and he doesn't know what's happening, he perishes. It's the law of survival.

The notion of "survival of the fittest" has a certain masculine allure. With the increasing abstraction of our modern struggle for survival, the tangible metaphor men create on the playing field becomes more and more compelling. The competitive drive, the urge to dominate through a demonstration of physical prowess, finds a readily accessible outlet in our highly ritualized battles:

> In high school I was a vicious competitor. I put a hundred percent into football. I really liked the physical contact—that feeling of smacking somebody, bringing him down. I don't know, I guess it made me feel superior to the other players. I didn't care how big they were, I just brought them down. I liked the combativeness of it. You'd wind up with a lot of aches and pains, like you had been through a war or something. Now I don't know where this comes from, but being male. . . . (Chuck Sipes)

The imagery here—the combativeness, the superiority—does appear to be "male," at least according to traditional connotations. Using a unique twist of masculine logic, we reduce the process of maturation to the task of knocking other men down in a make-believe game. Insofar as we assume that athletic prowess is indicative of manliness, we turn our games into ad hoc initiations which we assume will transform us into adult male *homo sapiens*—if only we can manage to come out on top.

In sports as well as in war, only the best and the strongest are supposed to prevail in the end. The common presumption which validates our athletic "initiations" is that merit, and merit alone, will determine success. At least in theory, the best will not only survive—they will actually win. In this sense competitive games promise to be improvements upon real-life battles. In sports, unlike warfare, the role of chance appears to be minimal. Everyone starts on an even basis, with an equal shot at victory. There is no such thing as political or technological advantage, and the rules apply equally to all contestants. An athletic contest therefore provides a seemingly fair and objective means for men to prove their worth. It's the pure essence of single combat, and the combat occurs out in the open where all can see and applaud. "May the best man win," we say—and then we assume that he does.

CHAPTER 7

The Role of Chance

But do these simulations of single combat really work? How real is the context they provide? Will the fittest survive, or will the best necessarily win?

All men, of course, are not equally endowed, so the race to become the "best" is not always as fair as we would like to believe. Was Alex Lash or Paul Z. born as well equipped physically as Chuck Sipes? Probably not. And native athletic ability is like any other form of class privilege; it effectively prohibits, for those who do not possess it, equal access to competitive success. This simple yet undeniable truth, whenever we bother to ponder it, inevitably alters the basic thrust of our athletic mythology, for it lessens the importance of individual volition and control in what we mean by "the best."

Any notion of "the best" must assume an objective means of measurement—and this is exactly what sports are supposed to provide. In theory, the objectivity of an athletic contest is ensured by its artificiality; since the event is removed from everyday life, its measurement of ability remains pure and untainted. In practice, however, athletic competition is not so pure and removed as we would like to believe. Extraneous variables unrelated to talent, drive, or character can make or break an athletic career. Listen, for example, to the personal testimony of a successful basketball professional, Al Attles:

I've never looked at my athletic achievements as anything extra special. I was pretty good, but there were a lot of pretty good people. I never thought in terms of playing basketball beyond college, and there were reasons for that. Small colleges, and in particular small black colleges, never graduated very many athletes into the professional ranks, because they really didn't scout them.

It was really a question of timing. I happened to take a year out of school before going to college, so that put me in a different class. In the year ahead of me there were three or four good players from the big cities, so if I hadn't taken that year off I would've been on the same team as these guys and nobody would've noticed me as much. And that was just about the time they were beginning to take a more serious look at black players. Before then they'd take one or two of the really great ones, but they wouldn't bother to take a look at guys like me.

So I was drafted by the Warriors in the fifth round, but that didn't give me much of a shot at making the team. Generally they only take the first or second round choice. But again, it was a question of timing. There was another player trying out for guard, and they said that the year before he was one of the best looking guards in camp. But he had to go up to the Army for a year and he probably lost that competitive edge. So his bad timing and my good timing made things work out. Maybe if I had been drafted into the NBA the year before or the year after I wouldn't have made it, because they didn't even need the kind of a guard I was.

Another thing about timing is the injuries. I've always had muscle problems from running; my thighs were kind of big, so I'd pull my muscles. Now I didn't have a contract when I reported to training camp, and I went through training camp and twenty games of the exhibition season and I never got hurt, nothing serious. If at any point something had happened, it would've been: "Adios. Goodbye.

You go home." I was just lucky, because later on I did get hurt, but by then I was already on the team.

So that's why I always look at being in the right place at the right time as being the single most important factor in our whole lives, which we have no control over. Of course with some people—like Wilt, you knew Wilt was going to be an NBA player as soon as he hit the floor and saw his skill. Sure, at any time he could have broken his leg or something, but all things being equal, if nothing special happened to change the course of history, you knew he was going to succeed. Okay, but for the majority of us I think it's the opposite. So you've got to keep it in the perspective of timing.

Al Attles's modesty is exceptional. Usually it is only the losers who like to point out the elements that are extraneous to the game: social forces, injuries, or chance in any form. But Al Attles is a winner. He was a respected player for many years, and he later went on to coach his team to a National Basketball Association championship. A successful career, indeed—and all made possible by fortuitous timing.

But what about Al's rival, the one who went into the Army? Or how about all those other hustling guards (the nation's playgrounds are full of them) who never even got scouted, or perhaps got injured at just the wrong moment? Where are they now? Is an athlete who was never seen and never called necessarily a worse basketball player than Al Attles, just because he didn't make it to the NBA?

And even more important: Is he any less of a man? Probably not, but the logical consequence of confusing athletic competition with maturation is to assume that he *is* less of a man. Of course this confusion is both common and understandable, for when we win we like to feel that we have convincingly proved our worth. But this same logic also implies that when we lose we are not the men we would like to be.

The role of chance figures significantly in many of our attempts to prove our manliness through individual achievement. The notion that the best or the fittest will inevitably prevail begins to break down in situations where fate, not just effort or courage, determines the results of our strivings. Witness, for example, one of Bob Beach's recent adventures up in the mountains:

Bob: **About a month ago I was climbing in Connecticut. I hadn't been climbing for a long time. I hooked up with the guy that wrote** the guidebook for the place, so somehow I felt that I was in safe hands—and also that I had something to prove to this guy, being the Yosemite local that I am. We did some routes together and I was feeling pretty shaky, but I got warmed up after a while. We went to this one route called Core Crack, about seventy-five feet high. It was a crack up to an overhang, and then an easy climb to the summit of the cliff. I started up. I climbed to the overhang. Not much problem. Then I climbed up some pretty easy ground and got to a ledge. At the ledge I placed two pieces of protection in the rock called wired stoppers. They're wedges that fit into the constrictions in the crack that will resist a downward tug but you can just lift them right out if you pull upwards. So I clipped my rope into these two pieces and I started climbing past. As I was passing these two wire stoppers, I didn't realize it but the friction just lifted them out of the crack. I was literally three feet from the top of the cliff and I said, 'Okay, reach for it.' I moved up and all the strength in my arm gave out. I had been climbing all day and I was out of shape and I couldn't tell how tuckered I had become. I pushed off in space expecting to fall four feet and then be held by the wirestoppers. I closed my eyes at the beginning of the fall, but I opened them after a second or so when I realized that those two pieces hadn't held. I kept going and going and going. When I opened my eyes I was a ways out from the cliff. I felt like I was a planet moving around the sun, just curving through space. I was rotating and I saw the position I was going to be in when I hit the ground. Then all this green came up and I was smashing through this tree, a big pine tree at the base of the cliff. One side of the tree was just blasted away by my fall; now it looks like it's been facing the wind for a hundred years. The rope caught in the top branches of the tree. If it hadn't caught, I would've hit the ground, and if I hadn't pushed off the cliff just right with my feet, I wouldn't have reached the tree. I went about seventy feet free-fall and stopped five feet off the ground.

Matt: That's pretty close to cratering.

Bob: I don't think many people have cut it that close. There was a moment of blackness. Life hasn't been the same for me since then. I always thought that one died at a really important time in their life, like right after they finished writing their memoirs. But no: it can just reach out and grab you on an easy climb on a day which is not particularly special.

This is one of those experiences that's a little too real for me. I don't want to find myself in a bar one day bragging about it. By translating it into words, by telling it again and again, it divorces me from the experience. It cheapens it. It's blasphemous to treat it as just another climbing story. I tried to get myself to cry about it, but it was a real block. Finally the next day I did. I still haven't completely worked it out. The first thought that came into my head after the fall was: 'I don't have a child in the world.' That's weird. It's something I never really thought about before. I wonder if that's a natural reaction or if I was just thinking too much or something.

I remember it was a Sunday and people were coming out of brunch at the school cafeteria. I went and just hung out outside. I wanted to feel what it was like to be dead, so I pretended that no one noticed me. I was quiet and just watched people walking in and out of the place. It was really easy to be dead. That was very strange.

Matt: Bob called home a few times that weekend, trying to get ahold of me. I finally talked to him on the phone and he was totally weirded out. He was telling me about how he was pretending to be dead and about how he had seen himself all sprawled out dead after he fell. I said, "Bob, be cool. Everything's cool." My mom said, "What happened? What happened?" We decided not to tell her 'cause she lets us use the car and stuff. If she knew what it was all about she wouldn't.

Bob: She would worry too much the next time I went climbing and it wasn't something I intended to stop—but I have been a little shaky lately.

Matt: Just lately, man. That's just 'cause you've been off at school being fat.

Bob: I don't think I'm going to be doing any free soloing again.

Matt: Yes you will.

Bob: You're right. I'll probably do it again. One thing that's affected me after my fall, one thing I've learned, is that I've made a promise to myself not to waste time—like sleeping late or lying in bed all day. If some friends want me to go out and do some adventuring, I'm not going to hang out at home and sit in front of the TV. In some ways that might be a bad attitude—like Matt and Steve now want to go down and do the Shield on El Capitan right in the middle of winter. On my general promise not to pass up any chance for adventure, I should go do the Shield with them. I don't know. It might just be my undoing. We'll see.

Matt: It's supposedly snowing pretty bad down there. But that'd be great to do the Shield. It'd make my Christmas vacation worthwhile, to pump out an El Cap route in the winter.

Bob: Kill yourself and freeze to death. I'm hoping that they'll chicken out—but if they go, I'm going with them.

Through an apparant act of fate, Bob was given a reprieve from his mistake—and a chance to respond to his fall. If climbing was once a challenge to his courage, it will challenge him even more in the future. Now he knows the risk; he is no longer in a state of innocence, and that alone would seem to add to his maturity. But why was he given a second chance? Because of a pine tree he had never seen. And what does that pine tree have to do with Bob's manly worth? There's no logic to Bob's good luck, just fortuitous circumstance.

In our attempts to prove our manhood, we like to assume more control than we really have. This assumption is tempting, for why should we even bother with our chosen tasks if we don't interpret the results as true indications of our merit? But the assumption is also dangerous. Success is not always a sure proof of manliness, while failure can be caused by variables that have little to do with our personal shortcomings.

Nowhere is this more apparent than in war. With the demise of single combat, a soldier is no longer in a position to control his own destiny. Witness, for instance, the story of Steve Graham, a seventeen-year-old dropout from school who joined the "Airborne" after being told by his recruiter that the Army would teach him how to become an airplane mechanic. Instead of working on planes, Steve soon found himself trekking through the jungles of Vietnam in search of an elusive enemy:

We were on a platoon-size sweep, trying to run anything up in the mountains down into this big valley. We did this for three days, with Nef walking point for our team. Nef was the grungiest grunt you could be. He had leather straps hanging off his wrist; he carried a big machete; he told lots of stories.

One morning me and Nef and my friend Doc were up on the ridge smoking a joint and the word came up from the lieutenant: "I want you guys down across that creek at the bottom in thirty minutes." So we went down a high-speed trail. We could see that people had been moving down this trail recently. We came into this little area where things had been crushed down, where quite a few people had been sitting. There were NVA [North Vietnamese Army] rations all around. Me and Nef and Doc moved on down the trail aways and finished our joint. Word came to move out again. I said, "Nef, be careful." He got up and started walking through this elephant grass.

There was no marking for this booby trap, 'cause I was looking. They had just left and set the booby trap on the way out and didn't mark it. The trail almost disappeared through the elephant grass and Nef tripped the wire. I heard the spoon come off the grenade, a very distinctive sound. I turned around to dive off in the opposite direction, but Nef was totally unaware that he had hit a trip wire. He called back, "Did you see what I dropped?" Because of his calmness I thought, "Well, he must have dropped something off his pack and that's what I heard." So I turned back towards him and said, "Man, you scared the shit out of me." Then this grenade went off as I was taking the step towards him. It was a very stupid thing. I didn't follow my instinct. I put too much trust and faith in what this guy knew. I mean, if *I* had tripped the trip wire I would've known it and I would've warned the guy behind me.

Anyway, he got blown one way and I got blown the other way. I never lost consciousness. I remember going through the air and landing on my right elbow and yelling, "Shit!" I looked down at my legs and they were just totally laid open. I tried to yell for Doc and I couldn't yell. It was like I was underwater. I couldn't hear nothing. I started relaxing and looking around. I could see branches falling off of trees so I knew we were being shot at, but I couldn't hear any of it.

It seemed like a lifetime for the helicopters to get there. They had to cut an area out of the jungle and bring the jungle penetrators in. They sat me on this thing and pulled me up to the helicopter. I remember looking down at everybody lined up. They all waved to me and I waved to them. It was a strange feeling: I knew I was going home, but I didn't know if I was going home alive or dead.

Up in the helicopter, that's when the pain started hitting. They brought Nef on behind me. He was dead when they put him on. They stuck a tube down his throat real quick and started breathing for him. I looked out over Vietnam and all I could see was graves. That's all I remember until we landed 'cause I passed out. Later, this one guy told me: "You were real lucky, 'cause you died." I just couldn't believe it. He said I had stopped breathing for sixty-three seconds.

They got us to the hospital and into this big ward with all these tables. It seemed like all around me was death, people dying. My hearing had come back by then and all I could hear was people screaming. This nurse was holding my hand while the doctors were working on my leg to try and stop the bleeding. I had blood transfusions in me 'cause I had lost so much blood. I hadn't been given any morphine or any pain medication at all. Things are really starting to hurt, and I'm starting to have a hard time breathing 'cause the blood is getting into my lungs. Finally they pushed a metal tube down my throat and sucked the blood out so I could breath again. That really hurt. It seemed like it hit the bottom of my lungs.

Nef was still with me in the hospital. He had died a couple of times but they managed to get him breathing again. Now he was blind, and I think part of his brain was gone. He had lost a chunk of his head in the explosion. We lay there together. Out of the corner of my eye I could see Nef's legs, little movements. He would lay there all day long complaining about these purple spots he saw in his blindness. It was almost funny.

After about a week they flew us to Japan. Nef finally died for good. They operated on me there, my legs and my throat. However long it took me to recover, they took me back into surgery. Six times they operated on me. I had to eat through a tube up my nose for about four months. A piece of shrapnel had shattered my voice box, severed a vocal cord, and lodged in my esophagus.

So that's why I still can't talk. This one vocal cord is cut, and the other one supposedly is paralyzed. There's a big air space there, so all I can do is whisper. It was hard to get adjusted to the loss of my voice. I used to sing. I had always thought that would be my career: in music, either singing or playing the guitar. And the everyday things, I was embarrassed by it. I'd have other people make my telephone calls, because whenever I'd try and call someone they'd think it was an obscene phone call or they'd just hang up. Or even when I'd go up to order a hamburger where music is played overhead in a speaker, I couldn't do it. I'd always need someone to order for me in a restaurant. And all the people: "Do you have laryngitis?" "I bet you had a hard night last night." All the time I was with my first wife, she did a lot of my communicating with the world. I just reclused myself.

I've definitely grown up through all this, I've grown older. Everything is going through change. All those things in my past have made me what I am, the same as anybody. I'm just living, like everybody else. But I do have a totally different aspect about life than I did before—and death. When I talk to other people about my views it usually ends up into death. That generally turns people off. I attribute a lot of it to Vietnam, because death was such an everyday thing. Someone is there that you like, and the next day they're not there anymore. Sometimes you can't even find any pieces of them. You realize how meaningless your life is. There's nothing for you to do. You make a name for yourself or make a bundle of money, there's no reason for that because everyone has to die—and has to die alone. That's the subject that I always get on, because it seems to be the most important subject to me ever since Vietnam. As I do things, that's always my philosophy; it's always in my mind. I start to get into something and work real hard, but then I realize it's just my own trip and it doesn't really mean anything.

People talk a lot about "delayed stress syndrome" from Vietnam. For myself, I have a hard time with depression and that death thing. There are certain things I can't do. I can't take care of business because business isn't important to me. It's not important for me to pay a bill or something, so therefore Holly has to handle all the bills and stuff.

Sometimes I think: "Why can't I really get into something? Anything: believe in God, do something I like, get a job helping other people, whatever." But I can't, I just can't make it important enough for me to do it. Everybody knows that death is scary, but then they just don't think about it anymore. They forget about it and go back to doing what they were doing. Somehow I can't forget about it that easily.

Steve's story—poignant, tragic, and profound—is not an uncommon one. Several of the men I interviewed had similar tales to tell of the physical and psychological horrors of war. Because of the age of my subjects, all of them who saw active service saw it in Vietnam. And the Vietnam legacy is now infamous: many vets came home injured, but even more came home confused. Steve Graham came home maimed in both body and spirit. The army did not "make a man" out of Steve; instead, it permeated his life with death. His initiation into manhood (if that's what it was supposed to be) can hardly be construed as successful.

A pure self-determinist might argue that Steve himself is to be held accountable for his own fate. He placed too much trust in Nef, and he paid the price for his poor judgment. This might be true, but it is not the only interpretation of Steve's tale. Steve went into the army for incidental and extraneous reasons; Vietnam meant nothing to him, but once there he became trapped in a drama that was not his own. He was in over his head, playing haphazardly in matters of life and death. If Nef hadn't tripped the wire, or if Steve himself had continued to duck for cover, he might not have been so seriously injured. But what about the booby trap a mile down the trail? Or the one the next day, or the day after that? On the most basic level he was simply playing with fate—and he lost.

Even those Vietnam veterans who came home in one piece often have strange tales to tell about fate, about the road not taken which might have ended in doom. Will Bell, for instance, returned from Vietnam with nary a scratch, but the nice, happy ending was in no way assured:

> **I was in communications. We were not per se combat troops, grunts, infantrymen, but because communications were so important we were often the first people to be at certain places. We would have to set up communication networks wherever we went. Once we were getting ready to make this move, partly by air and partly by surface. We flew down there to deliver all this equipment to the forward party. I didn't happen to be on the forward party, so I left and came back and I was supposed to go down there the next day. Well, that night the forward party was overrun. Everybody was either injured or killed. It was just one of those situations of war where there's too few individuals too far away from support.**

Why wasn't Will overrun by the enemy? Because his superiors did not happen to assign him to the forward party. Will's own fate, in this case, was certainly beyond his realm of personal control.

And even Evan R., who never saw active combat, could easily have been killed, through no special fault of his own, by the malfunctioning of his own aircraft:

> **Your buddies die on a regular basis. One fellow was out dropping bombs. He went to drop his bomb, pulled off, put the power up— and nothing happened. Engine quit. He jumped out and ended up breaking his neck in the parachute. Happens all the time.**
>
> **It's a very real thing. Airplanes break. I've had airplanes break under me, and the reason I didn't die is because I did things right. Sometimes, through no fault of your own, the airplane breaks, you can't do anything about it, and you die anyway. We used to call it "the breaks of naval air." Sometimes, when it's your number, kiss it off. That's it. You do everything you can and sometimes it's not your day anyway. You have to be able to handle that.[1]**

A fellow needs courage to confront this kind of danger, and he also needs just a little bit of luck. Evan R. is still alive today not merely because he was a better pilot than those who have perished, but also because the planes he happened to fly—planes built not by himself but by vast teams of engineers and technicians in faraway places—did not fall apart. At least in part, his survival is a matter of chance, and this gives a strange twist to the notion of individual valor: In what sense do we prove our manhood when the choice of who survives is something of a random affair? Is a pilot any less of a man if his plane happens to quit on him? Doesn't the element of chance interfere with the belief that military activity should somehow select the fit from the unfit, the men from the boys?

Naturally, we would prefer to think that the proof of valor is still a personal affair. It is little wonder, therefore, that many young males today have been attracted to the notion of guerrilla warfare as they try to circumvent the impersonal nature of the modern military, the dependence upon technology, and the consequent randomness of fate. (Witness, for instance, the widespread appeal of camouflaged clothing throughout our popular culture.) Third world countries struggling for independence have embraced guerrilla warfare for a strategic and practical reason—it's the only way they can ever hope to win a war when they are so outmatched by the superpowers. Americans, however, have embraced guerrilla warfare for a very different reason—it returns us to the primitive paradigm, transforming our military activity into a sort of real-life Survival Game.

By crawling around in the jungle and minimizing the impact of technology, we try to turn war once again into a true test of merit, where man is pitted against man and the best will inevitably prevail.

But does this popular image of guerrilla warfare match the reality? Guerrilla warfare is not simply men "having at it" with paint guns; instead, it is itself impersonal and technological. Rarely does a soldier who steps on a mine ever see the man who triggered the destructive device. The weaponry involved in standard warfare permits adversaries to be separated in space by many miles; the technology of guerrilla warfare permits adversaries to be separated in time as well. A guerrilla will set a booby trap and then disappear; by the time an enemy (or perhaps even an ally) happens to step on the trap, the fellow who set it might himself be dead. Steve Graham never did set eyes on the enemy who maimed him for life; indeed, it was his buddy, not himself, who happened to step on the mine. In the harsh but realistic words of Evan R., "Sometimes, when it's your number, kiss it off."

The randomness of destruction in modern warfare (even guerrilla warfare) is not a particularly new or startling realization, but it figures critically in our analysis of male initiations. As we noted in Chapter One, a crucial factor in primitive initiations is that they are structured to encourage success. A game of Russian Roulette is not so structured; there are too many casualties who fall by the wayside. Insofar as a stint in the armed forces exposes a young man to dangers he cannot control and has no power to overcome, the military functions only poorly (or at least randomly) as an initiation ritual.

Indeed, only a small handful of primitive societies have ever included the experience of actual warfare as a part of the rites of passage into manhood—and even then, the warfare has been limited and based upon single combat. In most primitive cultures male initiation rites are conducted as inside affairs, without reference to external enemies. The trials which the boys must endure are conceived in such a way that the initiands, by dint of their personal effort and endurance, will probably survive; real warfare, by its very nature, cannot be this well structured, for the results cannot be controlled.

Of course we too have a military initiation ritual which does not depend upon the whims of fate: Basic Training. In boot camp, as in primitive initiations, almost all of the initiands, not just the select few, are able to rise to the occasion and make it through to the end. The initiands achieve success according to their own merits and through their own efforts, but the ritual is structured in such a way as to ensure that most of the men will in fact pass the test:

Everybody was expected to perform at a certain level, no matter what. There were some guys, about a dozen or so, that were real overweight or just not physically inclined, not athletic at all, some real weak guys and some real obese people. But they were expected to perform right up to certain specs. Most of them eventually measure up, even the obese ones. They don't stay in boot camp forever, so they do get through there somehow. Almost everybody makes it. If you don't pass the tests, they give them to you over and over until you do pass. They can hold you over. You're stuck in there until you qualify with a weapon and pass your PT. (Will Bell)

In boot camp there is no outside enemy to drop bombs or fire artillery upon a random sampling of soldiers; there is little chance for technological failure to kill unsuspecting victims; there is no selective promotion that might favor a few worthy individuals while leaving the rest behind. The only real danger is an overzealous drill instructor.[2] Boot camp, although authoritarian and autocratic, is also strangely democratic in this one important respect: it is an initiation in which we all might succeed, and where most of those who enter will emerge at the end with a heightened sense of their own capabilities. Even the embittered Steve Graham is willing to acknowledge its practical success:

At the time you don't think you're learning anything, but you're learning a great discipline that later does come in useful. There's a whole psychological thing with Basic Training and AIT [Advanced Infantry Training]. They want to break you down into nothing and then start over again and brainwash you into what they want you to be. But that's the age-old story. That's how they have to do it to make it work. So I could see their point. It's a tried-and-true method.

There once was a time, only a generation past, when the classical form of initiation offered in Basic Training was almost universal. During World War II it was the common expectation that all able-bodied young men in America would undergo a boot camp rite of passage. This expectation was slightly modified after the War; during the 1950s and '60s, a stint in boot camp was still commonplace, though no longer universal. Whether or not a soldier saw action in Korea or Vietnam, all draftees and enlisted men shared this one well-defined experience: for six long weeks, the army provided them with most of the elements of a standard male initiation.

Not so today. Since we have had no civilian draft for over a decade, any form of military training has become purely voluntary. For most of us, the closest we will ever come to a warrior's initiation will be some form of simulated combat: football, baseball, or perhaps the Survival Game. But even in our makeshift substitutes—and particularly in the Survival Game—there are important lessons to be learned about the nature of war. Alec Jason's pretend warfare is just realistic enough to demonstrate that success as a warrior remains beyond the control of the individual and therefore cannot be construed as a sure proof of merit or manly prowess:

The unusual thing about the Survival Game is that virtually everybody loses. It's not like there's any champions like in other sports, some guy who always wins. We don't have that. There's no way you can not be shot often if you're going to be aggressive, if you're going to get out there and do things. You cannot come out unscathed, unless you're going to hide under a bush every game. So it's very hard to prove who's the best; you can't really distinguish yourself that way. You might shoot six guys in one game, but in the next game you'll get shot in the first five minutes by some little kid hiding in a tree because you happened to walk by him. Personally, I don't really care whether I win or lose; I'd rather win, but I just like to stay alive a long time and shoot a lot of people.

Sometimes we get people who are military buffs, real commando-type guys. They read all the magazines and they buy all the equipment and they think they're good shots and they're in great physical condition. They think, "I'm gonna be a terror. I'm gonna be the best." They get out there and what they come to realize is how vulnerable they are, even though it's only paint guns, because if you're walking up the trail and someone's well hidden there's no way—no matter how good you are, how smart you are, how well trained you are, what a good shot you are—there's no way you can prevent yourself from being shot. It just happens. I tell them, "You know in real war you could be shot from anywhere around here, from any of these hills or any of these trees. You just show your little nose out here and a guy'll

126

put a bullet through your head and that's it. You could get an artillery shell on top of you, you could step on a mine. It's not just a question of how good you are. If you're the best marathon runner in the world you will win every race, but if you're the best soldier in the world it doesn't mean you will survive."

So how can boys be turned into men if in fact they might well be killed? This is the basic message of war, in real life as well as in play: You can't always win, even if you display all the manly virtues. This simple fact implies that warfare is no more than a poor imitation of a male rite of passage. With men no longer facing off against each other in single combat, the choice of which soldiers will be destroyed and which will be saved is often made without any particular reference to individual skill or valor; the strong and courageous can perish as readily as the weak and cowardly. Modern warriors can be killed or injured by the malfunctioning of their own equipment (like Evan R.'s buddies who succumbed to "the breaks of naval air"), by the proper functioning of an enemy's equipment (like Steve Graham), or by the faulty orders of their superiors (like the unfortunate fellows in Will Bell's forward party). If merit alone cannot ensure success, the mere fact of personal survival does not say a whole lot about manliness.

This can also be said of our simulated battles. When a young man inadvertently mistakes athletic superiority for manhood, when he unconsciously confuses the task of winning with some sort of initiation rite, he places himself in the same tenuous position as when he allows himself to be persuaded that the attainment of manhood is dependent upon success as a warrior. Through no special fault of his own, an athlete can fail as well as succeed. Athletic competition might be less harmful than warfare, but both war and sports encourage a common deception: they hold forth an alluring image of manhood which is exclusive, not inclusive, and which in fact will never be achieved by large numbers of perfectly normal and deserving adult males.

When we fail to acknowledge the element of randomness, or God's whimsy, we become trapped once again by our private struggles, unable to see their roots in the flow of history which surrounds us. And our denial of the role of chance is but one instance of a general neglect of *context;* we tend to ignore all the external factors—social, economic, environmental, biological—that contribute to the propensity of an individual to succeed or fail. We assume a Puritanical sense of merit: the worthy will be turned into men, while the unworthy will be left uninitiated. Our fate, in this view, is thus within our individual control—those who *want* to succeed *will* succeed, and to hell with those who don't. But in fact we can never be in control of our lives to the extent that we would like. As individual mortals, we remain forever dependent on fate and circumstance, on the will of God and the acts of other men. Bob Beach can be saved by an unseen tree; Steve Graham can be maimed by a hidden mine. Our manhood can be threatened separately by illness or collectively by holocaust, and in neither case would an initiation based upon the ideal of competitive merit do us much good or offer us any solace.

CHAPTER 8

Zero-Sum Contests

The problem is not just that some might lose, but that many must lose. That's the logic of interpersonal competition, whether real or pretend. Insofar as we use competitive battles to prove our manliness, we build in failure as well as success. We trap ourselves within a peculiar male paradox: to affirm our masculinity we try to beat our rivals, while we simultaneously demand their approval for our superior strength and skill.

The psychological dangers inherent in this masculine logic are particularly evident in competitive sports. If Chuck Sipes had to develop the biggest muscles in the world to prove he was a man, what does that say about those who fall short of such a lofty ideal? In the hierarchy of sports, there is only limited room at the top. Those who make it might feel like men, but those who never get to the upper echelons, if they have bought into the Social Darwinism which permeates the athletic mystique, might well feel a certain sense of inadequacy: they have failed to become true men, for they have fought and they have lost.

Indeed, if we take athletic events solely on their face value, there are at least as many losers as winners. Football and baseball games are what we call "zero-sum" contests—every game that someone wins is lost by someone else. In tournaments the ratio for success is even worse; they are "negative-sum" events, for every contestant but one will emerge as a loser. No matter how high the level of competition, victory is never attainable by more than half the participants.

On the basis of demographics alone, the odds are stacked against us. For each professional athlete in any particular sport there are thousands of amateurs who peck away inconclusively at each other, tasting defeat as well as victory. And for most of us lesser athletes, the quest for dominance and superiority is never ending and ever frustrating. Perpetually, we must prove ourselves anew—and that leaves us always in doubt. Our masculinity is constantly being placed in jeopardy; our initiations (if that is what they are supposed to be) never seem to be finalized.[1]

At what level of success can a man finally relax? Not many aspiring athletes can truthfully say, like Chuck Sipes, "I don't really have to prove anything to anybody any more." Listen, for instance, to the story of Ken B., a confirmed amateur who is decidedly better than average but certainly not the best:

Back in high school and college, the biggest challenges for me were certainly in sports. I'd come up against them all the time, 'cause I played something every season. Every single week there'd be a game or a race or something, and I'd stay awake thinking about it. If I did well I'd strut, or if I did poorly I'd lie awake about it for days. I could ace a test and not think anything about it, but if I hit a couple of free throws in the last minute of the game, that would set me up for a long time. That's where I got all my emotional energy and juice. It just seemed more *important* as far as establishing who you are.[2]

Basketball was the big glory thing I was into. I liked the bright lights and the cheerleaders and the crowds and all the noise. In my senior year we had a pretty good team. We thought we had a shot at the championship, but I think we ended up third in an eight-team league. We weren't that far away from a couple of teams that were ahead of us, but we never did quite have that little something at the

end to beat them. We'd just sort of fold. That bothered me, even to the point of regret and shame. From the outside, it looked like we got beat because the other team was stronger, so it doesn't seem like the weaker team should have any shame about it. But if you're on the other side of it, if you're *in* it, you tend to think that you've failed in some way, or blew it—that you really *should* have won. That was our sense of it, anyway, that we let each other down, let ourselves down, let our girlfriends down, let the cheerleaders down.

At least in basketball, I never did expect to be any kind of a real star. I was short and white and couldn't jump particularly high. Realistically speaking, I always knew that the only reason I could start on that team was that the league wasn't particularly good. Whenever I went down to the playgrounds in L.A. and saw what these inner-city kids were doing, how tall they were and what they could do with the basketball and how tough they were. . . .

With tennis it was different. I had a head start in that 'cause my mom was a real good tennis player. She started me out when I was eight. So when it came time to play on competitive teams, I had a huge head start over anybody in my class. In my junior and senior years in high school I was number one on the team. In both those years I won the league individual tournament and went on to the C.I.F. (California Interscholastic Federation) tournament. I was real invested in tennis because I was good at it—and because everybody expected me to be good at it. Tennis was my turf.

But even when I was winning my league tournaments and having a lot of success, I was always afraid I was going to lose. When a ball would come floating over, I would tend just to float it back again rather than trying to put it away. I always thought that was kind of a chicken way out. Then when I tried to get aggressive I started forcing my shots. If I missed a few shots and lost my sense of confidence, I'd get more conservative and more nervous than ever. I'd worry about whether I'd double-fault, and then of course I'd double-fault. I wouldn't open up and take advantage of opportunities.

I don't know what it's like for other guys, for guys who are real successful in tennis. Maybe when they come down to an important point or an important match they take on a more arrogant stance. I don't know what their internal experience is, whether they have the kind of self-anguish that I always had at those moments—"Oh, God, can I do it?"—or whether they think, "I'm just great. Of course I can do it." I never really had that kind of blind self-confidence. I always had the sense that my outward success was precarious and that I might just blow it at any moment.

When I first got to college I went right up to the coach and started playing a lot of tennis. He ranked me third on the freshman tennis ladder, but it was just informal at that point because the season didn't start until spring. I played a lot of squash that winter to keep in shape, but when spring finally came I couldn't seem to make the adjustment back to tennis. I lost a couple of challenge matches on the tennis ladder and then I got into this losing frame of mind. I lost ten challenge matches in a row, dropping down the ladder from three to thirteen. It kept getting worse and worse. Every time I'd walk out onto the court I'd have this weird trip in the pit of my stomach and I wouldn't really see that good and I'd be sweating before the thing would even start. I was too tensed up: my neck was tight, my muscles were tight, and I would say to myself, "Oh no, here we go again!"

In between challenge matches, when it didn't count, I could still play well. I could beat a lot of those same guys in practice games. I could serve well, I could hit well, I could just beat 'em. But something was happening when it counted that was awful. I couldn't pull myself out of it. My ego investment was too extreme. It was very difficult for me to separate having a bad day on the tennis court and being a bad person. My sense of being personally okay was seriously threatened. It got worse and worse till finally I just quit playing competitive tennis for the next ten years.

So what good has come out of Ken B.'s spotty career in interscholastic sports? Athletic competition, which is supposed to help a young man establish his strength and self-assurance, seems to have had the opposite effect. Although Ken has in fact excelled in fields extraneous to sports (cf., chap. 3), his athletic activities have apparently had little to do with the development of manly ideals such as confidence, courage, or self-reliance. Even now, years later, Ken is still burdened with insecurities which seem exaggerated, not relieved, by his participation in sports:

Just last year a fellow came into town, Jack, who's a real serious player. It's a *big* part of his life. He makes his living at it, he's a professional. He heard I could play and he kept seeking me out as someone who could help him break a sweat.

I was real flattered, so I got serious about tennis again and we started playing together. He's younger and stronger and a more experienced player, so he always won. I don't think I've ever beat him. There were a couple of times when he got a little bit down and I got on a roll and we got to where a couple of points would become crucial. Then he'd always come on a little harder and I'd always not quite pull it off.

About a month ago we got out on the court and I started thinking: "All right, he's beat me every time for the last twenty times. Now *this* time I'm going to really have at it." I got myself worked up to a frenzy. At one point I got really mad at him because he seemed to be questioning one of my calls. That's very emotional for me—I hate the thought that somebody thinks I might be cheating. So I got in a stew. Then later in the set when it was still close—the games were tied—I put away an overhead and got ahead forty-fifteen. I went to serve and he stopped me from serving. He dried off his hand on his towel. I went to serve again and he stopped me again and said he had to change his sweatband. He walked clear across the court, and meanwhile I was there in this stew. I got so mad at him that I could hardly see the ball anymore. I said to him something like, "I don't need to learn any more about hitting tennis balls to beat you; what I have to learn is how to compete psychologically with this stuff." I can't remember my exact words, but it was some stinging phrase that I was sure would make him crumble. Of course he just thought I was acting weird and went on to trounce me.

I'm a fairly easy-tempered person, but this time I was in a stew all day. I was really wrought up, and I kept talking to people about it. I thought, "This is a little extreme here. Why am I so wired up? What's got ahold of me?"

Failure in war is tragic; in sports it's almost comic. The developmental quest for manhood becomes transformed into an absurd Sisyphusian task: we are forever trying to climb a ladder that has no inherent meaning. Why do we strive so hard to achieve such apparently pointless goals? What's in it for us, anyway? Or, more specifically: What *has* got ahold of

Ken B.? Why has this personable, sane, and otherwise rational young man allowed himself to take his games so seriously—even though he obviously knows better?

The actual games that Ken plays are fine; even the aggression is fine, the satisfaction of a primordial urge. The only problem lies in the interpretation of the results. The metaphor has become too real. Through sports, Ken hopes to determine his place on the pecking order: whom can he beat? Is he on the top or the bottom of the ladder? Or (as is much more likely) is he somewhere in between?

The promise of a competitive sport, for all aspiring athletes, is to provide a linear ordering of reality; we either win or lose, and that clearly defines us as better or worse than the others. We reduce the complex world of everyday affairs to a finite field with a well-defined set of rules, and on that field we try to pinpoint exactly where we stand with respect to all our rivals. The multi-dimensional tasks of life get reduced to the one-dimensional task of beating our opponent. By diverting complex questions of right and wrong into more comprehensible questions of winning and losing, sports can even supply us with a simplified sense of moral purpose. This simplification offers an antidote to some of the ambiguities of our pluralistic culture, where questions of meaning are hard to answer and a precise definition of rank is often difficult to achieve. Is a baker higher or lower than a butcher? Is he better or worse? Is he more or less of a man? It's hard to say—but when they face off head-to-head out there on the ball field or the tennis court, one will win and the other will lose and they will both know where they stand.

But even this simplified paradigm, in the end, often defies our quest for linearity—and that tends to cause us great concern. Like Ken B., we might win one day and lose the next, possibly to the very same opponent. Except for a rare handful of unbeatable champions, our place in the pecking order is forever in question. We climb a few rungs up the ladder, but we are always in danger of falling back down. Even Jack, the seasoned professional, must struggle to beat out his nervous rival. Success, once attained, must still be defended, so all that remains constant is the anxiety caused by uncertainty.

All this makes me wonder: What will become of young Alex Lash, the prospective major league pitcher? What are the likely consequences of the scenario he has presented to himself? Still in his adolescence, Alex wants, above all else, to make his way to "the top of the pyramid." He is high on hope, but he is hardly yet ready for the big leagues. He is only on his high school junior varsity; next year he will fight for a place on the varsity squad. He has not yet startled the sports world with his commanding strength and prowess, but he tries to believe in his dream nonetheless:

I'm very heartened by stories about players like Larry Bowa, who is one of the best fielding shortstops of all time and who didn't even make his high school team. He didn't play until college, where he was a walk-on. So I say, "Oh, there's hope."

But then I look at pitchers like Dwight Gooden and I say, "Jesus, by the time he was sixteen he was throwing a no-hitter every time out." I'm not; I'm barely surviving. I had an okay record—for the JV season I was two-and-three. I should have had about three more wins. This sounds like a cop-out or an excuse, but there are games where I left when we were winning four-nothing or seven-to-two and the next pitcher comes in and gives up nine runs. So I didn't win those games. Then I got a few really heart-breaking defeats, like a four-to-three game where I threw the ball away and two runs scored. That was our opening game.

I don't feel I pitched that badly. I feel I pitched pretty well. Still, it's a long way to the majors. I know I'm not a dominating pitcher, but I guess I am more intelligent than most of the guys out there playing baseball. I don't want to sound immodest, but I guess I could use that to my advantage. I know not to get down on myself. I know I have to keep myself calm, in perspective. Not saying, "I gotta blow my fastball by this guy. I gotta, I gotta, I gotta." Just think about what I'm going to pitch a little more. Think about who I'm pitching to and where I'm going to pitch him.

Size is a big factor, too. Right now I'm only five-nine. Hopefully I'll grow a little more. My dad's about six-two-and-a-half, almost six-three. So hopefully I'll be at least six feet. If I'm a little taller, I can get a little stronger push off the mound with my back leg. So that will help a little.

And I guess just a lot of work—a hell of a lot more than I'm doing now. Eventually I'll start working out in the off season, doing weight conditioning so my arm muscles don't turn to jelly. And working on my stamina—doing wind sprints, which I detest. The absolute worst thing about baseball is doing wind sprints, but I guess they have to be done. If I want to be a major league baseball player, I might as well do them.

Of course there are so many kids playing baseball, and there are so few major leaguers. So I know the odds against me are very high—maybe ten thousand-to-one that I'll even make it to the minor leagues. That's why I'm prepared to not do that—but I'd be very disappointed. This is still what I see myself doing. I tell myself, "If one in ten thousand is going to make it, it might as well be me."[3]

Alex seems to understand that the odds are against him. He knows that disappointment is a distinct possibility, although he tries to convince himself that he still has a shot at success. But if Alex does indeed become disappointed, it remains to be seen how he will cope with a shattered dream. Will his self-image be threatened? Will he develop alternate images of manhood which are still desirable but more accessible? Will he perhaps come to feel that "poring over old dusty volumes in a library" might not be so bad after all? Realistically, the true test of Alex's manhood will not occur when they call him in from the bullpen in the ninth inning in the last game of the World Series; instead, his manhood will be on the line when he is forced to adapt to the limitations of his own athletic talents. That is a far more common test; in fact, it is the ultimate lesson to be learned through sports.

The unfulfilled expectations of Alex Lash and Ken B. reveal the personal jeopardy in the logic of competition. The very nature of competitive struggles is to separate the winners from the losers; insofar as we interpret these struggles as personal initiations, we intend them to separate the men from the boys. Initiations such as these are bound to remain exclusive; they cannot possible live up to the classical ideal of ushering *all* young males into manhood.

And yet this sort of competitive ideology permeates so many of the makeshift initiations we have witnessed throughout this book. The avowed function of warfare is to generate losers, to kill or maim other men; the mutilation of Steve Graham, the Vietnam veteran, is in this sense perfectly normal, not exceptional. The classical initiation offered by medical school is itself tainted by its competitive context, for success is effectively denied to the many aspirants who will never be admitted. The allegedly non-competitive wilderness adventures of Bob and Matt Beach and David Smith are undeniably altered by our ubiquitous competitive mystique. And even our most intimate relationships with women are commonly transformed, during our adolescent coming-of-age, into counting coups and keeping score.

Is all this really necessary? Might there be alternate ways of looking at the initiation process which could lead to less competitive, and therefore more inclusive, definitions of manliness?

Many of us, I suspect, would like to believe that there are. Even our athletic contests, which we create consciously and specifically for the purpose of doing battle with each other, can be perceived through less competitive eyes. Sports can amuse and relieve; they can pleasantly distract. They can make us laugh and shout. They can inject vigorous dramatic tension into otherwise routine lives. And of course they can break down social barriers; they can give us common ground; they can help us belong.

On a more personal level, athletic challenges can be used to develop courage, endurance, and will; they help us push to our limits, and even beyond; they are a means towards personal fulfillment. They offer opportunities for physical expression in a technological world that threatens to deprive us of our sense of bodily strength and well-being. This, really, is what sports are all about. Even Chuck Sipes, who pursued and attained all the external rewards, understands that the entire edifice of interpersonal competition is based in part on a very personal reality:

> I enjoy the tightness, the pump, just the general well-being that I receive from doing something really physical. The firmness, and then the soreness that I receive the next day—I really like that. I like that feeling of strength.

And even Ken B., for all his anxiety, gets significant and positive results from his athletic endeavors:

> If I go through a whole week and don't do anything, if I don't run or play tennis or play basketball, if I don't work up a good sweat three or four times during the week, then I feel awful. And on the days when I do exercise, then the rest of that day I feel a lot better. I feel more settled down; I feel more focused; I feel less depressed. It eases a lot of that jangle; I can relax a lot better. It's just that thing of working it out, trying as hard as you can at something physical. When I'm in good shape I can feel it when I just walk around. Like walking to the mailbox or something, as I walk down the street I just

feel an extra bounce in my step. I feel just this *charge*—that's a big part of what I get out of sports.

So if we forget about the outcome of the games, we can still view any form of athletic activity as personally valuable in and of itself. Each and every participant can be strengthened by the process, regardless of whether he will eventually win or lose. And an increase in strength, particularly inner strength, is certainly integral to any definition of manhood.

Indeed, practices and training programs constitute reasonably close approximations of classical initiations: The athletes get hazed both physically and mentally, and sometimes they are even removed from their domestic surroundings for a specified period of time. Generally, these techniques produce the desired results. Just as boot camp ensures a greater ratio of success than does war itself, so do push-ups and wind sprints and even the constant harangues of a coach lead to the increased strength, endurance, and ability of most of the athletes.

And yet these personal gains, by and large, are not socially validated unless the players go on to win. The coaches who direct the hazing generally require more than an increase in strength, endurance, and ability; they want to finalize the initiation process with an undeniable proof of victory:

I had this cross-country coach who always said, "Pay for it. Leave it on the course. I'd rather have you guys fall down ten feet in front of the finish line than cross that line with anything to spare. Just leave it on the course. Don't take it home with you." He was the most drill sergeant sort of guy I ever had to deal with. He was really into this concept of being a man. He would talk about that a lot and fire us up for the individual challenge. "Nobody cares, nobody gives a good god-damn about this race—except you guys. The newspapers don't care, your girlfriends probably don't care, I doubt if your moms even care. But I'll tell you what. If you guys win this race and win this championship, twenty years from now *you'll* know and *you'll* remember. But if you leave it on the course today, if you come close to the championship and don't get it, *you'll* know and *you'll* remember." He was really into his version of the psychological approach. (Ken B.)

The emphasis in this pep talk shifts subtly from the beginning to the end. At first the runners are admonished to give it their best effort, even if they fall down ten feet from the finish line; later they are told that if they come close but fail to win it will haunt them for twenty years to come. The ideal of winning, in the final analysis, supersedes any notion of a more personal challenge. This, of course, is only to be expected. Coaches are not tribal elders, and they do not necessarily have the best interests of the athletes at heart. They are paid to produce measurable results, not merely to offer personalized initiations.

Most men, I suspect, inadvertently adopt an attitude similar to that of Ken's coach. Like Ken, they might understand on some level that the purest approach to athletic activity focuses on physical well-being and personal fulfillment— but that is not enough. Ultimately, it is hard to deny the persuasive force of interpersonal competition. We want to be "the best," and that's exactly what leads to trouble. At some point along the line, reality generally "rears its ugly head" and terminates our dreams, just as it did for Ken B. and Paul Z., and just as it might someday do for Alex Lash. This, in a sense, is our real initiation—and it's a negative one at that. There's no structured program, no genuine rite of passage, to help with our growth, just a profound and personal disappointment.

But what if we did not require victory in order to validate our growth? What if Ken B., Paul Z. and Alex Lash never even had a realistic shot at "success"? What if they were saved by some blessed ignorance of the rules of competitive gaming?

My first Special Olympics team I took down to Los Angeles to compete in the state tournament. I had five athletes; you're always counting to yourself—"one, two, three, four, five"—to make sure they're all there. On this particular adventure I had Michael Rice, who stands about six-four. He's a giant of a man. He and I started talking about, "We're going to kill 'em." He picked that up right away. Mentally disabled people pick up a phrase that you've tossed off callously and they'll begin to use it over and over. So in the airplane he begins to say nothing but, "We're going to kill 'em, Mr. Jones. We're going to kill 'em."

Joey Azaro is another athlete. Now Joey's got palsied arms that are all stiff and a wonderful smile. He's sitting next to me in the airplane, just grinning at the word, "kill." He's so excited about playing bas- ketball.

Audi Stansberry is Michael's best friend and Joey's best friend.

Audi is a great rebounder, but he doesn't know where to shoot the ball so he's always shooting at the wrong basket. But he does it with such grace and style that you have to take him on your team.

Then I had Jimmy Powers. He probably reminded me of myself because he's about two-feet-two tall. A great long shot, but he sleeps a lot.

And then I had Eddie Carter, the team lawyer. Eddie was always worried about: "We can't kill 'em. We don't want to kill 'em." And, "What time is it? We won't get there in time." He's always bustling around.

Anyway, we get into Los Angeles and I get my five athletes into their brand new black uniforms. In our first game we get blown away, but Michael Rice throws up his famous hook shot and he scores the last basket of the game. So my team jumps up thinking for sure they've won the game. We made the last shot so there's no doubt about it: We are champions, we killed 'em. My five athletes are jumping up and down doing their war chant. The actual score was like thirty-six to two. That was the first and only basket we made, but it didn't matter—it came at the appropriate time.

The next game we play East L.A., with these red devil uniforms. This team is really outstanding. Jimmy Powers makes one shot from about twenty feet and that saves us for the first half. I'm finding myself standing up and railing and yelling at Michael Rice, the best player I have: "Michael Rice, you dribble the ball down and do this and do that." I know what I'm doing, I can see myself in the mirror and I know I'm being stupid, but I'm lost. I can't help it. I'm so into the game that I'm a total fool and calling time outs and trying my best to change a physical situation that can't be changed.

So at the end of this game—we again get trounced terribly—my team gets off the floor and says, "We were great. Jimmy Powers was tremendous!"

I say, "Yeah, that was a good shot."

"We killed 'em, right Mr. Jones?"

"Well, we didn't quite kill 'em, but it was close." We had actually lost by sixty or seventy points; we just got murdered.

Then the official of the whole tournament comes over and he says, "Well, coach, here's some participation ribbons for your team. It might make them feel better. By the way, where's your team now?"

We look around and the team has already moved on to the next floor and they're chanting at the game in process: "You're next! You're next! You're next!"

The final game we play against San Diego, and everything you've dreamed about happens in slow motion. Michael Rice makes the very first basket, a tip-toe lay-up. Audi gets the ball and he shoots at the right basket. Unbelievable. Eddie Cotter stops being a lawyer and decides to play basketball and steals the ball and actually goes down and scores. It's like the floor tilting in your favor. It only happens once in a season.

Before this game Joey Azaro had never even *caught* the ball because he can't make his arms come down. He just runs up and down the floor like crazy, grinning, trying to scare the opponents. I usually give him a big defensive assignment: I put him on the tallest player and he just grins at his belt and circles around him in a great war dance. In this game the ball was bouncing free in the open court and I saw Joey go after it and I thought, "Oh, no, he's going to dive." Sure enough, midway down the floor he leaps through air, belly to the ground, lands on the ball and bounces about four times with the ball under his stomach and then rolls out of bounds. The official realizes what's going on and does a dramatic gesture: "Ball goes to the black team for good effort!" Joey gets up and smacks the ball back in. His first catch and his first throw. By now I've settled down and I realize the victories in this game are measured in inches, not in baskets, and they're measured in different kinds of qualities altogether. I'm very satisfied seeing what I'm seeing. Of course now we're winning. It's easier to be gracious when you're winning.

Anyway, the game comes to its dramatic end and my team is now jumping up because they've won. I go over to the other coach—winning coaches do this—and I say, "Gee, coach, I'm really sorry that I couldn't hold my team back and make the game more even."

The coach said to me, "Are you kidding? Look at my team." I looked over at the San Diego team and they were all jumping up and down: "We killed 'em! We killed em!" None of these teams could keep score, so it's absolutely irrelevant. The fact is you've played, you've played well, and if you're lucky enough the ball might have gone in the basket.

Coaching the Special Olympics, I realized that the level of native ability is lower than anything I'd ever imagined. It went way off the scale—so far off the scale that a brand new game had to be invented. How do you play with someone in a wheelchair who can only move with the assistance of someone else? Well, the opposing team has to part and let this person move down the floor. You could easily take the ball out of that person's hands, but will you actually do it? It's an unwritten law in our games—when Rose gets the ball in her wheelchair and she's moving down the floor, no one takes the ball out of her hands. All teams that play us instinctively know this, both regular teams and other Special Olympics teams. It's fun to see that recognition. Somehow, people know that the human spirit is more important than anything else.

The way we play, it's impossible to lose. We declare ourselves 45 and 0. That's part of our loudspeaker announcement before the games: "Welcome to the King Dome, where the R.C.H. Special Olympic team is undefeated, forty-five wins and no defeats." The other team goes, "What?" There's a moment when their faces drop, like maybe it's really true. Then they catch on. But in truth we *are* 45 and 0— we are wonderful and successful and happy. Because we believe it, it's true.

When these people say, "We are the champions," they are saying we are *all* champions. That's the big difference. They're not saying, "*We* are champions, we're number one and you're number eight." It's hard to explain, because that wasn't in my experience. I grew up striving to be "numero uno." But when you can't keep score, that's when bravery takes over, and a whole other set of virtues. Like Joey Azaro diving headlong onto a ball that's bouncing loose. I've seen Joey Azaro try to high jump. He never could figure out how to get his legs to go first, so he dived over this bar like an arrow going straight up in the air and then straight down. I thought, "He's going to break his neck." I've seen the same kid approach a ropes course real high off the ground. With his elbows he climbed up to the top of these things and then just rolled his body down into the net—because he wanted the experience. That seems pretty brave to me. (Ron Jones)[4]

In this "brand new game" played by handicapped athletes, there are winners without losers. The players still play hard, they still want to "kill 'em"—but there is really no "them" to kill, just the abstraction of an intangible enemy. Victory in this context is always assured. Joey Azaro can push to his limits and become a true hero without being dominated by players with superior talent.

A game such as this can only be played when personal development is divorced from competitive ranking. When we reach down below the last place teams, even below the players who know the rules, the anxiety of failure seems to disappear, freeing the players to focus their energies more constructively. Strangely, this is where we might find both freedom and equality, down so low that the very idea of ranking is entirely unknown. Here are people who are blessedly relieved of the burden of using games to prove their superiority over others. For these people alone, a game is still truly a game, a "positive-sum" event where everyone can come out on top.

But for the majority of us who are trapped in the middle, the ones who feel we are better than some but not so good as others, this game is harder to play. Our games remain "zero-sum" contests, and we are tempted to invest too much meaning in the results. No more than half the players will emerge as winners, and that's a poor percentage indeed. No primitive tribe would ever think of denying the status of manhood to fifty percent of its youths, but that, in effect, is what we are doing when we view the outcome of competitive sports as a measure of our manliness.

CHAPTER 9

Unmanly Guilt

Improperly construed initiations often result in failure, and this failure clearly bothers us. Manhood is not inherently better, by some absolute standard, than boyhood—and yet, significantly, the many males who don't yet see themselves as "men" are quietly but seriously troubled. Their self-perceived unmanliness, although deeply rooted in the social fabric of contemporary life, is commonly experienced as a personal and very private tragedy:

In high school the guys who were football players were always palling around together, and I always felt a little separate from that. I mean I had my own groups and my own interests, but I could never quite match that same camaraderie. On another level I never really wanted to subject myself to that, and I thought that some of it was a little nuts. I saw those guys on the school bus one time before a game. They had their uniforms and their helmets on and they were pounding on the seats in unison and chanting: "Kill! Kill! Kill!" The whole bus was just rocking. I thought, "Wow, these guys are crazy"—and at the same time I had a little longing to be a part of that group intensity.

When we talk about sports, we tend to focus on the politics of it, our careers, how we interact with other people. We're gregarious, we're herd animals, we're political animals. Our relationship with other people is what juices us—our relationship to the hierarchy, establishing your personal power in relation to other people. Carrying the banner for your school or your girlfriend.

As far as "manhood" goes, I think it's more in terms of this power over other people. I certainly remember feeling plenty of macho zing when I was fooling around with guys who were more wimpy than I was. On the other hand, I questioned myself whether I was as much of a man as a football player. It has something to do with toughness; physical strength was a lot of it. I always had real wimpy little arms, or felt like I did. I couldn't arm wrestle with the guys who were out there lifting weights. Arm wrestling is just one image I have for that. You're more of a man if you can put the other guy's hand down. If yours is always the one that goes down . . . well, then you have to find some other realm. You have to be able to run a long way or beat him in tennis or get better grades, although that's not really manhood. That was pretty wimpy to be a brain. At certain times you would really rather hide it. It didn't have very much to do with manhood in any kind of way that I could imagine. The image of the egghead brainy guy with the good grades, the little wimpy guy with glasses, you might as well be a girl.

So when I hear the word "manhood," and when I think of how it was in adolescence, I remember that it was a real question in my mind whether I could really be a man. It seemed like a real possibility that I might not. That sounds sort of absurd now, because by definition I am. Whatever I do counts. But that's honestly how I felt back then. If manhood was power over others, and if I was being powered *upon.* . . . (Ken B.)

The deep-seated fear that we might not ever become "men" is echoed by all sorts of American males—most notably, by those who have come to be called "non-veterans." Scarcely one young fellow in ten is now likely to see any form of military service, and the many who will never even set foot in boot camp often experience the absence of a military initiation as a threat to their manly status. The problem here is not that men can't win at their chosen games but that they don't get the chance to play the most manly game of all: war.

The status of the contemporary non-warrior began to shift in the Vietnam era. Vietnam altered the place of warfare and the prestige of the warrior within the texture of American society,[1] and it was Vietnam which seems to have introduced the notion of non-warrior guilt into our collective consciousness.

In Vietnam there were all sorts of extraneous elements which had little or nothing to do with a proof of manhood: the atrocities, the drugs, the corruption, the dubious politics, the questionable morality of our mission. These other variables posed a serious dilemma for young males in America who might, for whatever reasons, have hoped to prove their manhood through war: What do you do when the only war left to fight is regarded as morally untenable by a significant portion of the population? Does fighting on behalf of a dictatorial regime halfway across the globe carry the same emotional weight, and fulfill the same primal function, as defending one's homeland from the intrusions of foreigners?

Whatever our personal politics, there was no clear national consensus concerning the righteousness of the war. The soldiers who fought in Vietnam, whether they deserved it or not, were perceived by many American citizens to be villains rather than heroes. They received little social validation for their achievements in war,[2] and this was bound to have an effect upon the self-image of a warrior who might have hoped to prove his manhood on the battlefield. For many Vietnam veterans, the promised glories of the life of a warrior never materialized; instead of leading to some sense of proof or validation, the war seemed only to foster more self-doubt. All too often, Vietnam failed to facilitate a healthy transition from boyhood to manhood; Steve Graham, for instance, would certainly argue that it made the transition more difficult.

In a sense, Vietnam can be seen as an abortive rite of passage for an entire generation of American males, even for those who stayed behind. Although the war went on for a decade and dominated the politics of the times, only certain segments of the male population were actually subjected to the crude realities of front-line action. For millions of American males of fighting age, the Vietnam War was encountered merely as a serialized drama on the six o'clock news; the life of a warrior was experienced vicariously as a pattern of tiny dots projected electronically onto a television screen. If through warfare these youths were supposed to prove their manhood, they became mere spectators at their own initiation.

Theoretically, all men between the ages of eighteen and thirty-six were subject to military conscription during the Vietnam era. The draft appeared as one of the inescapable facts of life, right up there with death and taxes. But in truth the Selective Service System was a strained and awkward compromise between universal service and no service at all. The pathways through the draft were many and varied: a youth could preempt the draft by enlisting in the service of his choice, perhaps something as safe and innocuous as the National Guard; he could conjure up a doctor's letter or sneak by with some minor physical complaint (for one fellow I interviewed, it was nothing more than a case of acne); he could weasel through with a student or professional deferment; he could become a conscientious objector; he could flee to Canada or go underground or go to jail. Such choices—it was a truly pluralistic conscription, replete with many injustices of class and caste. By and large, the working class went to Vietnam while the educated elite stayed home. Not since the Civil War, when a draftee could literally buy his way out, has our country fought a war with such a class-biased army. In the end, when the draft turned into a lottery, the Selective Service System became a mockery of itself: boys would be turned into men not on the basis of endurance, strength, and courage but on the basis of a random drawing of the numbers between 1 and 365.

Although not all young men during those times had to face up to the realities of front-line action, they did all have to deal with the draft in one way or another. That was the one common test which each and every youth had to take: What would he do when Uncle Sam called?

As I looked at my approaching eighteenth birthday, it started to loom ominously. That was the critical point: What was I going to do when I turned eighteen? All those things happen right then—you become independent of your family in a legal sense, you graduate from high school, you're off on your own, and you're expected to register for the draft. That was the hardest time for me. Talk about hazing or duress, I put myself on the spot and I had to make a decision about what I was going to do. It was a decision about how I

was going to do. It was a decision about how I was going to live my life and what kinds of values I was going to affirm and who I wanted to be and what kind of a role I wanted to fill. (Charles H.)

———

I can remember sitting down on a rock and opening the letter and reading the greeting from Lyndon Johnson that I was going to go off to war. As far as my manhood was concerned, the biggest thing I had to do was to decide what I was personally going to do about this piece of paper I had in my hand. Was I going to go do this? Was I going to go to jail? Was I going to leave the country? Those were very heavy, serious choices to consider. That was a decision that had to be made by a man. Just dealing with that piece of paper threw me into manhood. (Thomas D.)

So in a sense it was not really Vietnam but the draft itself that formed the most basic rite of passage for an entire generation. But what a strange ritual it was, and how totally inadequate from a psychological point of view. There were many ways to get through the draft that required no challenge of endurance, no strength of character, no courage in the face of danger. Unlike traditional initiations, the draft entailed no built-in program to help a youth with his growth. There was no dramatization of manhood, no ritualistic hazing—just a letter from the President that called a boy in to take a test which he probably wanted to fail. It was a war of classifications—1A, 2S, 4F—which was best fought by aspiring lawyers and bureaucrats, not young soldiers.

If facing up to the draft was the basic test of manhood for the Vietnam generation, then how did America's youths fare on that test? How could they know whether they passed or failed? By what standards could they judge their performances?

Those were tricky questions. The young men were bonded by no uniform code of morality; they had no commonly accepted social or political purpose; America's pluralism extended to the very depths of their separate and individual psyches. Each young male, whether he went to Vietnam or not, had to develop his own personal reconciliation between the age-old tradition of a warrior's initiation and the bizarre historical fact that the war of the moment was publicly and constantly being questioned.

For some, like Will Bell, the politics meant little. These were the young men who assumed that military service was part of a time-honored male tradition, and they figured they might as well put in their time without undo fuss. Others, however, found a personally satisfying solution by resisting the draft and refusing to go:

> During my last two years of high school I first encountered the idea that the war in Vietnam could be wrong. That was really a shock because I had always taken it for granted that we must be right. As I looked into it further, I started to examine the whole channeling process that was involved in the military. I began to see how even the conscientious objector process supported the war in Vietnam because it didn't actively oppose it. I started seeing C.O. as a safety valve that continued the status quo. It never asked the question about whether the war was morally or politically correct.
>
> So a week or two before my eighteenth birthday I wrote my draft board a letter saying that I was going to refuse to register. That was the beginning of my three-year legal battle with the draft, which ended with being sentenced to a federal prison in Stafford, Arizona.
>
> Even now that whole thing with the draft still sets me apart. But I don't regret it, I don't feel any guilt. I feel real lucky in that respect. I have friends who were in Vietnam and they have a lot of problems with it. It's called various names: "post-Vietnam syndrome," or whatever. So many people feel sullied about their role in the war. We all did time in one way or another: I did my time, they did their time. But I ended up doing less time than I would have if I had been in the military, and I got out of it without feeling guilty. I feel good about that. I'd do it again if I had to. (Charles H.)

Vietnam seriously undermined the social sanction of a military initiation. A war resister might have been despised by the army, he might have been legally an outlaw, but he could still find himself a niche in some obscure corner of American culture. Charles H. did not act alone. During the Vietnam era, an elaborate underground network of anti-war activists was ready to accept resisters and deserters with open arms—and even to welcome them as heroes.

So this is a part of our Vietnam legacy: the dropouts from the military—indeed, dropouts from any segment of society—are not totally disgraced, since they can now find a home somewhere else. This simple truth has a profound impact upon the style and force of our initiations.

Our multitudinous options make it functionally impossible to create a difficult rite of passage while simultaneously ensuring that virtually all of the participants will remain and endure. The primitive model for successful initiations, based as it is upon a homogeneous social structure with limited choices, appears to break down when applied to a complex and heterogeneous society where we can leisurely browse among alternate beliefs and lifestyles.

This freedom of choice deprives our contemporary initiations of much of their power. The primitives made their initiations exceptionally difficult, sometimes to the point of masochistic absurdity—and yet they also made it virtually impossible for anyone to quit. There were several mechanisms to ensure against quitting: the unilinear expectations, the threat of ridicule, the remote location of the rituals. The participants didn't really have much choice in the matter; unable to fail, they were forced to succeed. Yet even as their success was effectively guaranteed, it could only be achieved by dint of individual effort, endurance, and courage, and so each separate individual experienced a sense of personal validation for his struggles. This basic strategy is not well suited to a pluralistic culture like our own. In a free and open society, we always have some choice between alternate paths; that's the defining characteristic of pluralism, and it impedes the development of autocratic initiations. Unlike the primitives, we are allowed to quit—and thereby fail—if we want. To mix popular metaphors: When the going gets tough, the grass gets greener on the other side of the fence.

But how do we reconcile this apparent freedom of choice with archetypal images of manliness? Traditional male expectations are not so easily abandoned, and they cannot be automatically negated by one messy war. Today, many men who came of age during Vietnam are not totally satisfied with the choices they once felt free to make. For those who neither served nor resisted, the ambiguities of the situation have never been adequately resolved:

I now almost regret that I didn't serve overseas during the Vietnam War. I think that there must be some parallel that war is to men what childbirth is to women. I've heard this from buddies of mine who are veterans, that there's no intensity of human emotion greater than being under fire.

Vietnam, unfortunately, was understandably unpopular: commu-

nist insurgency into a country punch-drunk and weary of decades of war can't be equated with World War II, where we had an obvious threat committed to conquering our very shores.

I managed to avoid the draft by managing to be conveniently absent from Santa Cruz County whenever the draft board convened a hearing of my "peers" (actually ten middle-aged hawks) to consider my claim of Conscientious Objector. I was traveling a lot at the time, and I'd send the draft board postcards from Bogota, Europe, or Mexico, asking for a new hearing on some other date.

I finally returned from one of my odysseys to find a card in the mail box declaring me ineligible for induction, as the Hearing Board was unable to hear my case for lack of quorum. Broke my heart. I think I just wore them out, and they went on to the next-most-available cannon fodder. (Stan B.)

———

Going into the physical, I had all sorts of things going for me: bad eyesight, allergies, asthma. I had a doctor's letter saying I had a bum knee. But I was still really nervous—matter of fact, my blood pressure practically broke the machine. In retrospect, it worries me how desperately I wanted to flunk that test.

The doctor's letter worked. I flunked the test with flying colors and I never went to Vietnam. Of course I was relieved, but I also couldn't help feeling like I had copped out. Failing an army physical—failing it so *desperately*—was not totally compatible with my feelings of incipient manhood (James W.)

Why does Stan B. "almost regret" not going to Vietnam? Why should he bemoan the fact that he was never forced to fight an ugly war in which he did not believe? And whatever became of James W.'s "feelings of incipient manhood" which were at least neglected, and perhaps even negated, by his devious escape from military life? We are talking now about "non-veteran guilt," as the media has labeled it. Many of those who never went to Vietnam describe an insidious sense of unreality to their lives, and they attribute this vague malaise to their failure to answer the call to military service:

Anyone who's been to Vietnam, it gives them a credibility to me. I listen to them more seriously. Because of the experiences they've had,

I've got to give them some respect for that. Whatever they say, it's got more meaning. It's more real. (Brian B.)

Objectively, it seems strange for such a surreal war to function as a reality check in the minds of the men who never fought in it. But this is not actually an affirmation of the Vietnam experience (after all, these men were never there)—it is an assertion of the timidity of a perpetually civilian life style.

Most young males today, like these non-vets from the Vietnam era, have not yet gone to war—and they probably never will. The draft is over, at least for the time being. The direct experience of traditional warfare is not a part of the texture of contemporary culture, so the dilemma of the Vietnam non-veterans has become common for most American males. A youth today is trapped between the archaic notion that men should be initiated as warriors and the objective reality that a warrior has little place in the modern world; he is reared with a strong military heritage (four major wars within the past seventy years), yet the methods by which he might live up to that heritage are no longer obvious.

The plight of the "non-veteran" is now well known, yet it is not often recognized as only one aspect of the general demise of traditional initiations. In fact there are many parallel ways in which young males today feel deprived, either consciously or unconsciously, of a meaningful rite of passage into manhood.

How many of us, for instance, have responded to David Smith's "call to adventure"? We might hunt and explore via video games, but not many young men actually make a habit of swimming from continent to continent or of climbing vertical cliffs. These kinds of personalized initiations are not quite in tune with our everyday lifestyles. On the most basic, physical level, adventure is literally not where we are at—the wild and exotic places in which these experiences generally occur are removed by hundreds or thousands of miles from our major population centers. Ironically, in order to reach an appropriate arena for romantic adventure, we must first confront traffic jams or crowded airports, and we must find a way to get free from school or from our jobs—we must, in short, engage in any number of routine and mundane hassles which seem to have little to do with a proof of manhood. The "call to adventure" is therefore not quite so pure and immediate as we might like to fancy, and many of us who hear the call never bother to answer.

And even if we do respond to the call, rarely do we sever completely the umbilical cord that ties us to civil society. It's not the same as the old days, when an adventurer was truly on his own. There are no more uncharted and unknown territories to explore, but only designated pre-serves. Our wilderness today is like a museum, a small reminder of what the rest of the earth used to be like. And our experiences in the wilderness are also self-conscious preserves, mere tokens from our primal past.

The paucity of adventuresome experiences in our everyday lives is both conspicuous and significant. Just as the absence of an experience with war has led to "non-vet guilt," so has the scarcity of real adventure within the context of our normal lives led to a sort of "non-adventurer guilt,"[3] a vague but insidious feeling that we are trapped by our civilized existence and that we are missing out on something *real*. Dick Byrum, for instance, is addicted to the wilds—but he must often revert to dreaming about the wilderness instead of being there himself:

I lead a pretty active fantasy life about having more adventures, visions of maybe doing a trip on foot or horseback from Mexico to Alaska, or doing a trip through the Sierras from one end to the other, taking no supplies, just my bow. Those ideas often occur to me. They'd be fun to do: the feeling of independence, being able to do it and not make a total fool of myself. Maybe be a little healthier for the effort, and probably a lot smarter. It's hard to define these things, why I want to do things like that. I don't want to lead too pedestrian a life. I want to do things that are fun, that have a little excitement attached to them. I'm looking forward to moving farther out of town. If I envision myself staying in town the rest of my life, it's a real grim outlook. But if I can hold out the hope that I can spend a significant amount of my time in the woods or someplace that's a little freer, without the people pollution. . . .

How many contemporary males, like Dick Byrum, lead this sort of fan-tasy life? I think a lot of us do—far more than will ever realize our visions.

Sean K., born and raised in a major metropolis, also regrets the lack of adventure in his life. Unlike Dick Byrum, Sean has never ventured very far into the natural world, and now, at the age of thirty-three, he feels that his failure to go adventuring has somehow impeded his development as an adult:

> **There's so much that I haven't gone through. It bothers me that I haven't been much of a risk-taker. I can't point to a whole lot of adventures that I've had. If I could take life over again, it would be better to have a group of friends and we could have gone to the mountains a lot, or canoing or something. Had some more adventures, learn more about being self-sufficient. That kind of stuff I missed; I literally missed the boat. I feel that youth passed me by without my going out and exploring the world.**
>
> **The fact that I haven't taken these risks affects my sense of adulthood. I feel like I haven't had enough life experiences. Somehow the act of taking risks, not foolish ones but just the risks people normally take, makes you grow. It's like getting from one place to another, and in the process you really grow. So I haven't done enough of that. I've just been a little too stationary during the time I could've gone out and traveled, and I feel a sadness about it now.**

Why, we might ask, doesn't Sean, who is still a young man, go exploring now? But Sean is currently facing problems of financial solvency which seem more pressing; a trip to the mountains might appear exciting and attractive, but it's not serious business. His real struggle for survival, even though it lacks adventuresome flare, is right here in the city. So Sean, like Dick Byrum, can only look wistfully into the distant hills as he pursues his everyday tasks.

And even Sean K. has more adventure in his life than many young males, for at least he lives on his own. Youths today seem increasingly unable to leave the comfort and security of their own family homes, let alone the supportive web of modern civilization. There are very real reasons why fewer young men are out on their own—most notably, the skyrocketing cost of housing[4]—but whatever the reasons, the fellows who stay at home often turn the vague self-doubts of contemporary non-adventurers into outright self-disdain. "I feel like shit," says twenty-three-year-old Alan F., a sales clerk in a hardware store. "I'm totally ashamed. But what can I really do about it?"

Twenty-one-year-old Michael V., like Alan F., feels bad about being stuck at home, but he is also candid about the comforts which his home still provides:

I hate it. I'm going to be out of here soon as I can. But there's no expenses, and I haven't really had any difficulties in the house. I basically lead my own life down in the basement. That creates tension in itself, because I'm in the house and then I'm not in the house.

Besides, I have like two different ideas about moving out, because I feel that I'm not really old enough to lead my own life responsibly. Most people my age aren't doing it; in fact, nobody I know my own age is out leading their own life with their own place and paying all the bills. Mostly they're going to school and their parents are supporting them or they're working little jobs.

I feel secure here, actually. I don't really have too many things to worry about. I don't have to worry about the six hundred dollar rent check coming up and what the phone bill is going to be. Not that I should worry about it anyway, because I could pay it. Everybody I work with is thirty-five with a wife and two kids and house payments and two cars, and they're all making it. So why can't I make it? I guess I'm not really motivated to go out there and search for a place and have to fork out all this money and then have to be there. Besides, I'd get lonely in my own place sometimes.

So I'm kind of skeptical about moving out on my own, although it looks like that's what I'm going to do anyways. I can't really decide at this point, but a decision has to be made.

Michael is clearly in limbo, not quite ready to be a man on his own. In a sense we are all like that. Insofar as we are cared for by society in safe and reassuring ways, we all still live at home. We generally feel (even if the feeling is illusory) that we are no longer perched on the edge of survival. We are vaccinated against disease, insured against calamity, protected from enemy nations. We hedge all our bets as best we can. Like Michael V., we assume that our bills will be paid.

The problem is we don't always *like* feeling this complacent. This is what we consciously deny when we go off adventuring, when we try to escape "too pedestrian a life," as Dick Byrum calls it. Like the fellows who feel trapped at home, we want to get out on our own. But can we? Do we? And how do we feel about ourselves when we stay at "home," secure within the confines of a pampering society? Have we become too soft to feel like men?

The plight of the "non-adventurers" and the "non-veterans" is also paralleled by that of the "non-laborers"—men who were never sent to the Australian mines for a taste of real work and who don't break a sweat on the job. In former times, only an elite handful of aristocrats were free of manual work, and these gentlemen had other ways of proving their manhood; today, more than half the grown males in America are engaged in sales, service, clerical, professional, or managerial jobs which require little or no physical exertion. These men might (or might not) be success-ful in their respective fields, they might (or might not) make a lot of money and enjoy some social prestige, but there is no escaping the fact that their jobs are not totally compatible with archaic notions of what constitutes "man's work."[5]

Particularly during adolescence, when masculinity and physicality are most closely linked in our minds, the manliness of manual labor can appear very attractive, while the absence of manual labor can be experi-enced as a threat to masculinity:

When I was sixteen, seventeen years old, I used to help out my dad in his men's clothing store. That was always an option for me, to go into the family business. There was money in it, at least some money, a successful business, but it had absolutely zero appeal.

Part of the problem was style. I preferred jeans and sneakers, clothes that let you feel your own body. We weren't selling that kind of stuff in my dad's store. His customers all wore ties and jackets and pressed slacks and leather shoes with slick soles. To me, dressing like that was pointless. The shoes slipped on the ice or fell off in the mud. The jacket and slacks ripped when you bent down to pick something up. The tie flapped in your face when you ran or it got caught in the gears of some machine and choked you to death. The whole outfit functioned like some sort of straitjacket which was purposely de-signed to prevent any sort of physical activity. My dad's customers looked enslaved inside their own clothes. Emasculated. I wanted no part of it. I wanted to be *out there* in the world, active and alive and doing real physical things.

I did a lot of gazing out the window when I worked there, out through those sterilized mannequins he had on display to the brazen workmen who were always digging up the street. That was a whole other world: jackhammers, wheelbarrows, overalls, unshaven faces, sweat, muscles. It was definitely more manly. At that point in my life,

I would've easily chosen to wield a jackhammer rather than just stand around and wait on my dad's dandy customers. (Jimmy S.)[6]

For the children of technology—the fellows from comfortable surroundings who, like Jimmy S., are not forced by objective circumstances to wield a jackhammer or work in the mines—the adjustment to the sedentary lifestyle of an advanced and specialized economy has been psychologically difficult. They are likely to perceive selling clothes or pushing papers as unmanly, despite the economic rewards these jobs promise to produce. Since the manly virtues which a modern adolescent still craves—strength, agility, endurance, courage—have strong physical roots, young males who find no means of asserting these virtues through their work are likely to lapse into a self-perceived state of unreality, much like the non-veterans of the Vietnam era who were never able to prove themselves in war. Deprived of both the war and the hunt, these modern-day youths sometimes feel like they are not given many avenues for the fulfillment of traditional male roles.

But is it really that manly to wield a jackhammer or spend one's life in the mines? Physical labor is often mindless, repetitive, and exhausting. It is menial, and the menial can easily become the demeaning. The social status of manual labor is minimal—and minimal status is hardly very manly. The workers must be subservient while on the job, and subservience is hard to reconcile with the masculine ideal of personal power.

Many blue collar workers have little sympathy with the romantic images of hard, physical labor. Peter M., a warehouseman who has literally broken his back lifting hundred-pound loads, has no grand illusions about the nature of his job:

Some of us might enjoy it, but not too many romanticize it. We do it because we have to—no other reason. Sometimes I feel good at the end of the day for doing a hard day's work, but often I feel lousy because it's just that—a hard day's work. I'm tired, and that's it. After I do a hard day's work, I just want to vegetate. I don't feel like going out and jogging like the Yuppies.

When Ted Kennedy was running for president, a crusty old coalminer came up to him and said, "I've heard you've never worked a day in your life. Well, let me tell you something: you haven't missed a thing." That's pretty much the way I feel about it.

The differing testimonies of Peter M. and Jimmy S. illustrate a basic dilemma modern-day males face as we try to assert our manhood through our work. If we opt for white collar careers, we must deal only with abstractions—numbers, words, papers—and we lose touch with that dimension of physical existence which still looms large in the psyches of young and aspiring males. If, on the other hand, our jobs are physical, they are often routine and demeaning, and they are unlikely to lead to wealth or prestige. In either case we are likely to feel somewhat powerless, and powerlessness, for a man, is easily interpreted to be emasculating.[7]

So how do we deal with this dilemma? How do we escape from "non-worker guilt"?

More often than not, we focus our attention keenly on our contemporary metaphor for a man's true work: the acquisition of money. Money provides an unofficial stamp of social approval, and it can even provide us with a sense of meaning or purpose where none might otherwise exist. If people are willing to pay us for what we are doing—and particularly if they are willing to pay us *well*—then our work must certainly be worthwhile. The language of money—what it means and why we need it—is understood by bankers and bricklayers alike. Money serves as a common symbol which, in its own way, brings us all together; it provides a simple measure of success that crosses over the provincial idiosyncrasies of our separate occupations.

And since access to money, in this day and age, is equivalent to survival, the acquisition of money constitutes an important component of any definition of modern manhood. Conversely, the lack of money leads almost unavoidably to unmanly quilt. How can a fellow really feel like a man if he is still financially dependent? A youth who wants to prove he has grown up must make at least enough money to get by in the world, and preferably enough to enjoy the power and prestige that money commands. The quest after money is the game we are all forced to play, whether we want to or not.

Since the money game is a game of numbers, it can easily be reduced to a linear scale. All transactions, all wages, all profits can be represented on a two-dimensional line. Any two numbers—any two paychecks, for instance—can be compared with each other; one is greater or less than the other. In a game such as this, it is hard to avoid the notion of winners and losers—and for those of us who lose, our personal sense of manliness is placed in jeopardy. Whatever our field of work, we can easily become trapped (just as we are trapped in competitive sports) between the hunger for personal success and the crude, simple fact that there is only limited room at the top. And so it is, for some of us, that our initiation into the world of adult work never seems to end:

> For me it keeps on going on and on. The uncertainty of it—at any moment you could be out on the streets. It's all tied up with money. I've got to keep on fighting for money and respect. The fire never stops; I keep running through it every day.
>
> I had an image, back when I was fifteen and living in the Midwest: I wanted to go East, I wanted to go preppy and Ivy League and all that kind of stuff. I don't know where I got all that. In fact I never went to prep school, but I always felt like I wanted to or should have. And so now I wonder why it didn't happen and what it could have been otherwise.
>
> After I got out of high school I took a year off and then went to the American school in Switzerland, where I met some tremendously wealthy people. I mean, these are old rich people, families that have been around for a hundred years and they have millions and billions and trillions of dollars. Company presidents' sons—the son of the president of Time-Life, the son of the president of Dow Chemical. So I'm in there rubbing elbows with them, and that very much fed what I was thinking about for myself—a very large ego, and I am going to succeed. Money, wealth, power, and influence was really where it was at.
>
> I gradually lost touch with those guys from Switzerland, but I single-mindedly started pursuing the idea of going to law school. I had a very traditional concept of law. Doctors, lawyers, professionals, those people all had the money and prestige that I was looking for. Being a lawyer fit my definition of manhood very handily. (Howard R.)

Howard did in fact graduate from law school and become a lawyer, but he did not manage to acquire much money or prestige. He worked first for Legal Aid and then for his father-in-law, but his "marriage went sour, and when the marriage went, the law business went." He went to Houston to help his mother with her nightclub, and he stayed on to take odd jobs as a bricklayer's helper, a carpenter's helper, an electrician's helper.

I finally came out to California because my brothers were here and California was just the place to be. There's a certain feeling of freedom and opportunity that's always in the air. It was just the thing to do, to come out here and start to make a go of it again. I started taking a home-study course for the bar exam; I sent away for all the books and got the material from the bar and paid all my money. I took the exam in '82 and didn't pass. I don't know how far I was away from passing, but I think on that particular occasion less than fifty percent passed.

Now, I don't know if I can ever pass the bar here; I don't know whether I'm ever going to try it again or not. I'd have to study a lot harder and sign up for the right to take the thing and then there's the likelihood of not passing. When I took it there was somebody I was talking to who had taken it fourteen times—that's seven years, because you can only take it twice a year. And these are smart people; these are people that were on law reviews in their law schools. And I was never that. I'm just a strong C+, B student—and these guys are law review and not passing the bar. Now you hear, well, only thirty percent passed this year.

I'm mad about that. There's something terribly wrong with that system, and I take it very personally that they are hurting me. I feel that very arbitrarily I'm being eliminated. They're depriving me of my pursuit of happiness. I went through law school. I did that, I went through the trial of fire and came out the other side. I got my degree and I practiced law and I'm a good lawyer. And now they make me run through the trial of fire again, and I can't make it.

I always heard that through your twenties, that's when you're getting up a head of steam and you're shopping around. You try two or three different employers; you don't want to look like you're shopping and hopping, but you should look around and get the one you want. When you're in your thirties, boy that's when you start to grind it out, and when you're in your forties that's where you start putting the cream on it. That's the way my life was supposed to be. But as I approach forty here, it's going to get even harder to get a job. That's what I was always told: "If you haven't done it by the time you're forty, you might as well forget it. People don't want to hire old people."

Now, I'm my own worst enemy in terms of daily flogging myself from that age fifteen script I used to have. Here I am, at age thirty-eight, doing what, relative to what I thought I would be doing? I thought I'd have kids that were in high school, and I'd have a nice big house, belong to a country club, have a couple of cars—a station wagon and a Mercedes. That's just the way life was supposed to be. Far from it. It's a sack of potatoes compared to that. I don't have anything. I don't have any clothes; I don't have a car that's worth anything; I don't have a house. What happened?

I probably should have gone into my own private practice when I first got out of law school, because that would have certainly put me somewhere other than where I'm at right now, financially. Maybe if I had gone ahead and made a million dollars or had a six-figure income from practicing law it would be different. Maybe I would feel something else. I don't even know what I *should* feel, at this point.

When my twentieth anniversary came around last year from my high school reunion, I didn't go. I just didn't want to be there and: "What are you doing? What's happening? Do you have a wife? Kids?" No, no. "A job?" No. No, no, no. Then when I think about meeting up with any of these people from the American school in Switzerland, I could *never* do that. I don't know what the heck they're doing, but they're living very well on their trust funds if they're not doing anything else.

Sometimes I can rationalize it out to think that I am a "good person," and really that's what is important. I feel very good about that, in terms of my own feelings about morality—at least how I intellectualize morality, if not practice it. In that way I'm a success; I feel that I'm on "God's side" in a sense. I'm not wasting my life. But at times I feel that I *am* wasting my life. Doing what I'm doing, waitering at the cafe, is not tremendously challenging intellectually. That's still the bone with me, the feeling that I want to have intelligence. I'm still chasing that thing down, proving that to myself one way or the other. And the material success has a lot to do with it, of course: If you're so smart, why aren't you rich?

I don't want to be digging ditches or pushing a wheelbarrow when I'm fifty years old. I'm not even talking about personal wealth anymore; I'm talking about *survival*. Literally, I don't know where next month's rent is going to come from. Prestige and power, I've abandoned those ideals. At this stage of the game it's a question of financial security, which has to do with marriage, with children, with the pursuit of happiness. If I don't have any security, I don't have the right even to think about marriage and the responsibility that goes along with it, and certainly not children. In a certain sense my relationships with women have to be kept shallow or at an arm's length or with that sort of disclosure up front: "There really can't be anything serious because I haven't the financial ability, and consequently the right, to participate in such an undertaking."

I'm trying my hardest to acquire that right. I always have three things going at one time, hoping that something will make it. I've never been one to sit back. I've been working full time, full speed ahead, ever since I was five. And that continues on, but somehow there are reasons why that doesn't succeed. Sometimes I think about going back to Ohio or going back to Houston and living under mother's roof again, which of course is very negative to me. I want to be in California; I want to make it here. My God, there are fifteen million people in California and they're all making it. Why can't I make it too?

Since Howard R.'s initiation never seems to end, it's not really an initiation at all—it's just life. Howard does not seem to have acquired the strong feeling of independence and self-worth so important to manhood. The consequences of his financial failure are profound. Marginal employment, like unemployment, leads to a feeling of powerlessness that is ultimately emasculating. Without significant work, or at least without significant remuneration for his work, he feels he cannot fulfill the traditional male role of supporting a family; he is not a good provider if he comes home empty-handed from the hunt.[8]

Sean K., like Howard R., feels the effects of low-status finances upon traditional male-female relationships:

I've been thinking about placing a personal ad in the paper, but what do you say about yourself in a little box? I definitely don't want to put in the usual stuff. Every ad wants the same thing; they want long walks on beaches, ethnic restaurants, quiet evenings in, walks in the rain. Everybody wants to get rained on for some reason. So I think about putting in a totally satirical ad: "I want to take long walks off short piers, McDonald's restaurants, walks in acid rain."

I find a lot of the ads that women put in intimidating because so many of them say that you must be professional, must love your work, must be financially secure. It just makes me want to go, "Fuck you, lady." Of course I wouldn't find it so intimidating if I was a professional and loved my work and was financially secure. Then it would be fine. Then I could just strut: "Hey, lady, here I am. I think we can make it. I think we have a lot of things in common. We're the perfect couple." Some people might place too much importance on those sorts of things, but they do say something about you. The images aren't just superficial. There is something more attractive about a person who has their life in order, who has all these things going for them.

Sean's question—what does one say in the "little box"—is but an updated version of the age-old male concern: How *do* we impress? There is a genuine pathos, a bewildering sort of sadness, to the sexual burden of men—and there is also a confusing paradox. Traditionally, we are the initiators of sexual activity, the ones who are expected to make the first advance; but what if we ourselves are young, innocent, and still dependent? How can the uninitiated initiate? How can a young male attract a lady to a nest which has not yet been built?

This is the dilemma which adolescent males must face as they first mature—and for those who have found no ready escape from sexual insecurity, the burden can become quite unbearable.[9] Witness, for instance, the testimony of twenty-one-year-old Sam S.:

Sex still makes me sick. Actually it's kind of like stage fright but a whole lot worse. I get real nervous and a little queasy before asking a girl out and also right before a date. Picking up the phone or ringing a doorbell requires an almost unbelievable act of will. But that isn't the worst of it. What really gets me is when we come back to her house or my house and it's time to try to make it. That's it, the anticipation—overwhelming nausea. If I'm offered something to eat at her house, I have to refuse. Sometimes I almost puke in the car beforehand. Not that I ever do, but the physical ordeal just to keep it together is incredibly intense.

Generally I bully my way through and maybe the girl never knows, or maybe she does, or maybe she feels the same way herself. I have absolutely no way of knowing. Once we get down to business and start in on it I'm fine, even if we don't go very far. But the thought that I have to make some kind of advance, and then she might turn me down, is unbearable. I think it's fear, straight fear. I've got friends who saw combat in Vietnam and they report the same kind of nausea before a maneuver. The fear of defeat.

Why such anxiety? Why should the possibility of failure (or even just temporary rejection) in sex produce the same fear as wartime dangers? The fragility of the male ego, as we all know, is nowhere more apparent than in our early sexual encounters. Our success or failure is dependent upon the will of another, but dependency is precisely what we are trying to overcome as we try to forge ahead into the world. We are testing our masculinity, and yet, as in war, we can't always control the results.

Of course our changing sexual roles have lessened the impact of the traditional male burden, for women can now initiate too. But the changes brought about by feminism and unisex have added a new and different dimension to our sexual initiation: Not only must we learn how to "get it up," but we must now learn simultaneously how to "tone it down." Naturally, these contradictory demands of modern masculinity can also cause considerable confusion, and we easily get stuck in the limbo between the two:

When Margo and I came out to settle on land in California, there was a feeling of newness and excitement to what we were doing with each other. It was a pioneer image, a real traditional thing we were playing out—and also a real traditional division of roles between us. But it felt real good to us, real secure. Even though we didn't have any money, we didn't have a place to live, we had nothing really—we had an old potato chip truck—we felt real secure in what each of us provided. Margo took care of the baby and she did the cooking and she did the cleaning, and she did it really well. I worked on the truck and built the house and those kinds of things. And made some money. So we felt like we had something that was real important. We each had our adult roles.

All this began to change when I became a fisherman because I was no longer there to provide my end of it. I was gone a lot. Even though being a fisherman was a real traditional masculine role, Margo got more into doing a lot of traditional masculine things at home: building things and fixing the vehicles and that kind of stuff. And it was right about that time that the women's movement started to happen, so she got a lot of support, too. It became all right to do all those things, more than all right.

It was a gradual process, but she became more and more independent, which was hard for me to take, actually. But at the same time I felt strongly that in a marriage each person should be able to develop in a way that felt good to them. So it was a struggle for me to let go of my areas of expertise, but I do feel, as I look back on it, that I did do that, that I was able to let go. I'm sure Margo has a different opinion.

Building the addition to the house was the big thing. She did that pretty much by herself. Not only was it taken away from me, but it actually got to the point where I wasn't *allowed* to work on the house. She felt that as a man, I would take over projects. And then there got to be these resentments of: "You didn't help me. I didn't want you to help me, but you didn't help me." That was a real source of irritation.

Meanwhile I was getting more into fishing. That was an image that I was good at and that people respected—and was still very masculine. So I really worked hard at that. I built a boat from scratch and then sold that boat and got a bigger boat. I became respected among the guys that I fished with and people in the community. The problem was that fishing only lasted for half a year; then I would come home and it was real difficult for me to fit in. I would grope for something—like fixing the cars. I *hated* fixing the cars (I still do) but I held onto that. Margo didn't like fixing the cars either, so she didn't mind if I held onto it. So: "At least I can fix the cars." And cutting the wood, I still did that too.

Then I sold my boat again and got a still bigger boat and got even more into fishing, was gone longer. Margo was real supportive of that, and as I look back on it I think she really wanted it—she really wanted me to be gone for six months out of the year. She liked that.

I was real afraid of change. I would go away for longer periods of time, and since Margo is a real active woman, whenever I came back everything would be different. It would blow me away. I was out on the ocean, battling with the ocean, and I had the image of Margo and the kids and the homestead. That's where I wanted to be; I didn't want to be out on the ocean at all. Then I'd come back and it would all be different. There'd be new pictures on the wall, everything would be changed around. There'd be acres cleared. I didn't *want* it cleared; I wanted all that brush, all the birds and stuff. I couldn't accept the change; I wanted everything to be the same.

She felt, "The boat is yours. You should let me do whatever I want with the land and the house." But the thing that she could never understand was: "Okay, you don't live on the boat. Once a year maybe you go on the boat, so what do you care? But I have to live in the house, and I care if it's . . . whatever." So that was a real big conflict.

Then when I sold the boat and I came back to live at home, it became harder and harder. We became locked into this power struggle. I went through a whole period of trying to become less aggressive and less willful and subservient to her. I got into doing massage, and that in itself became a real serving thing, which I wanted to develop in myself. And yet I felt like I was always being asked to be less and less of a dynamic person, that I wasn't allowed to express *my* creativity in the house or on the land. By that time she had mapped out the whole forty acres and there was really no room for me to do anything. Anything I wanted to do was seen as taking over one of Margo's projects, either a past project or a present project or a future project.

The fights became really petty, really down there. Like there was one arm chair at the head of the table—who gets to sit there? That became a big fight. Or who sleeps on the outside of the bed and who sleeps on the inside of the bed—that became a real big issue. Whether we'd have six inch heating ducts or eight inch heating ducts—that became a major, major issue in our marriage, and in my opinion was one of the main things that broke up our marriage.

Then she started her stable business, and she expected me to support her in the way that she had supported me in the fishing. I really tried hard to be able to do that, like I worked on building the stables and helped her to buy the land. But somehow I never could quite do it with the enthusiasm that was needed to make her feel good. I never felt that I was appreciated or that I had some say in what happened. I always felt that I had to keep my mouth shut and *work*.

That led to our both finding lovers, which was the eventual end of it. That gave us something to break up over. We both still had a lot of love for each other, but somehow we couldn't resolve a lot of the conflicts that we had. So we split up, and then we got back together. God, when I look back on it and talk about it like this, it seems like it took years and years and years to break up. Now we're broken up for good.

I believe strongly that people should be allowed to develop themselves within a relationship. The development of each person is really more important than the relationship, although I also feel that relationships to me are real important. So the process of change that I've seen in Margo through the women's movement I agree with. I think it was a good process for her. But at this point in my life I feel sort of lost, wondering what *my* process is.

I can see the good aspects of it for Margo, but I do feel bitter about it. I have definite longings for the good old days of well-defined roles. I don't know if I could really do that at this point in my life, but I don't see that the traditional roles are *per se* bad. They're only bad if the people involved in them are stifled to where they can't feel happy. (Shawn W.)

The feminist movement, even for men like Shawn who are sympathetic to its basic philosophy, can be experienced as an emasculating force, for it exaggerates that familiar sense of unmanly guilt. Shawn has been deprived of all his masculine props; he is no longer a builder and provider. Having lost his job, his family, and his home, he must now go out into the world and make it on his own—just as he had to do when he first tried to prove he was a man. At the age of thirty-five, he is forced to undergo a new and entirely different sort of initiation.[10]

Our attempts to deal with this new threat to our masculinity are not always graceful. Our apparent failures can make us bitter and resentful, thereby twisting our notion of what might constitute success. We become trapped by the negative logic of defeat. Instead of chasing love, we can easily chase after the raw power which we think will make us into men—and which will keep us from losing again:

I think the need to put myself through difficult emotional situations with women was a very important thing for me, far more important than joining the Marines. During the peak of the women's movement I was with a woman who was an extraordinarily bright lady. That was the time when women were beginning to assert themselves in a variety of ways that ranged from vindictive to unpredictable. The concept of "man" was an unacceptable one, and the language of most relationships had not to do with what *you* did but what *men* did.

My relationship with this woman broke up when she started going out with a gay lawyer. She was a very vigorous feminist who started a radical women's publication. For her, lesbianism was the only politically correct form of sexual behavior. For me, it was impossible to deal with that situation in any kind of positive context—men's group, private shrink, or otherwise. That relationship in itself was a rite of passage, picking a woman to live with and fall in love with when I knew in some sense it would never work. I was still struggling to become a male, a man—and this was an effort to reach maledom overnight. I picked this relationship simply because it was so hard, probably because it was impossible.

Looking back on it, I did it as a challenge to myself. It was part of an initiation process in the sense of trying to cram a lot of suffering and pain into a brief, difficult period so that you can come out of it having learned what it is to be a man for the next relationship. If one is going to go through some sort of sexual hazing, you cannot reduce it to a single flagellation ceremony. It's of necessity a longer process that involves the heart as much as it does the body. You just can't set yourself up for the proper form of suffering unless you do something like getting yourself deeply involved in a hopeless relationship.

I haven't quite learned to put all that aside. There've been a number of women since Sue with whom I've had very close relationships. The best was a woman named Dawn; I was with her for three or four years. It was a terrific relationship, but I still carried around the wound from my relationsip with Sue. I knew with Dawn it *could* work, but I never quite gave it the chance. I never really won the battle with Sue; it was a roller coaster ride with me screaming all the way. With Dawn, I purposely destroyed the relationship, which was for me the real entry into manhood.

There was probably something inside of me from my prior relationship that felt some sort of need to strike back at a woman I cared about a great deal, wanting to regain the lost masculinity that I suffered at the hands of Sue. Ending a relationship is that kind of strength. What I did in that relationship was to regain some sort of power over women, a silly concept in the end because of course you lose all the control by ending the relationship. But what you gain is the total independence that is a part of the masculine ideal. (Christopher T.)

Christopher has found a handy escape from the unmanly guilt so often produced by failure: he has decided to let his masochistic suffering harden him into a man, thereby regaining the "masculine" power of emotional independence, the ability to hurt others before they can hurt him. He's not particularly pleased with the tack he has taken, but at least it keeps him from the gnawing pain of not feeling enough like a man:

The problem that I feel I have in most of my relationships now is that I'm too powerful. I've lost contact with my emotional soft spots. I'm not reachable; I'm aloof and impersonal and capable of wrapping women around my finger, which is an offensive concept to me. I had no desire at the beginning of this to become an emotional warrior; I just wanted to be a survivor. But now I feel a little bit too able to manipulate the minds and sexual psyches of ladies, and to be uninvolved and also to give up the relationship if it doesn't look good.

The power that I have is what I once wanted, but now I have it without really wanting it. The idea that I can get control over an area of experience which should be spontaneous and open and free is something I reject. I don't like it in myself, and on some level I would like to feel as emotionally naive as I was once—but I don't suppose you can go back there.

Ironically, our changing sex roles have provided us with another seductive escape from the unmanly guilt created by our inevitable dependence upon women. Now that men have learned how to fulfill some traditionally female functions, we are easily tempted to believe that we can do it all ourselves:

The "Super Dad" fantasy is important to me in connection with my thinking, "What would make me feel like I was really a man?" It would be having to do it all, indefinitely: work, keep the house going, and take care of the boys. The image is this: Can you be changing the baby, answering the phone on some matter of business, and making sure that the oatmeal doesn't boil over all at the same time? That juggling of things, that's a macho kind of a thing for me, to be able to do that.

It's like: I don't need a woman. You're so macho you can not only get rid of the woman, you can *be* the woman. You don't need her; you *are* her. And you're him, too. You're feeding everybody. You're bringing home the bacon and frying it. That's Super Dad. Hey man, I'm doing it all. I don't need my wife. There's no more reliance on a woman because you're doing all those woman things too. You don't even have to pay a maid. As long as a real man doesn't need a maid, he can cook quiche all he wants. It's almost like androgeny is the perfect macho. You're a totally, utterly self-sufficient being; you can even have your own children. If you adopt the kids, you wouldn't even need a woman. You're taking care of some woman's children who couldn't take care of them herself.

I admit this whole fantasy is aggressive against women. Part of the aggression, at least in my own experience, is that Amanda has consistently been better at doing these things. She *can* do three things at once, and it's not even remarkable to her that she can do it. She has always just naturally done what needed to be done to keep the household going.

Amanda goes away for these two- or three-day trips. Like she's gone now, and she'll be back either Thursday or Friday, depending on how things work out. So she goes away, and I take care of the kids. That's where the Super Dad fantasy has its only place in real experience, when I'm left alone with the kids. I have to think through and execute the next forty-eight hours for three people, not just me but for those two little guys.

After it's over I feel stronger. I made it. And I see to it that the house is just immaculate when Amanda gets home, that all the dishes are done, that the kids are clean or asleep or whatever they're supposed to be doing, and everything is just so. I like to flaunt it. I like to go to the grocery store with both kids and handle them just right. Or changing diapers in public places. Women walk by and just adore me for being such a great father. They don't do that for moms, but for dads you get all these strokes. You can get just totally hooked on that stuff. And little old ladies, their husbands have never even seen kid shit. When you do stuff like that . . . .

One of the most affirming things as a Super Dad was when Willy for the longest time called me "Mom." He would call Amanda "Dad"; he just kind of had us the other way around. But for him to call me "Mom," what more would you want your kid to call you? It was such an emotional thing that I am acknowledged to be that role, that needful a thing in his life. (Nathan S.)

This modern myth of the Super Dad, this turn towards androgyny, is vaguely reminiscent of the urge among the males of the Busama and other primitive tribes "to eliminate the contamination resulting from association with the opposite sex." And it is directly reminiscent of one of the major functions of primitive initiations: the fathers of a tribe effectively manage to take the sons away from the mothers as they instruct the youths in the ways of a masculine world. Both primitive initiations and the myth of the Super Dad seem to contribute to the perpetuation of a male culture.

Today, the Super Dad fantasy extends the realm of male domination even further. We try to rear the daughters as well as the sons, and we try to rear them all right from the start. We don't have to steal the children away from their mothers when they come of age, for we never gave them up in the first place. The Super Dad proposes to procreate and to nurture, thereby assuming the total responsibiliy for the continuing existence of the species. "You can do *all* that," says Nathan S. "You got both a pecker and tits. By assuming both the male and female roles, we're taking God's place. The kids are *ours*. We made them. We're the Creator, God the Father and Mother."

Nathan, of course, is exaggerating. He affects a male bravado which doesn't really suit him that well. In fact he is a fine father and a devoted husband; he dearly loves and cares for his wife and children. But his posturing is not without significance. Just as our insecure sexuality during adolescence naturally leads towards certain types of macho behavior, so does the insecurity caused by our changing sex roles lead towards this new kind of overblown reaction. In both cases, our posturing indicates that we have not fully come to terms with the power of women in our lives; in this sense, our "initiations" are not quite complete. Even if we have left our mothers behind, women still threaten to control our emotional well-being. Our obsessive fear of slipping back to a state of dependency is a mark of how tenuous our manhood has become. Women seem to have us on the run. How many men, like Shawn W., have had their lives—and their sense of manliness—transformed by their failure to control their sexual relationships? Our defensive and reactive stance towards the power of the opposite sex is one further indication of our self-perceived unmanliness.

Still, the Super Dad mythology constitutes a marvelous adaptation to our threatened sexuality. At a time when an enlighted feminism has taken away many of our traditional props, at a time when many of our manly roles have become virtually obsolete, at a time when we have been placed on the defensive in what we perceive as a never-ending competition between the sexes, we have countered by aggressively usurping the roles once played only by women. We have somehow managed to redefine the rules so we still come out on top; ingeniously, we have taken the offensive by promising to alleviate our troublesome and frustrating interdependence.

The only problem, of course, is that Super Dad is merely a fantasy. If and when we undertake to prove our manliness by an exhibitionist display of our newfound nurturance, we are likely to find that there is more to postmodern masculinity than changing diapers or washing dishes, and that our need for women cannot be dismissed quite so glibly. Nathan himself knows this all too well:

I say: Act as if you really were Super Dad. Revel in it. Let them all believe that you really *are* macho. You know damn well you're not, but as long as everybody thinks you are, that's fine. If this is an initiation, you've got to make it look like you passed the test. If you go out on an initiation and didn't see God or anything else, you'll be damned if you come back and say you didn't. I mean, who knows how many Indian kids have made up their own names? "All I saw was a lizard." "We will call you 'Running Lizard.'"

Actually, I've never really had to be a Super Dad for any significant period of time. It would imply a disaster of some kind, either a divorce or Amanda dying or something like that. I don't want a disaster to happen, except for that strange fantasy of: "Could I really do it? Could I really pull it off?" For a couple of days I play at it, although I think if I had to do it for real I'd probably end up abusing my kids, or maybe fail at my job or have the house burn down.

And even if I did get all those other things done, what would I do with myself then? The whole thing is a myth from the start because so much of our lives is just living together. You could do the crossword puzzle by yourself, but it wouldn't be like doing it with her. It's all so

sterile. I mean, who could even think of test tube babies? I doubt it
was a woman's idea.

The androgynous ideal of Super Dad is only one of several redefini-
tions of masculinity that promise relief for unmanly guilt. Since much of
the trouble stems from a difficulty in living up to the masculine burden of
proof—through sex or money, through war or any of its simulations—
why not simply declare our burden to be obsolete? Why, we might ask,
do men have to prove anything at all? Why should we submit, in this age
of liberation, to the oppressive ideals of traditional manliness when those
ideals can no longer be readily attained?

I did lots of things for my family, being the good son. When I say,
"being the good son," I guess that was my idea of masculinity: having
it together, preparing myself to go out and earn money. Just being a
provider, and also being sharp and knowing lots of answers. That's
what I thought a man was supposed to do—anyway a middle class
man, a man who was striving up the ladder of success.
So I actually went through school and got out there in the business
world, trying to go up the ladder of success. All the time though, I
guess unconsciously, I felt a little uncomfortable about it. I didn't
know where I was going or what I was doing; I just wanted to go *up*.
I was expected to go up. The disappointment to my family, and to my
mother in particular, was that I wasn't a doctor. That would have
been such a nice thing. It would have brought more prestige to her,
to the family. I would have made lots of money.
I had a range of jobs: I did production control work, I was a
marketing manager, a sales manager. I had one job in particular for a
long time where I was director of administration for a cosmetic
company. I tried real hard to succeed, doing a lot of things that
weren't really what I wanted to do, that didn't always give me a
feeling of accomplishment. I would rationalize a feeling of accomplishment by either having acquired some personal power on the job
or getting a raise or getting a title or something like that. I didn't feel
I had any options. I was sort of blind, like a salmon going upstream.
I'm just going up the ladder. Where I'm supposed to go, I don't really
know. I'm supposed to be "successful," but what does that really
mean? I'm supposed to make money, but how much money is money?

Somewhere along the line I decided I wanted to get away from all that. Since that time, I've done a lot of consciousness-raising with other men, and it seems that we're all dissatisfied with ourselves. It could be because one guy has too small of a penis and the other guy has too big a penis. Whatever it is, the end message is we're not okay. One of the things we try to do with each other in our groups and our rituals is to reassure ourselves, to validate ourselves with each other that we *are* okay. There's so much out there in society that says: If you're not making a lot of money and you're not taking care of a woman and a couple of kids and if you don't have power over other people and if you don't have this and you don't have that, you're probably a loser. And who likes a loser? Well, I was buying a lot of that.

Sometimes it feels like I spend most of my life trying to de-program myself from all those expectations. I've gone to all these groups where men relate in an open way on men's issues. I've put a lot of time and energy into these meetings.

What I finally got into, which was very helpful for me, was witchcraft. I don't know what you think of when I say "witchcraft," but a lot of people think in terms of power over other people, turning princes into frogs and doing all these diabolical things. Well, that's not the kind of witchcraft we were doing. What we were doing was working on ourselves. Through these various techniques, whether it's trance or ritual or whatever, we were trying to get more in touch with ourselves and make a connection to the God and the Goddess. The God and Goddess is within us, which fits right into what I need: I don't have to look on the outside for my spiritual head, and being that it is the God and Goddess, my so-called male and female characteristics or qualities can be recognized and I can give expression to them and this is great.

The witchcraft tradition is mainly matriarchal, which was a flip for me. Coming from a patriarchal society, I all of a sudden found myself not in the gender that could rise up higher. I mean, I could never become a Goddess too easily, or I'd have a lot of convincing to do— even though the Goddess is within me as much as it's within anybody else.

The basis of witchcraft ritual goes back to Celtic tradition. There are a lot of old rituals that we would respect, but we would also utilize them so that they're meaningful to us right now. We would come together and decide on what our ritual was, what we wanted to do, what was the feeling of the group.

Commonly we started off with a salt water purification. We'd do a ritual over mixing the salt and the water, addressing it to the Goddess and the God, holding it up so that it can be purified. Then we'd pass around a bowl with the salt water and each person would, by breathing into the bowl or making a sound, purify what's in them that's bothering them. Through imagery they'd let out that blackness within us, that poison within us, that substance which is hurting us. Some people might just hold the bowl, others might be retching into their bowl, others might be crying into their bowl. Whatever it was, the salt water would purify it.

After we go through that and feel a little better, the men might want to do something to deal with the "no's" that are in us and get them out, the "no's" that we had been stuffing inside us. So we would set up a ritual accordingly. If it's at night and we have a fire going, we might all decide to dance around the fire and cast our "no's" into it:

"No, I won't be big and strong!"
"No, I won't take care of you!"
"No, I don't have to do that!"
"No, I won't work!"
"No, I won't grow up!"

—whatever the "no's" are that particular people are dealing with, just so that there is some way in which we can all put out these things that are working on us, and having the support of the group as we do it. And also seeing, "Hey, I'm not so crazy after all, 'cause there's my friend Joe over there doing the same thing." Just going around and around and around and throwing out all the traditional male roles, trying somehow to get out from under the oppression of the sex-role stereotypes we're supposed to live up to.[11]

Through our meetings we'd try to get into a different way of relating to each other. There's a bonding that goes on through the sharing, then from that a sense of community. It was very important for us to get together this way. I didn't grow up with the sense that it's really okay to share feelings with another man. I didn't have that with my father, and though I had male friends as I grew up, we never—or I never—allowed myself to be too vulnerable with them. I find most men have experienced that distance.

In all these groups of men, whether it's my witchcraft group or some political group, it feels so wonderful to me to have that time with men alone. We do what we call "Faerie Circles." We use the archaic spelling "F-A-E-R-I-E," and we use that name as a way of discharging any power to the word "fairy"—like the word "nigger" was used so much by black people that after a while it didn't have any power to it. Part of the ritual in the Faerie Circle is sending a kiss around and saying, "Thou art Goddess," and then sending a kiss around the other way and saying, "Thou art God." Can you imagine another man coming over to you and saying "Thou art Goddess" and giving you a kiss? Right! There's a lot of things that have to settle down after that, and that's why we do it. Now I can hug my brother and he may be gay and even though I'm not gay I'm not frightened that I have to have sex with him.

But that's a whole process that I've had to go through. The Faerie Circle feels so good to me because it's men coming together, having a connection, talking of their connection to the Earth and to the Goddess, to the male and female aspects of themselves, being open with their feelings, feeling free to get naked with each other. Just taking away a lot of those barriers. (Ed Lubin)

The notion of manhood here is radically altered, almost beyond recognition. It starts out with "No, I won't be big and strong"—a natural denial in a society where physical strength is no longer a prerequisite for survival. Then it goes on to "No, I won't take care of you"—another understandable denial of a traditional male role that has come to be experienced as a burden. Since both men and women are now encouraged to take care of themselves, and since our society places such a premium on individual survival, men increasingly have come to resist the expectation that they must take care of others.

But the rebellion against traditional expectations does not stop there. Other "no's" that are thrown into the fire or retched into the bowl include "No, I won't work" and "No, I won't grow up." Here, the self-conscious attempt to transcend the archaic image of manhood is in danger of becoming dysfunctional. What starts as a resistance to a particular definition of manhood gets reduced, in its extreme form, to a sweeping denial of *any* notion of manhood.

Ed Lubin's own position, however, does not seem quite that extreme; it is both tenable and consistent with the modern democratization of gender. If women can excel in traditionally male fields, then men are taken off the hook. They no longer have to apologize for not having "power over other people," for not "making a lot of money," for not "taking care of a woman and a couple of kids." Men who would formerly have been considered "losers" now might feel that they are in fact okay.

But are they really okay? Only when they tell each other that they are. The changing concepts of manhood do not seem to have altered the basic need for men to validate each other, to reaffirm to themselves that they are who they want to be. They still need that feeling of brotherhood, a sense of belonging to a community of men, even when the very definition of "man" is turned topsy-turvy.

But what about those of us who can't, or at least won't, buy into witchcraft or any other attempt to redefine contemporary masculinity? What if we are too conservative to abandon all traditional notions? What if we are just too self-conscious to join the Faerie Circle   or, for that matter, too shy to join even a college fraternity? What about those of us who can't seem to find *any* group of males, whether liberated or traditional, to validate our personal sense of manhood?

In my senior year in high school I was a back-up third baseman on the varsity. I didn't get to play a whole lot, but I did travel around with the team. We partied it up, a lot of locker room type stuff. Team spirit. There was real power in that. We developed our own set of jokes and even a sort of group language. We had a good team and that helped a lot, but really it was the feeling of togetherness that I remember the most, not the winning record. Just being with a lot of other guys with strong bodies and deep voices who liked to hang out together.

Then the season was over and we all graduated and that was the end of that. I went away to college and didn't see much of the team anymore. In college I wanted to create the same sort of feeling—find a bunch of guys who had a lot in common and did things together—but I never seemed to find the right guys. The obvious choice was fraternities, but they were always so hokey I couldn't get into it. I

wasn't after panty raids; what I wanted was some genuine kind of fellowship. The fraternity crowd seemed to like what they were doing, but to me it all seemed just plain dumb. I remember watching guys from the fraternities and half wishing that I could be stupid enough to be one of them.

Sometimes I ask myself even now: "Why can't I manage to get dumb like the rest of the guys?" Like going down to the bar and getting loaded and watching Monday Night Football. Maybe if I drank more I could find my personal tribe in some bar and my troubles would be over. That's where grown men get together to hang out, right? But then I see these guys in the bars making asses out of themselves just like the frat-rats in college and I figure I can live without it.

And what tribe would I join, the Bud tribe or the Miller tribe? They show you all these groups you're supposed to join just by drinking the right kind of beer. All over the country, there's supposedly these guys just like you drinking your brand and you have a sort of informal fellowship with all of them. The problem is, I'm not able to buy into that. Maybe I'm just too educated to be one of the guys. So then they come along with Lowenbrau and that should be my crowd, a higher class sort of gang. Well, that doesn't work either. It's too loose, too diffuse. I mean, who really believes in this stuff anyway?

What I do get into is going to see the Mets. I like that; I like yelling and cheering and stomping along with thousands of other people, lots of them men. That helps, but it's not quite personal enough to meet my needs. What I'd like to find, what I've always wanted to find, is a well-defined group of guys who are like *me*, maybe just an extension of me. And then we'd do stuff together, men's stuff—baseball, poker, maybe even hunting and camping.

The Mets games scare me a little too. Potentially it leads to fascism, so I generally catch myself before getting too carried away with it. I just get a little carried away, and that's all I can handle. Back in college a friend of mine went out to California on his summer vacation and visited Jim Jones's church (this was before he moved to Guyana) and came back with a glowing report. It was a real community, he said. They cared about each other. They even built a swimming pool for the kids right next to the church because it was so hot out there on Sunday mornings. I was tempted to check it out, but I'm glad I never did. Jonestown is what I mean by the potential of fascism.

I guess I have a sort of love-hate thing going with the idea of joining a group. I want the camaraderie with other men, but wherever I see it in action it seems to turn me off. Take the Shriners, for instance. They seem to be having a grand old time by dressing in funny costumes and marching in parades, but I could never imagine myself being a Shriner. Absolutely ridiculous. Even men's consciousness groups don't seem to do it for me. I'm probably as liberated as the next guy, but I want to be together with men to *do* something, to have fun, to be active—not just to sit around and bellyache about our problems.

This is all kind of embarrassing, to want a group of buddies and not to be able to find one. Is there something wrong with me? Sometimes I feel like I'm not really a man because I don't do things very much with other men. There's some kind of affirmation that I'm missing, some kind of support. I want there to be a group around me that's saying, "Yes, you're a man. You're a man because you're doing man-type things with the gang. You're a man because you're one of us, and of course we're all real men too." (Jimmy S.)[12]

A youth in primitive cultures did not have to choose which group of men to join in order to validate his manhood; his choice was automatic, for he simply joined with the men of his tribe. And since only the members of his own tribe were generally considered to be truly human, joining with the tribal elders and the tribal ancestors was equivalent to becoming an integral part of the entire human community.

Today, we don't have such easy and instant access to the universal brotherhood. We must pick and choose our own tribes—and for young men like Jimmy S. who cannot seem to find their appropriate fellowship, the complexities of a modern, heterogeneous society render membership in the adult male community questionable. This, in the end, is the most sweeping form of unmanly guilt: How can you become a man when you are not one of the men?

Our individualistic culture focuses upon personal survival and achievement; when we are trying to test our manliness, this focus borders on obsession. On some level, however, we *do* want more. Try as we might, we can't alleviate our unmanly guilt by ourselves. We need the support of other men to validate our achievements; we also need other men to connect us with a world that transcends the separate and isolate boundaries of personal existence. We too want to become "one with the ancestors."

But the ancestors no longer seem so willing to receive us, while our "tribes" are at best contrived. Perhaps this paucity of genuine bonding contributes to our readiness to confuse initiations with interpersonal competition. To rephrase a common saying: *"If you can't join 'em, beat 'em."*

PART III: THE MEN FROM THE BOYS

CHAPTER 10

The Competitive Edge

T he story that emerges from this inquiry has many facets. On the simplest level, our lack of a widely accepted rite of passage can leave us to swim troubled waters on our own, without an appropriate context to help us affirm manhood. But our problems go deeper yet. We still feel driven to create imitations of initiations, and these attempts to fabricate facsimiles commonly do more harm than good. The profound irony of growing up male in America is that we try to prove we are men in ways which reinforce rather than remove our childish insecurities. We are presented with ideal images for masculinity which, if attained, promise to turn us into the men we want to be. So we strive obsessively to achieve these ideal goals, only to discover that the spoils of this sort of manhood are actually quite limited. In order to fulfill our manly aspirations, we must first beat out our rivals. When in fact we fail to do this, we are left only with that insidious self-doubt: "If that was where manhood was supposed to be, and if I haven't been able to get there, then am I really a man?"[1]

In this manner, our highly competitive social fabric makes a healthy transition into manhood extremely hard to achieve for many, perhaps even most, American males. Interpersonal competition permeates both our formal and informal initiations, and it often serves as their defining characteristic. The task of a male initiation rite in any culture is to separate the men from the boys, but in our particular culture the practical effect of many of our so-called initiations is to separate the men from the men. Whether purposely or inadvertently, we create a polarized tension between winning and losing in which the success of some is dependent upon the failure of others. Our male rites of passage therefore tend to become dysfunctional and counter-productive. The self-concepts of young men, when based upon these competitive programs, are bound to suffer if they fail to emerge as winners.

This is not to say that competition per se is necessarily bad, but rather that it is being used inappropriately. Competition is an inescapable fact of life in a crowded world with finite resources, and perhaps it is even biologically programmed in the male *homo sapiens*—but that does not mean that competition is universally appropriate in all situations.[2] When our competitive struggles masquerade as initiation rites that are supposed to lead us into manhood, they lead to negative results; competition then becomes a restrictive and destructive force which simplifies, cheapens, and even interferes with one of life's most important transitions.

It can easily be argued, of course, that competition is an important component of socialization in an avowedly competitive society. This is certainly true. Since competitive initiations are quite in keeping with the overall values of American culture, they serve as effective means of teaching us what our society is all about. We learn the prevailing norms, and we learn to behave accordingly. Unfortunately, one of the predominant features of our society is a pervasive anxiety among males—and this we also learn as we struggle to adjust to personal setbacks which are ubiquitous but not sanctioned.

It might be argued as well that competition during the developmental stages is necessary to instruct young men in coping with a competitive society, to teach them how to win with grace and lose with dignity. The fellows will have to learn to compete sometime, the argument goes, so the sooner the better. Without some training, a youth would find it difficult to hold his own in an inescapably competitive world.[3]

This position also has substance, but only if the idea of "training" is taken seriously. What kind of training are we talking about here? Is the competition nothing more than an examination, to be passed or failed individually, or is it truly a developmental tool, complete with meaningful instruction in how to deal with the unavoidable implications of victory and defeat? Most often, the curriculum (insofar as there is any curriculum at all) gets shortened from "winning with grace and losing with dignity" to simply "winning with grace," and then, more simply yet, to just plain "winning." In its crudest and commonest form, the argument for competitive training treats the competition as an instructional instrument in and of itself. Through competition we supposedly learn, quite on our own, how to "go for it"—and then how to "tough it out" if we fail to make it. Excessive praise is heaped upon the winners, while the losers are given little help in dealing with the insecurities which are inevitably created by defeat.

The logical extension of this competition-as-initiation philosophy is simply to throw the young lads out on their own, to let them "learn the hard way," as the old saying goes. There's a tribe in East Africa, the Ik, who actually do this: Children from the age of three are sent out to forage for themselves, to compete with each other and with the adults for limited supplies of food.[4] But the Ik are a dying culture, forced out of their native land and deprived of a viable means of subsistence. The children might learn to compete, but that is about all they learn. These people are unable to make constructive use of the exceptionally long period of dependency which is distinctive to the human species; they are unable to teach, and therefore to comprehend. And this, in the end, is where "learning the hard way" leads us; we terminate all instruction as we retreat to the immediate problem of individual survival.

Of course we are not the Ik, for we do not throw the children out at three. But when we demand that youths compete with each other in earnest for limited rewards before they have been duly trained, we, like the Ik, are trying to short-circuit the crucial but difficult task of bringing an end to childish dependencies. In essence, we are trying to get by with no initiations at all.

Is this realistically possible? The point of initiations is to teach us something, namely, how our period of dependency can come to a satisfactory end. The simplistic demand to win or die, to sink or swim—that's not really a sufficient education. We need a better strategy than that, something that will not only provide a challenge but also give us the tools for meeting the challenge. And this is what true initiations are all about. They create a crucial link between nurturance and survival; they mediate between dependence and independence; they serve as a bridge from one natural stage of life to the next. To deny this period of transition, to claim that an individual can step immediately from one period to another with no particular tutelage or support—well, it's asking too much, and it's little wonder that young men who are told to jump right into the tough, competitive world, to face up to their rivals and be ranked, often fail to develop the personal sense of strength and self-worth that comes with genuine maturity.

And it is little wonder that this competitive interpretation of male initiations is not shared by most other cultures. There are few examples in the ethnographic literature of primitive tribes that rely upon interpersonal competition for their rites of passage. Instead of pitting one fellow against another—with the winner emerging as a man and the loser remaining in some sort of limbo—primitive rituals generally pit a man against the world; the competition (insofar as we can use the word at all) is only with oneself as the individual learns how to brace himself against hardship. Even the extreme rites of the Busama are noticably lacking in personal rivalry, whereas they do contain significant elements of instruction. The idea is to facilitate the developmental process by providing all young males with the opportunity to develop the strength they will need in their inevitable struggle for survival. When the men emerge at the end of a primitive initiation, they supposedly will be able to go into the world—yes, even into a competitive world—and be able to handle themselves well.

The contemporary misinterpretation of what constitutes a proper initiation is due, I suspect, to an implicit acceptance of that familiar Social Darwinism which was evidenced in so many of the interviews: life is rough out there, only the fittest will survive, so a man who wants to get by must first prove he is among the fittest. The primary function of our male initiation rites, in this view, is to separate the fit from the unfit.

This philosophy is based, of course, upon the model of natural selection. In nature, a creature who is weak or ill-adapted to its environment will perish, leaving only the strong and the hardy to carry on with the reproduction of the species. This might be an accurate description of the evolutionary process in the natural world, but the theory quickly breaks down when applied to human society. If only because of our human and humane sensibilities, weak or ill-adapted people do not always perish—they merely suffer. And since the weak can reproduce as freely as the strong, Social Darwinism offers no particular advantage for the development of the human species. The process of restrictive selection serves as a method of allocating privilege, but it does nothing to promote some grand evolutionary scheme. Only if the losers were actually killed would our exclusive initiations serve an evolutionary purpose—and most rites of passage do not go that far. Unlike the losers in nature, the candidates who fail to pass their bar exams or the baseball players who never make it to the major leagues are not likely to die in the wake of their failures; instead they live on, adjusting to failure as best they can, trying to find other avenues to success, but probably feeling less secure in their adult status than they might like.

What we are left with in the end, therefore, is not a functional evolutionary process but just a lot of insecure men. Men manifest this insecurity in diverse and often contorted ways. Some try to deny the validity of the traditional male virtues, thus altering their masculine heritage beyond recognition. Others take the opposite approach; they obsessively over-assert their masculinity, hoping to prove their manhood through a never-ending series of competitive struggles which pose, in their bastardized forms, as initiations. Then there are those who seem caught in a rift between these extreme positions: the "non-vets" ridden with guilt, the amateur athletes who lose as often as they win, the men who want real adventures but never actually have them. Denial, over-assertion, guilt—these are all understandable responses to the frustrations we are likely to encounter as we quest after an alluring but elusive image of what a man should be.

The frustrations of unfulfilled masculinity, I fear, are potentially dangerous. What if our male anxiety gets projected onto the political arena, where an overcompensation for personal inadequacy can easily get transformed into militaristic jingoism? In the wake of World War I, the severe emasculation of German males—militaristically, economically, socially—provided fertile ground for pathological politics. Of course our own situation is not that extreme; our insecurities are more subtle, and our jingoism (at least so far) is more tempered. But we do seem to be experiencing a resurgence of aggressive and uncaring social behavior which I think is attributable, at least in part, to the frustrations we so often encounter as we try to prove we are men.[5]

And these frustrations are not merely incidental; they are built right into the fundamental structure of initiations which actually *require* that many of the participants will fail. Howard R.'s law school professor stated it explicitly as he addressed the incoming class of students: "Look to the left; now look to the right. One of the three of you will not be here at the end of this program." This same dire prediction is repeated almost verbatim by countless professors and drill instructors who wish to instill the fear of failure into the hearts of their charges. Primitive tribes used fear tactics too, but never did they go so far as to deny the status of manhood to one-third of their young males. They simply could not afford such a sacrifice. Apparently we feel that we can, for we institutionalize failure without a second thought.

It seems ironic that here in our welfare state, where we try to provide guarantees that no one will ever go hungry, we make no such attempt to ensure a successful transition from boyhood to manhood. Primitive cultures, on the other hand, could not provide any guarantees against hunger, but they could make use of initiation rituals as a sort of psychological and sociological insurance policy—the men would always feel like men, and society could always count on them to do a man's job. Insurance is a hedge against the law of the jungle and the randomness of fate; primitives had no such hedge with respect to objective circumstances, so they were forced, at the very least, to make full use of their human resources. *All* of their young males—not just one-half or two-thirds or some other arbitrary fraction—had to feel and act like men. The men had to be willing and capable of performing their adult roles, even under conditions of hardship.

In our society, we have hedged against fate in other ways. Through welfare checks, unemployment benefits, or insurance programs, we take some of the heat off the individual in his struggle for survival. Since the individual will seemingly get by whether he's weak or strong, there is less of a need to provide him with the emotional tools he would require in a more serious struggle for survival. An uninitiated male who cannot hold down a job is as capable as a fully initiated man when it comes to collecting his unemployment benefits.

Since primitive tribes had a pressing need for their boys to become real men, they used their initiation rituals as educational tools that could engineer personal transformations.[6] The process was essentially dynamic—something would actually *happen* inside the boys which helped to spur their growth. Today, our initiation rituals are basically static. We assume a preexisting individual, and then we test him to see if he makes the grade. If he passes the test, we call him a man; if he fails the test—well, that's his problem. Society will simply look elsewhere for the men it needs, while the individual who failed the test will have to fend for himself as best he can. The actual change from boyhood to manhood is expected to occur individually and independently. Initiation rituals, when they occur at all, are used primarily to measure that change rather than facilitate it.

The images of manhood fostered by these sorts of initiations are also static and mechanistic. We tend to view manhood as the outcome of some external achievement, not as the development of inner strength. But what do we really prove by our superficial accomplishments? Is maturation like winning a stuffed animal at the carnival by succeeding at some meaningless game, or does it perhaps have something to do with a more significant and lasting process of emotional and spiritual growth?

CHAPTER 11

Makeshift Males

The transitional stage between boyhood and manhood, when occurring in such a competitive and superficial context, becomes filled with uncertainties and ambiguities. Some young males find ways to manage the transition successfully, while others try but do not succeed. Still others never even try at all, or perhaps they attempt to alter the very concept of manhood itself. Our pluralistic culture gives only a loose and pluralistic response to the problems faced by developing young men. And so it is that we have become a nation of makeshift males.

Of course this is only to be expected in a modern and complex society such as ours. Our heterogeneous culture can't possibly revert back to some primitive-styled homogeneity; we can hardly turn back the clock and all become hunters and warriors. Any modern adaptation of primitive initiations naturally has to come to grips with our technological and multifaceted lifestyles. The extent to which we might try to imitate the classical model for initiations is severely circumscribed by the obvious dissimilarities between modern and primitive cultures.

Indeed, when we do try to imitate classical themes and structures, we run the risk of reviving those aspects of primitive culture which are potentially disruptive in the context of modern society. Traditional initiations are based on a sense of tribal belonging that encourages chauvinistic and xenophobic attitudes; the tribal group is defined, at least in part, by the exclusion of outsiders. In the context of an elaborately organized and inescapably interdependent society, we can ill afford this kind of tribalism today. Witness, for instance, the youth gangs common in urban areas.[1] Gang initiations certainly provide a social context which is lacking in many of our freestyle variations; they are taken more seriously than fraternity hazing, while their consequences are apparently more "real" than those of athletic contests. But they also rely heavily upon generating feelings of "us" versus "them"—just as primitive initiations once did. Whereas chauvinism and xenophobia might have been functional in the context of tribal bands, these tendencies are clearly dysfunctional in the global village of the late twentieth century. The intent of our comparison between modern and primitive initiations is therefore not to encourage a blind return to some distant past but rather to point out that there are certain needs that were once fulfilled by primitive initiations and that are no longer being fulfilled today. Once we recognize that these unfulfilled needs result from significant social forces rather than personal shortcomings, we will be in a better position to develop alternate means of coping with that ever difficult transition between boyhood and manhood.

Why, we might ask, if primitive and modern societies are so different, should we bother to saddle ourselves with primitive conceptions of "manhood" as a separate and enviable ideal? Isn't there something to be gained by transcending the rigid and arbitrary barrier between "men" and "boys"? Aren't we all just "people"? Don't we really grow and evolve steadily, day by day? Why should we force ourselves to make such absolute distinctions between gradual stages of development?

Perhaps the primitives, after all, were too mechanistic. "Manhood" is not necessarily a definable state of being which is achieved once through a rite of passage and then in some sense owned. To become a man is a never-ending task which inevitably involves more than the completion of prescribed ritual.

True, very true. The construct of "manhood" is admittedly abstract; in fact it is *too* abstract, and that's why we try to use rites of passage, to help us get a grasp on it. It might be nice if we could abandon the concept of "manhood" altogether, but generally we can't. The notion springs from that fundamental task of male development: we must move from weakness to strength, from helplessness to responsibility, from dependence to independence. A change as radical as this seems to require an ideal image of something to strive for—and that's where the concept of "manhood" comes in.

That's where initiations come in too; they are concrete tools that help us come closer to our abstracted ideals. Proper rites of passage can and do facilitate the developmental process; on the other hand, when these rituals are ill-conceived or poorly defined, male development is likely to become more problematic. The issue is not whether we should or should not have initiations, because in fact we are going to have them in one way or another. If they are not readily offered, many of us will simply make them up on our own; we will construct some sort of facsimile to help us prove our manhood. The real question is this: What *kinds* of initiations do we fabricate for ourselves? Do they do the job we ask of them? Where do they really lead us?

Today, since we cannot readily affirm our manhood with a single, well-defined rite of passage, our initiations become severely fragmented as we seek to prove our worth in so many different ways and in so many different fields. And somehow, the results of these freestyle and piecemeal initiations are rarely as convincing as the single, all-encompassing initiation in a more homogeneous culture. Even when we are able to achieve some sort of personal success with respect to one particular field, our self-assurance does not always carry over into all the rest of life's many facets. Ken B., for instance, now feels he can cope with most of the medical problems that come his way, but that doesn't seem to help him much when he faces adversity out on the tennis court.

This segmentation of the initiation process has severe consequences, for many of the functions of traditional initiations are not adequately served by our separate and makeshift facsimiles. Primitive initiations were holistic in scope, preparing a youth for the full range of adult experience and possibility. In the words of Mircea Eliade, "Initiation, then, is equivalent to a revelation of the sacred, of death, of sexuality, and of the struggle for food. Only after having acquired these dimensions of human existence does one become truly a man."[2] The sacred, death, sexuality, and the struggle for food—that's a pretty full curriculum. In modern society this holistic approach seems to have been abandoned. Even the successful initiations we have just witnessed do not reach this far: John F.'s escapades with women had little to do with a revelation of the sacred; Chuck Sipes's bodybuilding did not help him directly to deal with death; Will Bell's experiences in the morass of Vietnam were irrelevant to his sexuality; Joseph A.'s fraternity pranks did not teach him much about the human struggle for food. The fragmentation of modern experience appears to impede a full and complete process of initiation.

Several of the most important facets of a classical, holistic initiation are seriously neglected in our modern renditions. The "revelation of the sacred," once the hub of it all, now occurs only rarely. Our formal religious training (when it exists at all) generally seems unconnected with the developmental tasks of incipient manhood. Images of "the sacred" appear in caricature form in Joseph A.'s fraternity story, while for Ed Lubin "the sacred" is treated rather self-consciously. In most of the rest of the interviews there is no concerted attention given to anything even approximating a "revelation of the sacred." Similarly, the issue of death is dealt with only in a few cases. Except for some of the war and adventure stories, where questions of mortality are paramount, most of the initiation experiences portrayed in this study include no confrontation with the ultimate.

In primitive times, the development of religious values and the coming to grips with individual mortality constituted a major focus for initiations. These were very real issues for young men who were more at the mercies of nature and who faced a precarious existence. But today, in a seemingly secure and secularized world where the life expectancy is over seventy years, the nurturance of deep spiritual values and a coping with mortality are not perceived as developmental tasks appropriate to youth, so they get dealt with only occasionally in our compartmentalized versions of initiation.

Yet it may well be argued, as Eliade has done for the primitives, that individuals who have not yet dealt with the themes of mortality and spirituality "do not yet fully share in the human experience."[3] Such individuals are incompletely developed as human beings; they remain "uninitiated" in a very basic sense. These are aspects of existence which must be confronted sooner or later—but it appears now that we would rather cope with them later than sooner. Commonly, we do not trouble ourselves with these themes until at least middle age.

This, of course, is part of what our modern "mid-life crisis" is all about: the postponement, for a couple of decades, of the developmental process of maturity. At the age of twenty, with the great bulk of our lives still lying ahead, virtually guaranteed, we do not see mortality as a particularly relevant issue. But by the age of forty we start to notice the body's inevitable decline, and we no longer perceive the future as indefinite. Since our finitude is now evident, it must finally be dealt with at middle age—precisely because we haven't bothered to deal with it before.

Significantly, there was no such event as a "mid-life crisis" in primitive society. This was not seen as a meaningful time of transition requiring structural and ceremonial support. Questions of mortality, finitude, and spirituality had already been confronted during an earlier initiation into manhood. Although any hunter or warrior certainly had to deal with the fact that his skill and prowess would decline over time, his previous initiation, in which he had confronted life's most fundamental realities, provided him with the strength and feeling of self-worth that would serve him well in overcoming the personal anxieties he might encounter with respect to the aging process. Furthermore, he generally enjoyed considerable authority and prestige if he managed even to *reach* middle age. It is little wonder, therefore, that there are no ethnographic accounts in the anthropological literature of a mid-life rite of passage among the primitives.

And so today, with the "mid-life crisis" ranking as one of our most important times of transition, we must face this passage without the aid of historically sanctioned traditions or precedents from previous cultures. Many of us, too, must face this passage without the benefit of a successful completion of a prior initiation. If our manhood was never fully affirmed during youth, this new time of transition presents even greater dangers to our personal sense of well-being. And the passage is made more difficult yet by the absence of any social structures to help us through. Just as Solon Kimbal noted for the modern transition from boyhood into manhood, this second passage must be accomplished "alone and with private symbols."[4]

Yet this mid-life passage is certainly in keeping with contemporary idioms. Just as each individual man must face up to the loss of his physical strength during the mid-life transition, so too must modern-day men collectively face up to the decline of physical strength as a defining characteristic of manhood.[5] It's as if our society as a whole is facing its mid-life crisis, where the classical image of man as a hunter and warrior—an image best realized in young adulthood—must now be transcended.

The modern mid-life crisis points to a further fragmentation of the initiation process. We have already seen that initiations are sectioned off into separate fields; we've seen that they are reflections of diverse value systems; we've seen that they are accomplished increasingly in private and individualized forms; and now we see that the very *time* at which the process of maturation occurs might be disjointed, with some tasks being completed during adolescence while others are not confronted at all until a much later stage of life.

This temporal fragmentation of the initiation process gets played out in many ways. Divorce, as Shawn W. so painfully evidenced, can be as important to the developmental process of maturation as a man's early sexual encounters. The decline of our athletic prowess at the onset of middle age presents at least as much of a personal challenge as do the athletic events in which we participate during the prime of our youth. Similarly, as Howard R. has clearly demonstrated, facing up to a limited career presents as true a test of manhood as do the standard apprenticeships undertaken at an earlier age. And even in war, the readjustment to civilian life can be as trying as the experience of battle; fifteen years after the war has ended, many Vietnam veterans like Steve Graham are still struggling with their participation in "normal" life. This second round of tasks is as important to the realization of manhood as the earlier challenges, and yet these new tasks are not often encountered, let alone overcome, until men are well past the age of their first, and more traditional, initiations.

The whole question of age raises other issues relating to our contemporary images of manhood. Today, we do not generally emulate our elders or hold them in high esteem. In none of the diverse interviews presented above did elders (loosely defined as older men who are the purveyors of wisdom) play a significant role. We now see age as an adversary rather than an ally in the developmental process, a regrettable reality which is to be avoided if possible, or at least suppressed. The primacy of youth within our culture serves as a significant impediment to any simulation of a classical process of initiation, for without tribal elders who are universally respected and revered, an initiation is likely to suffer from a loss of viable authority—and since the initiation is not appropriately sanctioned, it is unlikely to have as meaningful and complete an impact upon the participating individuals.

The modern image of manhood, colored as it is by our collective phobia of the natural aging process, becomes unduly restricted. We implicitly think of "manhood" as equivalent to *young* manhood, roughly between the ages of twenty and forty. After that, we tend to think that manhood starts on a gradual decline, as if the onset of hemorrhoids, the loss of hair, and a weakening of body tissues somehow manage to negate the manly virtues and reverse the maturation process. This is indeed ironic, for the physical strength of youth, which we now equate with manhood, is no longer objectively necessary for our social and economic functioning.

Strangely, modern images of manhood also seem to preclude certain elements which we now associate only with childhood: curiosity, wonder, dreaming. These elements did not figure significantly in any of the stories we have just read about the coming of age in America. Yet in primitive times, dreaming was considered to be one of the primary functions of grown men, for it was largely through dreams that men could gain access to the spiritual domain. Often, it was through a dream that a man's true name would be revealed, a name that marked his new status as a mature individual. Today, we are more likely to associate dreaminess with immaturity, not maturity; there is little room within our modern image of manhood for an unconscious or non-literal dimension. Intuition, spontaneity, wonder—they are all expected to disappear as useless appendages of youth when we set out to prove we are men.

These restrictive conceptions of manhood are further reflections of our segmented experience. Both the wisdom of old age and the intuition of youth are excluded from our narrow, separate, and secular images of what it means to be a man. Whether we prove our manhood by our athletic or sexual exploits, by going to war or climbing mountains, or by any other selected but isolated achievement, the generalized sense of *maturity*—a state of being which successfully incorporates our own particular existence within a greater reality[6]—is not easily attained through our fragmented simulations of a rite of passage.

The most severe consequence of our atomized adaptations of manhood rituals is that we isolate ourselves from each other. Through our fragmented initiations we hope to prove our manhood quite on our own, following individualized paths. The cult of the individual is central to our culture, and the drive for individuation is particularly strong during the transitional stage between boyhood and manhood. The primary tasks of adolescence, according to all contemporary notions, are self-definition, identity formation, differentiation.[7] This is undoubtedly true within the context of American culture, and it is therefore quite natural that our paths to manhood, as evidenced by the stories presented above, are so varied. We like to define ourselves separately, each in our own peculiar way.

And yet we should be aware that this approach to the developmental process is culturally specific, not universal. The primitives viewed the transition from boyhood to manhood in more communal, and less individualistic, terms. Raymond Firth, the prominent British anthropologist, describes the function of primitive initiations as follows:

Entry into adult life involves the realization of social obligations and the assumption of responsibility for meeting them. What initiation does is to set a time on the way to manhood . . . and by bringing the person into formal and explicit relation with his kindred, confronts him with some of his basic social ties, reaffirms them and thus makes patent to him his status against the days when he will have to adopt them in earnest.[8]

The task of adolescence, according to this notion, is to foster a sense of belonging, not individuation; the individual is to become an integral part of tribal life, not a man apart. Our own freestyle initiations, by contrast, do not pay much attention to our interconnectedness or to our collective roots in the human community.

But can manhood really exist in a social vacuum, without reference to any social context? The isolationist image of manhood, in which each individual stands alone and pristine in his separateness, suggests that we have become trapped in the very first stage of the initiation process—the "separation" phase, as Van Gennep called it. The major task of modern adolescence is allegedly differentiation and individuation—but when are we supposed to go through the second and third stages of a classical rite of passage? We might like to think of our informal hazing and our competitive striving as versions of the crucial "transition" stage, but there is a paucity of instruction during these activities, so they don't really fulfill much of a transitional purpose. The third and final "incorporation" stage we treat almost jokingly. Do we really take our fraternity pledges and bar mitzvahs and graduation ceremonies that seriously? Can we truthfully say that they turn us into men?

Recently, it seems, we have discovered a historical precedent for our isolationist notions: the "vision quest," a form of initiation common among certain tribes of American Indians. The vision quest offers a perfect model for a rite of passage in an individualistic culture: the Indian simply rides off into the wilderness alone, seeking his own challenges and ready to receive any divine validation of manhood that happens to be tossed his way. That's the way we would like to have it. Among the Indians, the vision quest was only one of many steps on the arduous path to manhood; for us, the vision quest itself is all we really want or need. We happily dispense with the religious preparation and communal ceremonies that were used by the Indians in conjunction with their private journeys.

In a recent movie, *Vision Quest,* a young man who has just turned eighteen figures it is time to prove his manhood. The task he chooses for himself is to take on an undefeated wrestler in single combat. Where, we might ask, is the "vision" in this "quest"? What makes this routine sports film into a vision quest, even though it's totally devoid of any spiritual content, is the avowedly individualistic nature of the challenge. The special appeal of the vision quest idea is that each person is left alone to "do his own thing," whether it's to win a wrestling match or climb El Capitan. Ed Lubin, the male witch, can undertake a vision quest just as readily as Chuck Sipes, the international body-building champion. This is what our freestyle initiations are all about—we seek our own challenges, we create our own proofs. This is the very essence of our contemporary approach to initiations: We choose our dragons freely and separately, and then we go out and slay them.

But the vision quest model, the privatization of our initiations, fails to provide any structural support to help us with our personal struggles, and so it does little to help ensure success in our difficult time of transition. If we happen to possess a strong and durable body like David Smith, the adventurer, or Chuck Sipes, the body-builder, we might well succeed in our private tasks—but if we are not blessed with their exceptional strength or endurance, we might just as well fail, or never even bother to try. It is a purely laissez-faire approach to the process of maturation.

Unfortunately, our individualistic leanings force us to take our failures more personally than we should. It is hard for us to accept that our personal inadequacies (or what we *feel* to be inadequacies) are often due, at least in part, to the disparity between the dominant values of our culture and the realities of our social institutions. We are simultaneously tempted by traditional images of manhood and deprived of viable means of fulfilling those images successfully—and yet we still tend to blame ourselves when we fail to resolve this obvious contradiction.

Our individualistic initiations blind us to our social interdependence. We tend to go off on our own private journeys with no particular sense of a social (or spiritual) context to our personal struggles. It is this inability to accept and appreciate our interconnectedness, I suspect, which lies at the root of our secret guilt, of that vague sense of self-perceived unmanliness so common in contemporary males. A fellow is not necessarily less than a man because he refuses to fight in his country's war of the moment, or because he goes off to fight and happens to step on a mine, or because there are no wars in which he is even allowed to fight.

It is not my purpose here to argue for or against our personalized and freestyle initiations, but only to observe their effects upon us. In these pages we have seen young males play games and climb mountains and fight in wars (both real and imagined) in their attempts to affirm their manliness. This diversity of personal encounters with manhood taxes the very notion of initiations: in what sense can all these experiences be considered genuine rites of passage? The inability to define our modern rituals with accuracy and precision is not a flaw in analysis but a reflection of confused experience. We don't even *know* what constitutes a true and proper initiation, so we conjure up our various imitations. In lieu of accepted ritual, we make do with what we can.

I am not trying to be defeatist, but only realistic. I am not saying, point blank, that we are all a bunch of unfulfilled males (the results of my study would scarcely bear this out) but only that the achievement of "manhood," even by our own separate and private definitions, is sporadic and problematic in contemporary society. It is a pluralistic critique of a pluralistic society: Some men make it and other men don't. This, of course, is obvious. On the surface such a critique might not seem very forceful, but its power lies in the realization that frequent failure is actually necessary, that it is required by the very structure of our initiation facsimiles. Many of our contemporary initiations (both formal and informal) not only *allow* for failure, they *demand* it. Individual failure in this context is not merely incidental—it is tragic.

What we need, really, is more than just "a few good men." We should try to see manhood not so much as a special reward for selected individual achievements but as a normal stage of life accessible to all males—as normal and ubiquitous, for instance, as boyhood. Is this possible? Ironically, this sort of thinking is actually a living reality for Ron Jones's handicapped athletes:

A common Special Olympics experience is what happens when you prepare the athletes to race. I had painted pink lines with a spray can down one of the streets where I work and was very excited about giving the kids a sense of a real track with lanes and a starting line and a finish line. We worked a lot on how to start and finish a race. I had everyone all lined up in their favorite stance and they were all jiggling around in anticipation of this race. I ran down about fifty yards and strung a line across from a telephone pole to myself. I told them, "I'm going to say, 'On your mark, get set, go,' and when you hear me say 'go' you run as fast as you can down to where I am and run through this line. Does everybody understand that?"

"Yeah, yeah."

"OK. Don't start yet. Now . . . on your mark . . . get set . . . go!"

I look at this surge coming at me, running and stumbling, and lo and behold this one guy is breaking out in front and this other woman is breaking out and it looks like I've got two really fast athletes. I begin mentally to cheer for the winner—"Come on! Faster! Faster!"—and I even start coaching—"Pump those arms! Lean!" I've got someone fast, maybe the championship of the world. So I'm out there yelling encouragement and all of a sudden I realize that this champion I've been yelling at has come to a screeching halt about five feet from the finish line, thrown both arms skyward, and then turned back to the other racers coming towards him. As the others reach him he hugs them and holds them, and together they wait for the final runner who's literally wobbling down towards them. Then all of them, eight of them, grab each other's arms and cross the finish line together. My first impulse was to tell them, "You're supposed to *race,* to *win.*" But what I was starting to understand was that it was a sharing of victory as opposed to getting a victory. The idea that you would share something with your friends was more important than listening to this frantic coach yelling about pumping your arms. Coaches like you and I, or athletes like you and I who think we know the game—there's another game being played which I think is a little better. Surely it's more enjoyable.

So what do these folks know that we don't know? A race for them is not intended to select a single winner while turning all the rest into losers; it functions instead as a means for all the participants to experience their own power, both individually and collectively. Fulfillment is inclusive, not exclusive. Manhood, too, is naturally inclusive. We all want to get there somehow; we all want to cross that line.

Notes

1. Hogbin, H.I., *Kinship and Marriage in a New Guinea Village* (London, Athlone Press, 1963), 30–31.
2. Jack Sawyer, in the article which is alleged to have ushered in the male liberation movement, refers to the "burdens" of masculinity ("On Male Liberation," *Liberation*, 15 [1970]: 32.) Four years before the idea became transformed into a movement, Myron Brenton wrote a book "about the invisible straitjacket that still keeps [the American male] bound to antiquated patriarchal notions of what he must do or be in order to prove himself a man." (Myron Brenton, *The American Male* [New York, Coward-McGann, 1966], p. 13.) Well before that, the Beat writers of the fifties railed, in their own fashion, against the responsibilities required of American manhood. The best-known and most prolific proponent of male liberation in the seventies, Herb Goldberg, bemoans "the endless, impossible binds under which he lives, the rigid definitions of his role." (*The Hazards of Being Male* [New York, Nash Publishing, 1976], p. 17.) A mere list of book titles from various

authors serves to accentuate this theme: *The Male Ordeal, The Male Predicament, The Male Dilemma.* On the more positive side, there are titles which suggest relief from the male ordeal/predicament/dilemma: *Male Liberation, Male Survival, The New Male.*

3. Writers as diverse as Lionel Tiger and George Gilder have suggested that many of the dictates of the male role have a biogenic base, that economic and ecological determinants have resulted in a particular genetic programming for the male *Homo sapiens.* My own presentation of the contemporary male experience, however, is not dependent on a biogenic base; sociogenic interpretations would work equally well. For pragmatic purposes, I think it is irrelevant to argue whether the male experience is genetically programmed or socially engineered. The apparent reason for becoming involved in this sort of theoretical debate would be that a biogenic interpretation seems to render the masculine roles more "real"—universal and immutable attributes of the human condition which resist any conscious attempts at alteration. Whatever we find in man's "true nature," we assume, cannot be changed. But genetic programming is the product of evolution and, like social programming, is subject to evolutionary change. The real question is not *whether* man's "true nature" can change, but how *quickly* it can change. Can social programming evolve faster than genetic programming? Presumably so, but when we talk about tens of thousands of years of social programming, we can only guess at how adaptable or resistant the various male characteristics might be. It might even be argued that biological characteristics of maleness, at least on the individual level, are more pliable than sociological characteristics: "According to the California Gender Identity Center, for instance, it is easier to surgically change the sex of a young male . . . than it is to change his cultural conditioning." (Gloria Steinem, "The Myth of Masculine Mystique," in Joseph H. Pleck and Jack Sawyer, eds., *Men and Masculinity* [Englewood Cliffs, N.J., Prentice-Hall, 1974], p. 135.)

CHAPTER I

1. I do not wish to claim that all, or even most, pre-modern cultures practice initiation rituals, nor that those cultures practicing them conform absolutely to some universal norm. It should not be the

intent of cross-cultural studies to hide or deny the magnificence of human diversity, but rather to search for significant and useful patterns, so that the presence of one element can predictably lead to others.

2. Arnold van Gennep, *The Rites of Passage,* tr. Monika B. Vizedom and Gabrielle L. Caffee (Chicago, University of Chicago Press, 1960). First published in 1908, van Gennep's work provides a widely used framework for the discussion of rites of passage in any culture. Also in 1908, Hutton Webster, van Gennep's American contemporary, supplied another cross-cultural survey of male initiation rites in *Primitive Secret Societies* (reprinted by New York, Octagon Books, 1968). Although Webster did not break initiations down into three phases, the rest of his analysis closely parallels that of van Gennep. Taken together, these two classic works provide a broad framework for all subsequent treatments of male rites of passage in primitive societies

3. Van Gennep, *Rites of Passage,* p. 75.

4. Ibid., p. 77.

5. Mark Hanna Watkins, "The West African Bush School," in *Education and Culture,* ed. George D. Spindler (New York, Holt, Rinehart, & Winston, 1963), p. 436.

6. Thomas A. Leemon, *The Rites of Passage in a Student Culture* (New York, Teachers College Press, 1972), pp. 6–7.

7. Baldwin Spencer and F. J. Gillen, *The Native Tribes of Central Australia* (New York, Dover, 1964), p. 251. First published in 1898.

8. Henri A. Junod, *The Life of a South African Tribe* (New Hyde Park, N Y, University Books, 1962), vol. 1, p. 84. First published in 1912.

9. Cf. Raymond Firth, *We, the Tikopia* (New York, American Book Company, 1936), p. 465.

10. Cf. Mircea Eliade, *Rites and Symbols of Initiation* (New York, Harper, 1975), p. 28.

11. Since a name is equivalent to an individual's spiritual existence, the utterance of the name in a non-spiritual context is like "taking the Lord's name in vain" in Christian culture.

12. Leemon, *Student Culture,* p. 9.

13. Junod, *South African Tribe,* p. 92.

14. Eliade, *Rites and Symbols,* p. 3. Emphases are those of Eliade.

15. Ibid., p. 3. Another spiritual interpretation, based upon Jungian archetypes, is found in Joseph L. Henderson's *Thresholds of Initiation*

(Middletown, Conn., Wesleyan University Press, 1967), pp. 102–3: "Initiation as a rite has been shown to transcend the worldly plane of existence and to have its chief concern in relating spiritual height to psychological depth."

16. Lionel Tiger, *Men in Groups* (New York, Vintage, 1970), p. xvi.

17. Ibid., pp. 57–58. Note that for Tiger's evolutionary argument to work, he must demonstrate that male bonding leads to a breeding advantage for the bonded males. For this demonstration he cites primate studies that show "that in all but two species, lemurs and hamadryas, male bonds exist between dominant members of a troop or community of primates, and it is the members of the dominant bonds who have sexual access to estrous females." (Ibid., p. 61.) Tiger thus concludes that "bonding among most primates is a clear correlate of productive copulation," although he fails to note that this line of reasoning renders his "man-the-cooperative-hunter" argument irrelevant, since not all the male-bonding primates evolved into cooperative hunters.

18. "[I]nasmuch as among the chief constraints of specific evolution are economic factors, and given the significance of hunting in human evolution, I choose to interpret male bonding . . . as dependent upon economic-ecological rather than nonmaterialist psychological factors in evolution. . . . It seems preferable to me to derive psychological factors from economic constraints rather than the other way around, particularly when the data about hunting economy are as persuasive as writers in the field have come to conclude." (Ibid., p. 130.)

19. Cf. John W. M. Whiting, Richard Kluckhorn, and Albert Anthony, "The Function of Male Initiation Ceremonies at Puberty," in *Readings in Social Psychology,* ed. Eleanor E. Maccoby, Theodore M. Newcomb, and Eugene L. Hartley (New York, Holt & Company, 1958).

20. Whiting et al. support their hypothesis by showing that elaborate initiation rituals tend to occur primarily in those societies in which the baby boy sleeps with his mother and the father is banished from the mother's bed during the post-partum period. Since the baby in this case has had his mother all to himself, he is likely to rebel when his father takes his place in his mother's bed during the time of weaning. Apparently, this situation "so magnifies the conditions which should produce Oedipus rivalry that the special cultural adjustment of ceremonial hazing, isolation from women, and symbolic castration, etc., must be made to resolve it." (Ibid., p. 363.)

Three years after formulating this post-partum hypothesis, Whiting rephrased it with less emphasis upon Oedipal rivalry and more attention to sex role identity: "In societies with maximum conflict in sex identity, e.g., where a boy initially sleeps exclusively with his mother and where the domestic unit is patrilocal and hence controlled by men, there will be initiation rites at puberty which function to resolve this conflict in identity. This hypothesis suggests that the initiation rites serve psychologically to brainwash the primary feminine identity and to establish firmly the secondary male identity." (John W. M. Whiting, "The Absent Father and Cross-Sex Identity," *Merrill-Palmer* Quarterly 7 [1961]: 90.)

21. Cf. Bruno Bettelheim, *Symbolic Wounds* (Glencoe, Ill., The Free Press, 1954).

22. Cf. John W. M. Whiting, *Becoming a Kwoma: Teaching and Learning in a New Guinea Tribe* (New Haven, Yale University Press, 1941), p. 106.

23. Bettelheim, *Symbolic Wounds*, p. 109.

24. Watkins, "Bush School," p. 431. Despite all the attention given to the harshness of hazing rituals, in some cultures the adult males treat the novices quite tenderly, adopting a sort of feminized nurturance. In the Andaman Islands the youths are actually fed and massaged by the grown men (A. R. Radcliffe-Brown, *The Andaman Islanders* [Glencoe, Ill., Free Press, 1948], pp. 98–99), while even in the Busama tribe, where the initiation rites are unusually severe, the men carry the novices on their backs, like a mother with her papoose, during a part of the ritual (M. R. Allen, *Male Cults and Secret Initiations in Melanesia* [Melbourne, Melbourne University Press, 1967], pp. 26–27)

Almost twenty years after Bettelheim first formulated the "symbolic wounds" hypothesis, George Gilder repeated it succinctly, although without attribution: "In ceremonies shrouded in mystery, with women excluded, the men ritualistically reiterate the processes of childbirth. The boys are brought into a great womblike structure; they are sometimes maimed in the genitals, as if to provide them with symbolic vaginas; they are administered blood, as if through an umbilicus; they are fed, as if from a mother's breast—all before being issued in a great tumult of sound and movement into the world of men. The apparent purpose of the ritual is to assert that even though the women perform the indispensable marvel of producing babies, it is the men who can create men of boys. These initiation rites, found in hundreds of cultures, are evidence that the creative ventures of man emulate the organic creativity of women." (*Sexual Suicide* [New York, Quadrangle, 1973], p. 83). Gilder takes this line of reasoning one step farther than Bettelheim: men have good reason to emulate women, he claims, for the social role of men is at best dispensable and at worst disruptive. Women, not men, are the purveyors of civilization and culture, so it is in the best interests of society that the males try to emulate the females.

25. Definitions of the male initiation might vary in some respects, but all definitions seem to include the exclusion of the uninitiated, whether women or children, as one of the basic features.

26. The choice of antagonists, of course, is an indicator of the severity of gender conflict and sex-role division (cf. Allen, *Male Cults*), and particular ritualistic elements can often suggest which antagonism is dominant. When we read that a Bantu boy, having just been circumcised, "may run after the operator, beat him with a stick, and try to tear off his head-dress," we naturally suspect an emphasis upon generational conflict (Guntur Wagner, *The Bantu of North Kavirondo* [London, Oxford University Press, 1949], vol. 1, p. 352); on the other hand, when we read that "if a [Thonga] woman should glance at the leaves with which the circumcised covers his wound and which form his only clothing, she must be killed," we might suspect a more gender-related conflict (Whiting et al., "Male Initiation Ceremonies," p. 360).

27. Cf. Firth, *Tikopia*, p. 467.

28. Ibid., p. 466. To support the idea that traumatic hazing leads to bonding and therefore serves as a means of socialization, Cohen points to animal studies which show that "any sort of strong emotion, whether hunger, fear, pain, or loneliness, will speed up the process of socialization. . . . We may also conclude that the speed of formation of a social bond is dependent upon the degree of emotional arousal, irrespective of the nature of that arousal." (Yehudi A. Cohen, *The Transition from Childhood to Adolescence* [Chicago, Aldine, 1964], pp. 110–11; cited from J. P. Scott, "Critical Periods in Behavioral Development," *Science* [1962]: 138.)

29. Cohen, *Transition*, p. 104. Cohen goes on to claim that initiations occur primarily "in those societies in which children are brought up

to be anchored in the wider kin group" rather than the nuclear family (p. 113); initiations are thus seen as a means of transferring allegiance from the nuclear family to the larger group which the initiand must eventually join.

30. Frank W. Young, "The Function of Male Initiation Ceremonies," *American Journal of Sociology* 67, no. 4 (Jan. 1962): 382. This article serves as the most succinct single application of symbolic interactionist thought to the subject of initiations. Young has elaborated upon his analysis in a book, *Initiation Ceremonies* (Indianapolis and New York, Bobbs-Merrill), 1965.

31. Young, "Function of Male Initiations," p. 391. It is important here to note the distinction between genuine rites of passage, which include all young males, and initiations into exclusive fraternal orders, where selective membership is instrumental in the maintenance of hierarchical structures. This distinction is elucidated in Walter E. Precourt, "Initiation Ceremonies and Secret Societies as Educational Institutions," in *Cross-Cultural Perspectives on Learning*, ed. Richard W. Brislin, Stephen Bochner, and Walter J. Lonner (New York: Wiley, 1975).

32. Young, "Function of Male Initiations," p. 391.

33. Ibid., p. 382.

34. It would be difficult to adopt one of these theories to the exclusion of the others, since they deal with overlapping variables; perhaps they should be treated as complementary rather than contradictory interpretations. In the words of Joseph H. Pleck, "Given the strong interrelationships among the many cultural variables that predict initiation rites, at present no theoretical explanation is compelling." (*The Myth of Masculinity* [Cambridge, Mass., MIT Press, 1981], p. 131.) Another summary of the various theories can be found in Precourt, "Educational Institutions," pp. 232–35.

35. "The essence of this approach, it should be noted, is the analysis of the function of rituals for groups, not individuals." (Young, "Function of Male Initiations," p. 391). In *Initiation Ceremonies*, Young rejects "the individual as a unit of social analysis relevant to the explanation of structure." (p. 164)

36. This interpretation is certainly compatible with Whiting's later formulation of the male identity hypothesis, and it does not directly contradict any of the other theories mentioned above. What is unique and important in this formulation is the relationship of dramatic

events, which are publicly conceived and thoroughly social, to the tasks of personal development.

37. Whiting, "Function of Male Initiation," p. 360.

38. Cf. Leeman, *Student Culture*, p. 7.

39. Firth, *Tikopia*, p. 430.

40. In the words of Hutton Webster, "With the tribe as a secret association consisting of all initiated men, it follows that initiation is practically compulsory. Failure to undergo the rites means deprivation of all tribal privileges and disgrace for life. The uninitiated are the 'barbarians' of primitive society." (*Primitive Secret Societies*, pp. 24–25.)

CHAPTER 2

1. Popular wisdom credits Jean-Jacques Rousseau with the "discovery" of adolescence in the late 18th century and G. Stanley Hall with its "rediscovery" in the early 20th century. It is important to note, however, that Rousseau and Hall in no way invented or created adolescence; they only "discovered for the modern world the distinctive human plight that arises when a child assumes the sexual and moral responsibilities of adulthood." (Louise J. Kaplan, *Adolescence: The Farewell to Childhood* [New York, Simon and Schuster, 1984], p. 51.) Rousseau and Hall helped to reveal that the problems of maturation were no longer being resolved in the classical manner, thus leading to a new look at personal development. After Hall, our conceptualization of "adolescence" took on its modern slant, with a label that connoted a troublesome and ill-defined middle ground, of some duration, between childhood and adulthood. A typical modern view of adolescence is provided by Eugene Mahon: "If becoming a man means crossing the river of childhood to enter the land of maturity, adolescence can be thought of as the search for the proper vessel to set sail in and complete the journey." ("The Contribution of Adolescence to Male Psychology," in *The Psychology of Men*, ed. Gerald I. Fogel, Frederick M. Lane, and Robert S. Liebert [N.Y., Basic Books, 1986], p. 229.) The "proper vessel" to which Mahon refers was once supplied by formalized rites of passage; today, there must be a "search" to find it.

2. Margaret Mead, "Adolescence in Primitive and in Modern Society," in *Readings in Social Psychology*, ed. Eleanor E. Maccoby, Theodore M.

Newcomb, Eugene L. Hartley (New York, Holt & Company, 1958), p. 349. Even as recently as the early nineteenth century, most youths in this country left home for jobs or apprenticeships by the age of fourteen. (Joseph F. Kett, *Rites of Passage: Adolescence in America 1790 to the Present* [New York, Basic Books, 1977].) For these lads there was little contradiction between familial dependency and a masculine ideology which demanded more independence from the nuclear family; there was no gap between the attainment of physical maturity and the opportunity to perform adult labor; there was not much room for an "unplaced" youth, for this would be an indulgence which society (and the youth) could simply not afford. When a youth in pre-industrial America could handle "a man's work," he *did* a man's work.

3. Dan Kiley, *The Peter Pan Syndrome* (New York, Dodd, Mead & Company, 1983), p. 22.

4. Ibid., p. 23.

5. Barbara Ehrenreich, *The Hearts of Men: American Dreams and the Flight from Commitment* (Garden City, N.Y., Anchor/Doubleday, 1983). Other writers have noted the trend towards male irresponsibility, and some point to the lack of a rite of passage as a contributing cause. George Gilder notes that "nearly every society known to anthropologists provides special rituals of initiation and passage for its boys," and he then regrets that our society "is blurring or destroying all the lines of male demarcation, replacing the usual series of tests and rituals with a no man's land—a sexually neutral arena where one becomes an 'adult human being' by 'doing one's own thing.'" (*Naked Nomads: Unmarried Men in America* [New York, Quadrangle, 1974], p. 27.) But for Gilder, this lack of a manhood ritual is hardly the major cause of irresponsibility; he believes, with Hobbes, that men are *naturally* nasty and brutish and propelled by their disruptive sexual energy; this is the original condition of the male *Homo sapiens*. Men can scarcely hope to transcend this state by affirming their manhood through viable rites of passage (since, in his view, all masculinity is inherently irresponsible); instead, their only hope is to be tamed and civilized by women.

6. Some conceptions of "initiation" would exclude bar mitzvahs by definition. Cohen, for instance, would require the following characteristics for a ritual to be counted as a true rite of passage: "The rite must be universal for the members of the sex for which it is pre-

scribed. . . . The rite must be conducted in a group and not focused on a single individual. . . . The opposite sex is usually excluded from witnessing the rite, whether or not it includes genital mutilation or exposure." (Cohen, *Transition,* pp. 102–3.) Bar mitzvahs obviously do not qualify by any of these criteria—nor do many of our modern variations of initiations. We have no universal rite that includes all males; many of our "initiations" are highly individualistic (as we shall observe in ch. 4); secrecy and the exclusion of women can prove troublesome in an open and democratic society (as we shall see in ch. 5).

7. Introduction to Van Gennep, *Rites of Passage,* p. xvii.

8. Ibid., p. xviii.

9. *The Nation,* May 12, 1984, p. 588. Myron Brenton likewise alludes to this dilemma of American masculinity when he discusses "how to reconcile the sedentary, overrefined present, which is marked by an extreme lack of physical challenges, with the age-old image of the male as hunter, builder, hewer of wood, and drawer of water—a male who, in short, establishes a primitive contact between himself and his surroundings." (*The American Male* [Coward-McGann, N.Y., 1966], p. 16.)

10. Lucinda Franks, *Waiting Out a War* (Coward, McCann & Geoghegan, N.Y., 1974), p. 53.

CHAPTER 3

1. Of course not all soldiers perceive their military experiences in such a positive light, as we shall see in later chapters. Among social scientists, there are also serious differences of opinion concerning the psychological impact upon the developing individual. Some writers (cf. Hilmar Wagner, "The Impact of Military Service upon the Male Adolescent," *Adolescence* 10, no. 37 [1975]: 31–34) claim that military service provides "an opportunity to grow up;" others feel that life in the military is psychologically "dysfunctional," leading even to "impacted sexuality." (cf. R. Wayne Eisenhart, "You Can't Hack It Little Girl: A Discussion of the Covert Psychological Agenda of Modern Combat Training," *Journal of Social Issues* 31, no. 4 [1975]: 13–23. In the wake of Vietnam, there is now an extensive literature documentating the psychological traumas of a military "initiation" which are detri-

mental to the developing personality.) Without passing judgment, however, virtually all observers can agree that "militarization translates into socialization into a masculine domain." (William Arkin and Lynne R. Dobrofsky, "Military Socialization and Masculinity," *Journal of Social Issues* 34, no. 1 (1978): 166.) It is likewise clear that basic training provides the first and most decisive step in that socialization: "Basic training is a rite of passage for a young American 'boy'. . . . Ultimately, basic training is where the most profound changes must be made; it functions as the military's agency for primary socialization." (Ibid., p. 158.)

2. A parallel and more detailed account, with a distinctly anthropological perspective, is provided by Melvin Konner, *Becoming a Doctor: A Journey of Initiation in Medical School* (New York, Viking, 1987). Konner agrees with Ken B. that the third year of medical school is the most intense, that it is "the year in which the most important phase of socialization is largely completed, when the adoption of the values of physicians is affected" (p. xiii).

CHAPTER 4

1. The historical relationship between the frontier spirit and the masculine mystique is explored in Joe L. Dubbert, *A Man's Place* (Englewood Cliffs, N.J., Prentice-Hall, 1979); Mark Gerzon, *A Choice of Heroes* (Boston, Houghton Mifflin, 1982); Peter N. Stearns, *Be a Man: Males in Modern Society* (New York and London, Holmes and Meier, 1979); Joseph F. Kett, *Rites of Passage: Adolescence in America 1790 to the Present* (New York, Basic Books, 1977). In a sense, all historical works dealing with the social and psychological impact of the closing of the frontier are relevant to American conceptions of masculinity.

2. David Smith's search for "a more primitive aspect of myself" is in keeping with poet Robert Bly's call for men to rediscover a mythic "wildman" —an essential maleness—which has been suppressed not only by an over-civilized society but also by the recent feminist demand than men be "good." ("What Men Really Want," *New Age Magazine,* May, 1982.) Bly feels that the hairy beast inside us is seeking release, regardless of what mothers, grandmothers, or feminist lovers want us to be; the "new male," he claims, must provide release for this primitive aspect of masculinity.

3. For a full written account of David Smith's personal adventures, see David Smith with Franklin Russell, *Healing Journey: The Odyssey of an Uncommon Athlete* (San Francisco, Sierra Club, 1983). Dr. Smith is currently a keynote speaker on risk-taking and can be reached through Sierra Club Books.

4. David Smith's emphasis upon his own individual achievements is compatible with Ehrenreich's critique of the contemporary male; solo adventuring, a transitional activity appropriate to the young and unattached, can be seen as an "escape from commitment" when pursued as a way of life. (Note that Smith's initiation did not even *start* until Smith was twenty-six.) Traditional hunting is more than just a fantasy—the man actually returns home with meat to feed his family and tribe. But this is not the aspect of hunting which excites the contemporary male; it's the adventuring—and the independence which goes along with it—which captures his fancy.

5. The apparent incongruity between mountain climbing and social climbing seems to trouble many a mountaineer. In Ken Wilson, ed., *Games Climbers Play* (San Francisco, Sierra Club, 1978), there are several interesting articles written by climbers who voice concern over the competitive "hierarchy" and climbing ethics.

CHAPTER 5

1. A similar story of informal validation for adolescent sexuality ("Sam's Secret Sex Society") is reported by Perry Garfinkel: "We met once a week at Sam's house after school before his mother came home from work. Membership requirements? You had to have a penis and be curious about how it worked. We were about twelve or thirteen and just finding out all the potentialities of our bodies. Sam's father was a fisherman so he'd bring his father's tackle box up to his bedroom. First we'd time how long it took to get a hard-on. Then we'd see how strong they were by hanging fishing weights on them. Each event was worth a certain number of points. The guy who accumulated most points made Grand Master and we had to do things for him, like finish his homework or shine his shoes. The club finally got disbanded when a teacher intercepted a note in class announcing the next meeting." (*In a Man's World* [New York: New American Library, 1985], pp. 104–5.)

2. Many authors have observed the parallel between college fraternities and primitive initiations; Tiger, for instance, alludes to fraternities in support of his male bonding hypothesis (*Men in Groups,* pp. 186–89). For an in-depth study, see Thomas A. Leemon, *Rites of Passage in a Student Culture.*

3. Although I have phrased this summary of the function of initiations primarily in Eliade's terminology, I think the wording is also consistent with Tiger's male bonding hypothesis and the structural-functionalist's emphasis on socialization—and there is nothing to contradict any of the other hypotheses presented in chapter 1. I use here the broadest possible terminology in order to give maximum leeway for the obvious comparisons with college fraternities.

4. This focus upon sexual imagery is reported in other fraternities as well: "In one, for example, pledges stand naked in front of an open fire in which branding irons are conspicuously heating. The pledges are blindfolded, told they will be branded, the branding irons are drawn from the fire and plunged, with a hiss, into a cold bucket of water as cold irons are jabbed against the buttocks of the candidates. Another fraternity strips pledges and ties bricks to their penises. Blindfolded, the pledges are told to throw the bricks without knowing the strings have been cut." (Garfinkel, *Man's World,* p. 104.) Tiger relates another fraternity "parody" of sexuality: "Before the ceremony pledges are required to find a variety of objects with sexual connotations. These are brought to the ceremony. Included are a five-inch nail and a bottle of Vaseline. Pledges are ranged in a circle facing in. Behind each pledge is a senior member of the fraternity. In a progression articulated with various vows and statements, the pledges remove all their clothes. They are handed their nails and Vaseline and told to grease the nails and pass the nails back to the seniors behind them. The room is now dark. Then they are told to bend over, in effect presenting their buttocks to the seniors. The right hand is placed on the right buttock and the left hand extended back to the senior, to receive the nail. A can of beer is placed in the hand, the lights come on, the pledges dress, and a drinking party begins. It is difficult to avoid mentioning the superficial parallel between this ceremony and the pattern, among some primates, of dominant males briefly mounting subdominants; this appears to define or redefine status." (*Men in Groups,* pp. 187–88.) In military initiations, where the

215

"elders" enjoy the privilege of legal sanction, the symbolism tends to be less friendly and even more blatant: "One night three men who had been censured for ineffectiveness in their assigned tasks were called forward in front of the assembled platoon, ordered to insert their penises in the breeches of their weapons, close the bolt, and run the length of the squad bay singing the Marine Corps Hymn. This violent ritual ended as the drill instructor left and the three men sank to the floor, penises still clamped into their weapons. We helped them remove the rifles and guided them to their beds. There was considerable bleeding as the men cupped their wounded penises with their hands, curled into balls, and cried." (Eisenhart, "You Can't Hack It," p. 15.) This passage lends itself to two interpretations, both of which may be held simultaneously: (a) it gives empirical credence to Whiting's Oedipal/castration hypothesis, and/or (b) it demonstrates the extent of violence occurring in secret, all-male societies which are unmitigated by the feminine constraints that Gilder claims are necessary to temper uncivilized (and potentially psychotic) male behavior.

5. At first glance, it might seem that the aura of secrecy contradicts the notion that initiations work best as public events. Ironically, however, secrecy is a sure indication of social importance. Secret societies utilize outsiders, from whom the secret is hidden, to cement bonds among insiders; secrecy gives special meaning to their shared symbols and events. In Georg Simmel's classic words: "The strongly emphasized exclusion of all outsiders makes for a correspondingly strong feeling of possession. For many individuals, property does not fully gain its significance with mere ownership, but only with the consciousness that others must do without it. The basis for this, evidently, is the impressionability of our feelings through *differences*. Moreover, since the others are excluded from the possession—particularly when it is very valuable—the converse suggests itself psychologically, namely, that what is denied to many must have special value." (*The Sociology of Georg Simmel,* trans. and ed. Kurt H. Wolff, [Glencoe, Ill., Free Press, 1950], p. 332.) Simmel also notes how important it is that others are aware that a secret is present: "The sociological characteristic [of secrecy] is that the secret of a given individual is acknowledged by another." (Ibid., p. 330.)

6. The same can be said of the "Playboy rebellion" documented by Ehrenreich. The explicit sexuality of *Playboy* magazine is intended to

confirm a manly status which implicitly legitimizes the childish indulgences so proudly pronounced in the name itself. Boyhood and manhood exist simultaneously; they are complementary rather than contradictory aspects of Playboy masculinity. To "kill the child" in order
to recreate the man would seem to contradict the basic thrust of our
youth-oriented culture, as epitomized by the mass media. The
boy/man connection is clearly evident in so many TV advertisements,
particularly the Miller Lite "tastes great—less filling" ads which self-
consciously validate patently immature male behavior.

CHAPTER 6

1. The notions of "single combat" and "the right stuff," of course, were
   popularized by Tom Wolfe in *The Right Stuff* (New York, Farrar,
   Straus, and Giroux, 1979). Wolfe provides the following background:
   "Single combat had been common throughout the world in the pre-
   Christian era and endured in some places through the Middle Ages. In
   single combat the mightiest soldier of one army would fight the mightiest soldier of the other army as a substitute for a pitched battle between the entire forces. . . . The Old Testament story of David and
   Goliath is precisely that: a story of single combat. . . . With the decline
   of archaic magic, the belief in single combat began to die out. The
   development of the modern, highly organized army and the concept of
   "total war" seemed to bury it forever. But then an extraordinary thing
   happened: the atomic bomb was invented, with the result that the
   concept of total war was nullified. . . . During the Cold War period
   small-scale competitions once again took on the magical aura of a
   'testing of fate.'" (Bantam edition, pp. 101–3.) The term "single combat" is now popularly used, as I use it here, to refer to all forms of
   individualized battle, whether the outcome is intended to determine
   the fate of a nation or simply to validate personal performance.
2. Descriptions (and critiques) of the military bureaucracy are too numerous to cite. For one readable and reasonably comprehensive account, see Adam Yarmolinsky, *The Military Establishment* (New York,
   Harper and Row, 1971).
3. For a particularly incisive application of the sports-as-war metaphor,
   see William Arens, "The Great American Football Ritual," *Natural
   History,* Oct., 1975.

4. Cf. Peter J. Stein and Steven Hoffman, "Sports and Male Role Strain," *Journal of Social Issues* 34, no. 1 (1978): "The athletic role is the prototype of the male role. It separates the men from the boys" (p. 148).

5. Note the similarity here with the versions of "manhood" fostered by college fraternities and *Playboy* (see ch. 5).

CHAPTER 7

1. Not all pilots are able to handle "the breaks of naval air" with this philosophic perspective. In *The Right Stuff*, Tom Wolfe describes the devious psychological games many pilots play while trying to convince themselves it could never happen to *them*.

2. It cannot be denied that overzealous drill instructors do present a very real danger, particularly when they neglect to encourage *all* the initiands to succeed: "In boot camp one recruit had a good deal of difficulty keeping up with the rigorous physical regime. He was a bright, intelligent young man who had volunteered, yet lacked the composite aggressive tendencies thought to comprise manhood. He was slender and light complexioned, not effeminate by civilian standards, but he was considered so in boot camp. He was continually harassed and called 'girl' and 'faggot.' We, his fellow recruits, began to accept the stereotyping of him as effeminate.

"In the midst of a particularly grueling run, when Pvt. Green began to drop out, we were ordered to run circles around him. Two men from the formation attempted to carry him along. His eyes were glazed and there was white foam all around his mouth. He was beyond exhaustion. He fell again as the entire formation of 80 men continued to run circles around him. Four men ran from the formation and kicked and beat him in an attempt to make him run. He stumbled forward and fell. Again he was pummelled. Finally four men literally carried him on their shoulders to the base area where we expected to rest. We were then told, 'No goddam bunch of little girl faggots who can't run seven miles as a unit will get a rest.' We were ordered to do strenuous calisthenics. The weak 'effeminate' individual who had caused the additional exercises was made to lead us without participating, counting cadence as we sweated. The tension crackled in the air, curses were hurled, and threats made. As we were made to exercise for another full hour we became so exhausted that stomachs began to cramp and men vomited. Pvt. Green was made to laugh at us as he counted cadence.

"The DI looked at Green and said, 'You're a weak no-good-for-nothing queer,' then turning to the glowering platoon, 'As long as there are faggots in this outfit who can't hack it, you're all going to suffer.' As he turned to go into the duty hut he sneered, 'Unless you women get with the program, straighten out the queers, and grow some balls of your own, you best give your soul to God because your ass is mine and so is your mother's on visiting day.' With a roar 60–70 enraged men engulfed Green, knocking him to the ground and kicking and beating him. He was picked up and passed over the heads of the roaring, densely-packed mob. His eyes were wide with terror; the mob beyond reason. Green was tossed and beaten in the air for about five minutes and then literally hurled onto a concrete wash rack where he sprawled, dazed and bleeding." (Eisenhart, "You Can't Hack It Little Girl," pp. 16–17.) In this account the fate of one individual has been sacrificed to cement the allegiance of the many. This is a clear violation of classical form: the purposive sacrifice of particular novitiates is not often reported in the ethnographic literature on primitive initiations.

CHAPTER 8

1. Stein and Hoffman claim that the equation of athletic prowess with manliness is stressful to athletes and non-athletes alike: "Both athletes and non-athletes experienced role strain. The athletes' preoccupation with and emphasis on high-level performance and winning were the underlying reasons for their experience of role strain. The non-athletes, on the other hand, were faced with their inability to make it in the pervasive child's world of sports. They experienced role strain and feelings of failure and nonmembership in the world of their male peers." ("Male Role Strain," p. 148.) In the words of Myron Brenton, "The straitjacketing effect of athletics occurs when so much emphasis is placed on it as a masculine value that it has . . . a distorting effect on the men who participate in it and a distorting effect on society's view of men who do not. . . . In terms of the stereotype, athletics becomes not a choice but a compulsion." (*American Male,* p. 65.) Male liberation literature abounds with personal testimonies by non-athletes

concerning the feelings of inadequacy and inferiority fostered by the pervasive male emphasis on sports, but athletes are clearly affected as well. According to Stein and Hoffman, athletes have all sorts of causes of stress: ambiguity of norms, decreasing internal and external rewards for performance, structural insufficiency of resources, role conflict, overload of role obligations, role-intrinsic anxiety, and physical injury.

2. J. S. Coleman ("Athletics in High School," in *The Forty-Nine Percent Majority,* ed. Deborah S. David and Robert Brannon [Reading, Mass., Addison Wesley, 1976]) summarizes the results of several studies which confirm this personal testimony. In a study of ten high schools in the midwest, athletic stars were more visible and enjoyed a higher status than scholars. The school experience appears to augment this value system, for incoming students were more likely to aspire to athletic stardom at the end of the year than they were at the beginning. In the leading cliques at four schools, every member went out for either football or basketball (or both). Athletics in these schools, even in the minds of non-athletes, ranked far above any other item as an attribute of popularity. In another study of a large school in New York, eight fictitious characters were presented to the subjects, and all the fictitious athletes had higher acceptability ratings than the non-athletes. Brilliance had little effect on acceptability, and studiousness actually reduced it.

3. Over two years have passed since the time of this interview, and as the book goes to press there are further developments to report: Alex Lash was on the mound when his high school varsity won the city championship last spring. Could the dream be coming true? Perhaps, but there is still a long way to go to reach the world of professional baseball. This fall, Alex writes back from college: "Ah yes, you ask, what about baseball? Well, I'm almost eighteen now, instead of almost sixteen, and I know what kind of effort and time commitment college sports demands. Which means that I'm gearing up, physically and mentally, for JV tryouts in the spring. If I make it (as a pitcher, of course), fantastic, and if I don't, then I have plenty of things to do to keep me busy, and as they used to say in Brooklyn, 'Wait 'til next yeeah!' So baseball is still in the game plan, and if you asked me what I plan to do after college, or, more precisely, what I want to be when I grow up, I'd have to say 'A baseball player.'"

4. A fascinating and greatly expanded written version of this story can be found in Ron Jones, *B-Ball: The Basketball Team That Never Lost a Game*. To receive a copy, send $4.00 to Ron Jones, 1201 Stanyan Street, San Francisco, CA, 94117.

CHAPTER 9

1. There are many who would argue that the Vietnam War was a pivotal point in the entire American experience, but that is beyond my scope. The literature on Vietnam, including a wealth of first-hand material, is now too numerous to mention. The discussion that follows is based on my own interview material combined with the commonplace knowledge shared by the conscious body politic of the Vietnam generation.

2. The now-famous wall in Washington, D.C., with the names of all those who were lost in Vietnam, is of course a belated attempt to supply that recognition. Clearly and consciously, it is an act of compensation for a prior neglect.

3. My use of the word "guilt," both here and in the chapter title, is a play on the popular notion of "non-vet guilt" referred to above. In common usage, "guilt" traditionally implies the existence of an aggrieved party upon whom some sin has been committed, but in an era of self-absorption the aggrieved party can simply be oneself. We now feel "guilty" for such victimless crimes as eating chocolate cake while on a diet or failing to go jogging on Thursday, so it is easy to feel "guilty" for not living up to self-perceived manly expectations.

4. A partial list of socio-economic causes for the delay in leaving home might include: (a) the standard assumption that one must graduate from high school (rather than get an early job); (b) higher costs for live-in colleges, with a corresponding increase in the enrollment of local junior colleges which make it possible for students to stay at home; (c) the decreasing importance of the armed services, which used to get most young males out of the house; (d) high rates of teenage unemployment, making separate living arrangements economically unfeasible; (e) the astronomical cost of housing, particularly in urban areas which traditionally attract young workers who are just starting out on their own.

These causes might help to explain why fewer young men are out on their own, but they do not explain why these men are so displeased with their situation. The compulsion to leave home is a culturally specific phenomenon deeply rooted in American versions of individualism, not a universal requirement of the male psyche: "In many peasant societies, the problem is staying home—living with one's parents until their death and worshipping parents and ancestors all one's life. In traditional Japan, the expression 'leaving home' was reserved for those entering monastic life, who abandoned all ties of ordinary existence. For us, leaving home is the normal expectation, and childhood is in many ways a preparation for it." (Robert N. Bellah, Richard Madsen, William M. Sullivan, Ann Swidler, and Steven M. Tipton, *Habits of the Heart,* University of California Press, Berkeley and Los Angeles, 1985, p. 57.)

5. The emasculation of white-collar work is described most forcefully in C. Wright Mills's radical classic, *White Collar* (New York, Oxford University Press, 1951): "The white-collar man . . . is more often pitiful than tragic, as he is seen collectively, fighting impersonal inflation, living out in slow misery his yearning for the quick American climb. . . . When white-collar people get jobs, they sell not only their time and energy but their personalities as well. They sell by the week or month their smiles and their kindly gestures, and they must practice the prompt repression of resentment and aggression." (pp. xii–xvii.) Mills notes that white-collar work is sedentary and dependent, in marked contrast with the active self-reliance which once characterized a man's work in America. Although Mills wrote before the analysis of gender became a pronounced theme in social criticism, his critique of white-collar work can be easily adapted to a discussion of contemporary masculinity.

6. The fascination of middle-class youth with working-class lifestyles and values has become a culturally significant obsession, symbolized by the immense popularity of Bruce Springsteen and of Sylvester Stallone's characterization of Rocky. As Ehrenreich observes, Hollywood has now "located 'traditional' masculinity in the working class, much as it had once been located in the filmic west." (*Hearts of Men,* p. 136.)

7. The equation of powerlessness with emasculation, made implicitly by Mills, is made explicitly by Karl Bednarik: "The danger originates within the male world itself [not from feminism], in the male tech-

nological machine which permits a few 'Big Brothers' to make the vital decision for more and more people. . . . This means that for the majority of men, the traditional male role is jeopardized; the ordinary male is pushed increasingly into play activity and a female pattern of consumer behavior." (*The Male in Crisis: The Emasculation of Contemporary Man by the Technotronic Society and Superstate He Has Created*, trans. Helen Sebba [New York, Alfred A. Knopf, 1970], p. viii.) Like Mills, Bednarik takes his analysis to its logically radical conclusion: "Unless man is willing to be feminized, he must bring about a new distribution of authority in society; he must learn to exert the democratic responsibility due him as a mature man" (p. xi).

8. By most definitions and within most cultures, the right to have a family is a critical component of full adult status. In the words of S. N. Eisenstadt, entrance into the adult age span "coincides with the transition period from the family of orientation to that of procreation, as it is through this transition that the definite change of age roles, from the receiver to transmitter of cultural tradition, from child to parent, is effected. One of the main criteria of adulthood is defined as legitimate sexual maturity, i.e., the right to establish a family, and not merely the right to sexual intercourse." (*From Generation to Generation* [New York and London, Free Press, 1956], pp. 30–31.)

9. Mirra Komarovsky, in a study of male college seniors, reported that most of his subjects suffered from "the distinctly masculine role strains," with 72 percent of the troubled youths experiencing some problems in the sexual sphere. (*Dilemmas of Masculinity: A Study of College Youth* [New York, Norton, 1976].) For those who were still virgins, "the failure to live up to role expectations with respect to sexual experience . . . undermined their self-esteem" (p. 109).

10. For more complete discussions of the male response to feminism, based on extensive interviews, see Anthony Astrachan, *How Men Feel* (Garden City, New York, Anchor/Doubleday, 1986); Eric Skjei and Richard Rabkin, *The Male Ordeal* (New York, Putnam's, 1981); Anne Steinmann and David J. Fox, *The Male Dilemma* (New York, Jason Aronson, 1974).

11. This concept of "traditional male roles" serves as the cornerstone of the men's liberation movement, and it figures prominently in all the movement's literature. Herb Goldberg, for instance, polemicizes: "The male . . . has yet to fully realize, acknowledge, and rebel against

the distress and stifling aspects of the many roles he plays—from good husband, to good daddy, to good provider, to good lover, etc." (*Hazards of Being Male,* p. 19). The idea of "role," of course, is borrowed from the theater, where it is intended to distinguish between the actor himself and the character he portrays; modern sociology has taken this as a handy metaphor (now raised to the status of dogma) for referring to social expectations placed upon individual "performers." For the men's movement, the postulation of a male "role"—"distinct from men themselves and imposed on them to their disadvantage" (Ehrenreich, *Hearts of Men,* p. 125)—has been crucial, for it has given men an external object to resist. The logic of radical politics requires something to rebel *against*; for white, American, middle-class males, the object of oppression was hard to locate until the idea of the "traditional male role" was discovered and popularized. Now, the objectionable "roles" can be tossed into the fire, allegedly liberating rather than consuming the individual "actors."

12. Tiger regrets the lack of "empirical study" and "field research" which might verify his male bonding hypothesis (*Men in Groups,* p. xix). But testimonies like that of Jimmy Stein, although they cannot easily be quantified, indirectly lend support to the basic thrust of Tiger's argument: the importance of male bonding becomes all the more evident in its absence.

CHAPTER 10

1. Gregory Rochlin observes: "The unique vulnerability of failed expectations is the fatal flaw in the masculine ego. It grows up in the shadow of a socially promoted and compliantly willing self-fashioned Herculean ideal. The expectations make the ego thrive. But they also feed its worm. It makes a readiness to turn on oneself in despair. . . ." (*The Masculine Dilemma,* Little, Brown, Boston, 1980, p. xi.) Rochlin, however, sees this as a permanent condition irrespective of age: "The testing of masculinity knows no bounds. Hence, the warrant to prove oneself remains a lifelong necessity. It is the case as much in manhood as it was in boyhood. It gives rise to many of man's anxieties and failures as well as to his often extraordinary achievements. We shall find this the timeless case in a boy's adventures as in a man's enterprises." (Ibid., p. xi.) Personally, I see the need for proof as more relevant, and more pronounced, at particular stages of development.

During youth, "the warrant to prove oneself" is tied very closely with the need to demonstrate gender, and this gives it a special thrust. In the absence of proper initiations to offer instruments of proof, the "testing of masculinity" might well be experienced just as strongly in later years. Perhaps this is the situation we live with today, but I doubt whether it is universally so. Where a youth's masculine status is dramatically and emphatically validated through a rite of passage, the "adventures," the "enterprises," and the "testing" might still be pursued—but without the air of desperation that comes when gender has never been adequately affirmed.

2. There is nothing in my argument that contradicts the view (offered by Ardrey, Lorenz, Gilder, and many others) that man is naturally aggressive, territorial, and therefore competitive. What I am calling into question are the psychological and sociological consequences of centering initiations around this male tendency towards competition, of pitting peer against peer and then calling it a rite of passage. With Tiger, I see classical initiation rituals as focusing more upon the equally important need for male bonding, with competitive/aggressive impulses, insofar as they come into play during a rite of passage, being directed only towards outsiders (whether uninitiated women and children or men from another group) in order to cement the bonds among the initiates. I readily admit that this insider/outsider dichotomy is often accentuated during initiations, for it encourages the male solidarity and tribal belongingness that initiations intend to foster; I also admit that classical male initiations are therefore conducive to ethnocentrism, militarism, and oppressive versions of patriarchy (see ch. 11). These dangers are real—but they are not directly relevant to this study precisely because our modern versions of initiations are not often fashioned in the classical mold; a critique based upon these dangers would be more appropriate to some other time and place. The problems we have created for ourselves are somewhat different: our competitive initiations tend to exaggerate rather than alleviate male insecurity, and the greater our insecurity, the more prone we are to overcompensating for our weaknesses by excessive and aggressive male posturing.

3. Gilder, while discussing primitive cultures, offers a clear and explicit formulation—and I think a mistaken one—of the competitive interpretation of initiations: "The group is formed and sustained by rites

of competition. One wins admission by passing tests, meeting standards, and excelling in contests that embody the purposes of the unit. Whether in a hunting party, a military company, a juvenile gang, a football team, or a rock group, membership has value because it is earned. Leadership is revered because it epitomizes the same values. Thus bonding, hierarchy, excellence, and excitement are all assured in the process by which boys and young men gain entry. In fact, it is the process by which they become men as well." (George Gilder, *Naked Nomads,* p. 88.) In a typically American fashion, Gilder confuses "hierarchy" with "initiation." He fails to account for the fact that *all* males gain admission in a traditional initiation; whatever hierarchical demands are made upon men in primitive society, any desire to prove superiority over other men within the group does not interfere with the "admission" which is administered during a rite of passage. Membership does indeed have value because it is earned—but not because it is earned competitively at the expense of others. Interestingly, Gilder relies heavily upon modern-day examples to support his competitive interpretation ("a juvenile gang, a football team, or a rock group"), although this passage occurs within the context of a discussion of hunting and gathering societies. He naturally has to resort to modern examples, since he can find no ethnographic evidence to support his position. Primitives did not have "rites of competition;" they had rites of passage. The practical need for male bonding, as formulated by Tiger and reiterated by Gilder, would clearly contradict an approach based upon interpersonal rivalry.

4. Cf. Colin M. Turnbull, *The Mountain People* (New York, Simon and Schuster, 1972).

5. The dangerous political manifestations of male insecurity are talked about often in men's movement literature. Two classic expressions of this theme are: Gloria Steinem, "The Myth of Masculine Mystique," *International Education* 1 (1972): 30–35 (reprinted in *Men and Masculinity*), and Mark Fasteau, *The Male Machine* (New York, Delta, 1975). Fasteau's historical critique, "Vietnam and the Cult of Toughness in Foreign Policy," is reprinted in *The American Man,* ed. Elizabeth H. Pleck and Joseph H. Pleck (Englewood Cliffs, N.J., Prentice-Hall, 1980).

6. For a treatment of some of the implicit and explicit curricula offered during initiation rituals, see Precourt, "Educational Institutions."

During recent years, there has been an increasing interest within the ethnographic literature in the transformational processes of primitive initiation rituals. Gilbert H. Herdt documents instances in which the impact upon personality structure can be both pronounced and confusing (*Rituals of Manhood: Male Initiations in Papua New Guinea* [Berkeley and Los Angeles, University of California Press, 1982]). Suzette Heald explains that circumcision among the Gisu of Uganda can best be understood in terms of a molding of personality into the specific traits deemed appropriate to Gisu adult males ("The Making of Men: The Relevance of Vernacular Psychology to the Interpretation of Gisu Ritual," *Africa* 52, no. 1 [1982]). Heald notes that this function of initiations is overt, not hidden—that it is in keeping with the way in which the Gisu themselves perceive the ritual. Heald also observes: "If rites of passage are regarded not only as transition markers but as transformational experiences, then the possible effects on individual consciousness, and indeed on character structure, loom large. It is then no longer sufficient to see initiation rituals simply as formal markers of status or as part of the regulatory mechanism whereby social classifications are maintained and social life made predictable and orderly." ("The Ritual Use of Violence: Circumcision among the Gisu of Uganda," in *The Anthropology of Violence,* ed. David Riches [Oxford and New York, Basil Blackwell, 1986], p. 83.)

CHAPTER II

1. By focusing my attention on mainstream Americans I have systematically excluded street gangs from this study, but their strong resemblances to primitive initiations remain obvious. Had I based my study upon them I would naturally have come up with a different analysis and a different set of problems. Tribalism would probably have emerged as an issue of considerable concern, but it is not that much of a concern for the subjects of this particular study precisely because of the noted absence of significant and appropriate "tribes" within mainstream society. Where tribes (such as fraternities) have been self-consciously generated, their contrived pettiness has probably minimized the dangerous effects of tribalism. The subjects of this study who were members of fraternal organizations or sports teams, when reflecting upon their experiences, did not seem overtly antagonistic

towards outsiders. Although the potential for chauvinism is certainly present in any ritual based on a rigid separation of insiders and outsiders, it is reasonable to suspect that the less significant the ritual, the less serious are the inherent dangers.

2. Eliade, *Rites and Symbols,* p. 39.

3. Ibid., p. 3.

4. Van Gennep, *Rites of Passage,* p. xviii.

5. The decline of the importance of physical strength as a masculine attribute is mentioned often; for an explicit and succinct statement, see John H. Gagnon, "Physical Strength, Once of Significance," in *Men and Masculinity.*

6. The specific wording of this definition of maturity is my own, but it has many close parallels. Mahon, for instance, states that "the young male, . . . developmentally incomplete at the outset, hopes by the end of adolescence to have aligned the inner structures of his mind with the outer structures of reality and society in a manner that can be called 'mature'" ("The Contribution of Adolescence," p. 230). Mahon goes on to note that this process "has been called an identity crisis, a trial mourning, a second birth, a second individuation, a psychological moratorium, and probably many other things, as investigators have attempted to put names on its multifaceted surfaces." But whatever particular name (and theory) we choose to adopt, there can be no denying that some kind of synchronization of the self with the world is an indispensable component of maturation.

7. A typical textbook definition is offered by Robert E. Grinder: "Adolescents are described as attaining maturity by asserting themselves as distinct human beings" (*Adolescence* [New York, Wiley, 1978], p. 42). Edgar Friedenberg (*The Vanishing Adolescent* [Boston, Beacon, 1959]; *Coming of Age in America* [New York, Vintage, 1965]) holds an even more individualistic conception; not only must adolescents define themselves as "distinct human beings," but they "must differentiate themselves from their culture and must question it and themselves in order to learn who they are and what they really feel." (Grinder, *Adolescence,* p. 36.) The conception of the "individual" as distinct from his "culture"—and necessarily in opposition to it—is significantly American.

8. Firth, *Tikopia,* p. 437.